Marketing to Women Around the World

Marketing to Women Around the World

By Rena Bartos

HARVARD BUSINESS SCHOOL PRESS
Boston, Massachusetts

The paper used in this publication meets the requirements
of the American National Standard for Permanence of Paper
for Printed Library Materials Z39.48–1984.

Harvard Business School Press, Boston 02163

Library of Congress Cataloging-in-Publication Data

Bartos, Rena.
Marketing to women around the world.

Includes index.
  1. Women consumers. 2. Marketing. 3. Women—
Employment. 4. Women in advertising. I. Title.
HC79.C6B34   1988   658.8'348   88-24379
ISBN 0-87584-201-1

For Harold—
and for Jim

Contents

Contents

Preface

A BOOK on marketing to women around the world seems like an inevitable and natural continuation of the studies of the women's market in the United States that I began in the early 1970s. At that time, news of working women and the continuing presence of women in the work force began to be noticed by the press. I wondered whether working women constituted a new or different marketing target and whether marketers and advertisers should consider them when approaching the women's market.

Although this was only fifteen years ago, it is remarkable to recall that working women were truly invisible in marketing and advertising plans. Most advertisers thought of women consumers as housewives. The usual target definition was "any housewife, 18 to 49." Occasionally, advertisers would recognize young, single women, usually described as "girls," as the natural target for cosmetic and fashion products. These two perceptions of women consumers dominated marketing approaches to women in those days.

My studies of the dramatic demographic and attitudinal changes among women led me to challenge some of the assumptions that lay behind the conventional definitions of the women's market. It is a truism that effective marketing and advertising must be built on an understanding of the consumer. I had assumed that marketers would be the first to identify social change and build that change into their marketing procedures. Instead, many marketing practitioners become so immersed in the specifics of their particular product categories or functional specializations that they do not always relate consumer behavior in the marketplace to the larger forces of social change. They often accept the conventional wisdom of their peers and predecessors on how to define the consumer groups that are the ultimate targets of their marketing efforts.

I found that communicating my findings about the changing women's market required a constant challenge to marketers' assumptions about women. I discovered from the very beginning that the subject of women elicited an emotional response far greater than warranted by their potential as an interesting marketing target. In the early days of my study, almost every client in the United States who saw the presentation or participated in a meeting on the subject inevitably took me aside afterward to tell me about his wife, his daughter, or a member of his professional staff. Apparently, the subject touched people deeply.

I observed the same reaction overseas. Before discussing the subject on international platforms, I had assumed that the changing role of women was a peculiarly American phenomenon. In almost every country I visited, however, people told me stories about the situation in their own country. Many speculated that the patterns I found in the United States were beginning to appear in their countries. They wondered if I thought it was merely a matter of time before comparable developments would occur in their markets. It was this intense interest in many parts of the world that led me to recommend to my management that they extend the study of "The Moving Target" to a number of countries around the world.

That study was authorized. The conceptual framework developed for the study of the women's market in the United States was applied in a number of international markets. Ten countries participated in this project:

North America	Canada	Far East	Australia
	United States		Japan
Europe	Great Britain	Latin America	Brazil
	Italy		Mexico
	West Germany		Venezuela

The principle that effective advertising and marketing must be built on understanding the consumer is particularly relevant to the international marketplace. The stereotypes and assumptions that marketers in the United States used to hold about consumers in their own country are compounded when they move overseas.

Some believe that consumers are fundamentally the same around the world and that strategies that work in one market can be transported to others.

Some concede that rapid change has occurred in the United States, but believe that consumers in other parts of the world are still motivated by traditional values.

Still others believe that there are such strong cultural differences between countries and regions that every marketing effort should be based on indigenous cultural patterns and life styles.

It has been said that all advertising is local. Ultimately, each advertisement communicates with consumers one at a time. This is equally true of local advertising programs and of far-flung multinational campaigns. I believe that since advertisers do communicate with consumers one at a time, it is essential to consider the national and cultural contexts within which they hear or see advertising images and buy or use products. In national or international advertising the essence of communication is understanding. In order to communicate, advertisers must listen. They must learn how consumers live, what they believe, what they aspire to, and the cultural context of their lives. On the one hand, advertisers must try to identify the universals, because many human emotions and needs transcend national boundaries. On the other hand, they must be sensitive to cultural differences. They cannot take a rubber stamp or pattern book approach to international or multinational communications.

In recent years there have been some profound changes in consumer life styles in the United States. The changing role of women, the aging of society, and trends toward delayed marriage and nonmarriage, smaller families, and single parents, as well as the impact of the baby boom generation, have redefined the consumer marketplace. In many cases we see parallel developments in other countries around the world. But even as we compare consumers in one country to those in another, we would be making a grave mistake if we assume that the United States model will take root elsewhere. Even if some of the demographic patterns and surface manifestations appear similar, trends in other countries will not necessarily have the same character, occur with the same intensity, or at the same pace as they do in the United States.

We should not confuse apparently similar behavior with similar motivations and attitudes. For example, the flood of women entering the work force in the United States has been termed "the outstanding phenomenon of the Twentieth Century."[1] We can compare the proportion of women working from one country to the next. It is relatively easy to obtain statistics on the total number of women in the work force in countries around the world. Their motivations for work and their perceptions of the male and female roles, however, may vary widely.

In 1976, the American Marketing Association conducted a study tour of three countries in Eastern Europe. In Budapest we met with high-ranking commissioners of finance, consumer affairs, and so on. One of the Americans asked how many Hungarian women were in the work force and how this affected marketing and advertising in their country. The commissioner of consumer affairs (a woman) answered that 90 percent of the women in Hungary work and all have three jobs: professional work, keeping house, and raising their children. I commented that we have had more of a social revolution in the United States than they have had in their country because there is a move toward sharing home responsibilities and a sense of partnership among working couples, particularly among the young. There was a moment of silence. Then one of the male commissioners said, "Let's face it. We're all a bunch of male chauvinist pigs!"

The J. Walter Thompson Company conducted a study of the women's market in Australia, and found that women's aspirations and attitudes toward achievement and self-fulfillment were parallel to those of women in the United States.[2] But in a seminar in Melbourne at which I had shown some advertising from the United States, a man in the audience accused me of an anti-male bias because one of the commercials featured a young father diapering a baby. This particular ad elicits warm approval in the United States, but was apparently shocking to the men in Melbourne.

In Japan, more than half of the women work, but for the most part they are in lower-level jobs and tend to be subordinate to male colleagues. They are not visible in the executive suites. On the other hand, Asian women in Singapore are very visible and have career opportunities similar to those of men. A Japanese woman who lives in Singapore is chairman of a major company there. She has a prominent Chinese husband. She explained the difference in the situation of Japanese and Chinese women by saying that "the Chinese treat their wives as partners."[3]

There are signs that Japan is catching up. I have observed changes in Japan in just a few short years. During my first visit there in 1977, I was taken to dinner in a pleasant, traditional Japanese restaurant by two colleagues, one an American and the other an Englishman. I was the only woman in the restaurant. It was full of groups of Japanese men having dinner with each other. My colleagues explained that this was the custom and that Japanese wives never go out in public.

I returned to Tokyo in 1986. One evening I was taken to dinner by two Japanese colleagues, a man and a woman. On this occasion, the gender ratio in the charming French restaurant was similar to what it might be in the United States. There were tables of two women with a man, couples, and one table with two women having dinner together. The difference between 1977 and 1986 might be explained in part by the choice of the restaurant: nevertheless, women were more visible than they were only a few years ago. It may not be coincidental that Japan has recently passed an equal rights amendment and women in that country now have equal rights under the law.

I also observed marked changes in Latin America. In the late 1970s, I visited the J. Walter Thompson office in Mexico City, where I conducted a seminar for a number of clients and professional staff. The audience was totally dominated by men. I showed some commercials that were particularly well liked by American consumers. One was a charming ad for a car. The spokes-person was a young woman who explained that women buy cars for the same reasons that men do. In a number of vignettes she explained features of the car such as fast getaway, quick pickup, and economy. Each was illustrated by a slightly humorous episode. In the final scene the young woman called for her boyfriend and gave him some flowers as they drove off. In the final line the boy says, "Well, I still have to be home by ten."

This was an obvious spoof on usual dating practices. The advertisement was appreciated and enjoyed by all segments of women in the American study. When I showed it to our clients in Mexico City, there was a marked gasp from the audience. When the managing director of the office thanked me for the speech, he felt called upon to comment that no woman had ever given him flowers, and I responded by saying that I had personally never given flowers to a man. We were both trying to soften the obvious shock felt by our clients.

Just three years later I revisited Mexico City and conducted another semi-nar on the same subject. There were two noteworthy differences: the audience was approximately one-third female. It included women representing our cli-ents as well as women executives from the J. Walter Thompson office. This time the audience reacted to the commercial with appreciative laughter rather than shock. Just a few weeks ago I had a note from the gentleman who origi-nally assured the audience that no woman had ever sent him flowers. He re-minded me of the time I "set back machismo in Mexico by fifty years."

Once this project was underway, the part that I had assumed would be the simplest to implement, the comparison of basic demographic data from country to country, turned out to present an unexpected challenge. I learned that *there is no such thing as a simple demographic fact in international research*. While some of the countries we studied have excellent sources of government statistics and census information, some of them do not. For the most part, we were able to obtain the relevant census statistics from Canada, Great Britain, West Ger-many, and Japan. A good deal of census information is also available from Italy and Australia. However, such large scale statistics are almost impossible to come by in the Latin American countries—Brazil, Venezuela, and Mexico.

In order to supplement the demographic information supplied by my col-leagues in the international J. Walter Thompson offices I sought supplementary data from a variety of sources. I consulted with Doris Walsh, the editor of *International Demographics* magazine; Barbara Torrey, chief of the Center for International Research at the Census Bureau; and Joanne Vanick, who heads statistical analysis at the United Nations. I learned that many of the answers I was seeking simply had not been asked or included in the published census reports in those countries. I decided that if I were ever to complete this book,

I would have to report on the data available, not on the data I wished I had. In some countries where I have not had authoritative government statistics or official data available for a particular issue, I have taken information based on survey samples. Although the surveys purport to be projectable, in many cases their projectability is limited to particular age parameters or other limitations.

The demographic facts basic to the concepts of this book are: occupation, education, marital status, and presence of children, as well as the occupations of their husbands.

Such data are available only from a handful of countries. In the course of this book I will comment on the information areas that did not come from official governmental sources, and I will urge that marketers in those countries where data are lacking to strongly request that future censuses of the population in their countries include these kinds of basic demographic data. I believe that this information would be of enormous value to marketers, to advertisers, and to students of society as a whole. And, of course, if and when it becomes available, we will have better and more definitive data about women around the world.

Acknowledgments

MANY people in many parts of the world contributed to the development of this book. Since this is the direct culmination of a project sponsored by the J. Walter Thompson Company, I begin my acknowledgments with deep gratitude to Don Johnston, former chairman of the J. Walter Thompson Company. His encouragement and support of all the activities relating to the study of the women's market in the United States and around the world helped bring the project to fruition.

I also want to express my sincere appreciation to Harry Clark (Harold F. Clark, Jr.), former executive vice-president of the J. Walter Thompson Company and currently partner in a communications consulting company, Smith Clark Associates, in Princeton, New Jersey. It was Harry who urged me to develop a formal proposal for a book on the international women's market.

My thanks to the many dedicated and talented professionals in every country represented here for contributing information and insights about the women's market in their countries.

Starting in North America, a sincere thank you to Griff Thompson, former director of research of J. Walter Thompson Canada, currently vice-president of Canadian operations, Audit Bureau of Circulation, and to Renee Auer, former project director at J. Walter Thompson Toronto, currently a research analyst at Colgate-Palmolive, Limited.

In Latin America, my heartfelt gratitude to Astrid Cohen, account planning director, J. Walter Thompson de Venezuela, for her tireless dedication in coordinating the study in ten countries in Latin America; to Celia Schiavone, research director of J. Walter Thompson Publicidade Limitada (Brazil), for implementing the study of the consumer marketplace in Brazil; and to Andrew Robert Fenn Fenning, vice-president, director of strategic planning for Latin

America, J. Walter Thompson Publicidade Limitada (Brazil) for his involvement and contribution to this project. My thanks to Elizabeth Beristain, director of account planning and research for J. Walter Thompson de Mexico S.A., for her contributions to the study of the consumer marketplace in Mexico.

My deepest appreciation to Judie Lannon, vice-president and director of research at J. Walter Thompson Company Ltd., for her perceptive contribution to the understanding of women in Great Britain. My sincere thanks to Linda Fuller, former project director at J. Walter Thompson Company Ltd., and currently associate director and head of qualitative research at Communication Research Limited in London.

My sincere gratitude to Robert Schutzendorf, director of J. Walter Thompson West Germany, and director of account planning, for his help and cooperation in developing the information about women in West Germany. My thanks to Jacqueline Winter, a member of the Account Planning Department, for her patient assistance in clarifying the German data.

My most sincere appreciation to Anna Scotti, president of J. Walter Thompson Italy, for her enthusiastic support, and to Vanna Bonvini, formerly managing director of European Marketing and Research Bureau Italia, and currently comanager of Abacus Research.

My deep gratitude to Kazuo Kobayashi, president of the Japan Market Research Bureau, Incorporated for his tireless and highly professional analysis of the Japanese women's market. My sincere thanks to Kazuko Ohye, director of qualitative research of the Japan Market Research Bureau, for her insightful analysis of the attitudes of Japanese women.

My particular thanks to Maxine Krige, former research director of J. Walter Thompson Australia Pty. Ltd. (Melbourne), and Robert B. Langtry, former research director of J. Walter Thompson Australia Pty. Ltd. (Sydney), for developing the study of women in Australia. Maxine is currently a partner in Jenssen Krige and Associates in Brighton, Victoria, Australia, and Rob Langtry is currently with McCann-Erickson in North Sydney, N.S.W., Australia.

Although a decision was made not to include the report from South Africa, I must express my sincere thanks to Barbara Ross, former research director of J. Walter Thompson Company South Africa (Johannesburg), for her groundbreaking study of the moving target in South Africa. Barbara is currently group manager of research, Nasionale Tydskrifte Ltd., Sandown, South Africa. My thanks to Timothy Hamilton-Russell, chairman of J. Walter Thompson Company South Africa, for his support of this project.

A number of people gave invaluable assistance in guiding me to international information sources. My sincere thanks to Mary Gegelys, former director of the Information Center of J. Walter Thompson Company in New York for

Acknowledgments

her help. I am particularly grateful to Doris Walsh, editor of *International De-mographics*, for her untiring assistance in guiding me to possible sources of international data.

I am grateful to John G. Keane, director of the Bureau of the Census, for his help. My appreciation to Barbara Torrey, chief of the Center for International Research at the Census Bureau, for her assistance. A sincere thank you to Joanne Vanick, who is in charge of statistical analysis at the United Nations.

In addition to the many dedicated and talented people who contributed to this book, there are others here in New York who assisted in the processing of the data. My sincere thanks to Amy Abramson, who assisted me in the analysis of the demographic data. My thanks to Amy for her patience and dedication in attempting to clarify some of the complexities in the international data. Amy is currently a project director at Saatchi & Saatchi/DFS/Compton.

My thanks also to Denise Yuspeh Hidalgo for her invaluable assistance in analyzing the attitudinal aspects of the data. My particular thanks to Bruce Simons, Dina Mead, and Scott Cosgrove of the Computer Imaging Department of J. Walter Thompson Company for their patience and dedicated assistance in translating the numerical information into graphic form. And, above all, my deep gratitude and thanks to my treasured secretary, Peg Lang, for her infinite patience and dedication throughout the development of the manuscript. The completion of this book would not have been possible without her at my side.

Introduction

THE purpose of *Marketing to Women Around the World* is to describe the similarities and differences among women in ten countries and to document how women in different parts of the world are like or unlike their American counterparts. The dynamics of the marketplace and the attitudes and behavior of women vary from country to country, and I therefore focus on the marketing and advertising implications of the role of women in each country. In order to achieve a meaningful cross-national comparison, I have tried to deal with a consistent set of topics or issues.

In general, I discuss demographic trends, attitudes, and marketing behavior, but the nature of the sources and the extent of data available varies from country to country. The conceptual framework of the book is parallel to the one I employed in *The Moving Target*.

The Evolution of the Conceptual Framework

Working Women versus Nonworking Women

In the earliest stages of my study of working women, it seemed logical to compare them to nonworking women. Even an approach as basic as this revealed strong differences in consumer behavior and levels of education and income. The comparison suggested that working women who had been ignored by marketers might, in fact, represent an opportunity segment whose business should be cultivated. In those simple days I entitled my first analysis "Working Women: The Invisible Consumer Market."

Introduction

Working Women versus Housewives

As my studies continued, I realized that not all nonworking women were housewives. It became necessary to separate full-time homemakers from other nonworking women who were out of the work force, either because they were too
young and still in school or too old, retired, or disabled, or a combination of
these. This fairly obvious discovery led to the creation of what I call the occupational profile, which clearly differentiates working women, full-time homemakers, and "others," that is, schoolgirls and retirees. This brought the contrast
between working women and housewives into sharper focus and provided the
basis for further analysis.

The Life-cycle Concept

About that time I realized that neither working women nor housewives were
monolithic groups. I realized that women's needs as consumers and their patterns of living vary enormously depending on whether or not they are married
and whether or not they have children in their households.

This fairly obvious observation led to the development of the life-cycle concept, which divides women into four life-cycle groups: those married with children at home, childless wives, unmarried women with no family responsibilities, and unmarried women who are raising children on their own. Under
"unmarried" I included all women who are currently not married, that is, the
never-married or single woman, as well as the formerly married, that is, the
woman now widowed or divorced. The purpose was not to analyze their emotional lives but to identify factors in their living situations that would affect how
women buy and use products.

I then used the life-cycle concept in my comparison of working women and
housewives. This proved to be very productive. It gave a more realistic framework for comparing the market behavior of working women and full-time
homemakers. It also revealed that in some product categories or activities the
presence of children or the fact of marriage defined the direction of consumer
behavior. This comparison enabled me to be more precise in defining the relative marketing value of working women and housewives. For example, although in some product categories married women with children behave very
differently from their childless counterparts, within life-cycle groups working
women were universally more active consumers than the full-time homemakers.

About this time it became clear that this was not merely a study of the
working women's market but rather a study of the entire spectrum of women,
working and nonworking. In many cases this required a comparison of women's
market behavior to that of men. In order to encompass this complex and constantly changing set of consumer segments, I retitled the study from "Working

Women: The Invisible Consumer Market" to "The Moving Target," which seemed to more properly reflect the dynamic nature of the changing marketplace.

The New Demographics

An additional dimension was added to my analysis of the women's market by the development of the perspective that I term the New Demographics. This concept evolved from a pair of questions asked by the Yankelovich Monitor, an annual study of social trends and values. The questions were based on the attitudes to work held by both nonworking and working women.

The housewives in their sample were asked if they ever planned to go to work. Approximately half of the housewives said that they did plan to go to work within the next year, within the next five years, or "sometime." On the other hand, working women were asked whether their work is "just a job" or a "career." This was not a matter of job definition but of how they felt about their work. Their responses segmented women into four groups: "stay-at-home housewives," "plan-to-work housewives," "just-a-job working women," and "career women." At that time the unanswered question was whether the attitudes they expressed would be translated into differences in their behavior in the marketplace.

As a first step to answering that question, I asked the Yankelovich people to compare the demographic characteristics of the four groups of women as well as their attitudes and values on a number of other issues. They found that stay-at-home housewives were really out of step with the other three segments. Although plan-to-work housewives were defined as "full-time homemakers," the reality was that their attitudes and values were far closer to those of working women than to their nonworking neighbors. There were differences between the just-a-job working women and career-oriented women as well, which, in part, were a reflection of the fact that career women were the best educated and tended to take the most nontraditional perspective on many issues.

Applications

The challenge at that time was to find out whether these differences in demographics and attitudes translated into differences in marketplace behavior. Beginning in 1975, these questions were incorporated into a major market and media study called the Target Group Index. The first results were striking. The four segments of women did, in fact, have very different patterns of market and media behavior. Since the life-cycle concept had proved so productive, I coordinated the two and examined the life-cycle patterns of women within each of the New Demographic segments. This resulted in a sixteen-cell analytic model, which I began applying systematically to various aspects of marketing.

The Qualitative Dimension

The reanalysis of market and media behavior gave a quantitative framework for tracking the behavior of the New Demographic and life-cycle segments. But it didn't answer how women felt about the products they used and why they behaved as they did. This led me to return to qualitative research.

One basic study of the New Demographics simply explored how women felt about their lives, their attitudes toward their work, and how they approached the various aspects of life that provide the context for many products and services: keeping house, personal grooming, travel, cars, financial matters, and so on. The discussions were designed to gain some understanding of the context for these various areas of behavior rather than to elicit specific brand and product information. The qualitative study provided rich insights for the creative people who were beginning to try to communicate with these previously unexplored consumers.

About that time I was asked to speak about the changing women's market on a number of platforms and, of course, to communicate about the continuing study to our account groups and clients. Some of the questions that emerged from these symposia were:

Does this mean that they require separate strategies?

How should we advertise to the new working or career woman?

Do we need to show her in her occupational role to reach her?

How do housewives feel about seeing "new" women in advertising? Are housewives turned off by seeing working women in ads?

My fundamental answer to these questions was to build the New Demographic and life-cycle framework into the marketing process and to obtain the responses of the various segments of women to creative concepts. However, many people in the marketing community sought the security of an instant answer to their questions. This led me to undertake further research, in which we obtained the responses of the New Demographic segments of women to a variety of advertisements—another example of how the quantitative framework of behavior can be enriched by applying a qualitative study of the responses of the varying consumer segments.

Spreading the Word

Since this approach to the women's market was unique, I was invited to speak on the subject at a number of professional forums and seminars. I was invited to write an article on the women's market by David Ewing, then the managing editor of the *Harvard Business Review*. The article, entitled "What Every Marketer Should Know about Women," was published in the *Review* in 1978. The conceptual approach I took there was ultimately expanded into a book, *The Moving Target: What Every Marketer Should Know about Women*, published by the Free Press in 1982.

The International Aspect

Since the J. Walter Thompson Company is a large, international advertising agency, I visited many of our international offices as part of my responsibilities. I conducted seminars and presentations for our clients and professional staffs. Very often I also gave public presentations to the professional communities in those countries. I spoke on a number of subjects, but I always found that the subject of "The Moving Target" evoked the most intense interest and response.

As a matter of fact, some of the people in the international offices asked me to explain how they might be able to do parallel studies of the women's market in their own countries. So I developed a "how-to" document, "A Do-It-Yourself Workbook for Developing a Moving Target Presentation." I set forth the conceptual framework on which my own analysis had been based and gave very specific suggestions on how this might be replicated in other countries. This became the framework for the analysis of the women's market conducted by my colleagues in the international J. Walter Thompson offices, which is the basis of this book.

I
Women and Work

The surge of women entering the work force has revolutionized the way we define the consumer marketplace in the United States. The challenge to the international marketer is to determine whether these changes have occurred in other parts of the world or whether this is a uniquely American phenomenon.

In this section I examine the extent to which women in ten countries participate in the work force, and how the present compares with the past. I will also examine why women do or do not go to work.

Chapter One, "The Quiet Revolution," deals with the basic demography of women's participation in the work force. It compares women's present workforce participation with that in the 1960s. The occupational profiles of women in each of the countries indicate that all nonworking women are not housewives. The analysis separates full-time homemakers from other nonworking women who are out of the mainstream, because they are still at school or retired or disabled, and enables the marketer to determine the ratio of working women to housewives. Isolating full-time homemakers from other nonworking women is a more actionable way of defining the women's market than merely comparing working women to nonworking women as a group.

Chapter Two, "Why Women Work," explores the economic, emotional, and psychological reasons why women work. Women work for economic necessity as well as for the "second paycheck" that enables them to supplement the family income. Yet, there are motivations beyond the paycheck that attract women into the work force: social stimulation, involvement with the outside world, an enhanced sense of self, and, for some, the sense of professional achievement and personal fulfillment.

Chapter Three, "Will It Continue?", examines whether women's presence in the work force is a temporary phenomenon or part of a trend. It examines the relationship between women's education and their presence in the work force as well as the trends toward women's increased participation in higher education. It also reports on the changing aspirations of housewives who are currently out of the work force but seek broader horizons beyond the boundaries of their homes and families.

Chapter Four, "Why Women Don't Work," examines the other side of the coin: housewives who have no desire to enter the work force. It examines their perceptions of their role in life, their feelings about their homes and families, their concerns about the stress of attempting the dual responsibilities of work and family, and their sense of their own limitations of education and energy.

The results of these investigations have led to several recommendations for marketers.

Action Implications

1. The most basic use of these data would be to define or redefine the target group. Since many marketing and advertising efforts are aimed at housewives, it is imperative to isolate full-time homemakers from other non-working women. The occupational profiles reported in Chapter One differentiate between full-time homemakers and the "marketing non-combatants," the schoolgirls and retired women. I define the combination of housewives and working women as the universe of "active women." I recommend that any existing studies of the marketplace be reanalyzed from the perspective of working women, in contrast to that of housewives.

2. If the occupations of women have not been included in demographic questions of comparable studies, then I recommend they be included in the future of all studies of the women's market so that the consumer behavior of working women and housewives can be built into strategic thinking.

3. In the long term, researchers want to improve the basic data sources available to marketers. The occupational profiles of women are available from official government sources in the United States, Japan, Great Britain, and Italy. In Canada, Australia, West Germany, and Venezuela, however, it is necessary to project information from survey data sources onto the census definition of the proportion of working and nonworking women. It is possible that this information is, in fact, available from the censuses in those countries, but it was not accessible in any published source. Therefore, I suggest that marketers in Canada, Australia, West

Germany, and Venezuela request that the occupations of women be included in future studies of the population so that researchers can isolate the full-time homemakers from other nonworking women.

This kind of information was not available at all in Brazil and Mexico. Therefore, I recommend that marketers in Brazil and Mexico request that this basic data be incorporated in future studies of the population.

one

The Quiet Revolution

THERE is a simple demographic fact at the heart of a quiet revolution that has changed the consumer landscape in the United States. That fact is the number of women who flooded into the work force in recent years. I have pointed out that "it would be too narrow and simplistic a view to assume that that unprecedented flood . . . is the only real change that has taken place. The dramatic increase in the number of working women is one symptom of a more fundamental change in women's self-perceptions." [1]

The challenge to the international marketer is to learn whether and to what extent the quiet revolution has taken root in other parts of the world. In the following pages I shall document the most obvious manifestations of the quiet revolution, the presence of women in the work force, and the most obvious manifestation of change, the extent to which their presence in the work force has increased.

How Many Women Go to Work?

From 27 percent to 55 percent of women in the ten countries studied go to work. Although there are more working women in the United States than in the other countries, there are countries that have higher levels of working women. Relatively more women in the Eastern bloc and Scandinavia go to work than in any of the countries reported on here.

The highest proportion of working women is in North America. Fifty-five percent of all in the United States and 52 percent of women in Canada go to work. [2]

The level of working women in Japan, Great Britain, and Australia [3] is also

Figure 1.1

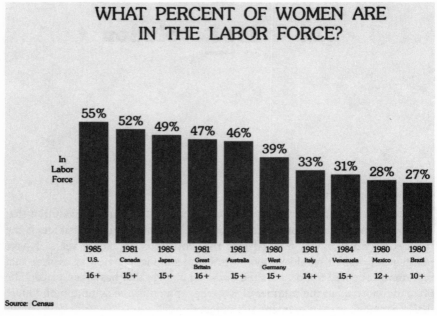

WHAT PERCENT OF WOMEN ARE
IN THE LABOR FORCE?

Source: Census

high. From 49 percent to 46 percent of women in those countries are working women.

West Germany is in the middle. Thirty-nine percent of women in Germany are in the labor force.[4] There are relatively fewer working women in Italy; just 33 percent of Italian women work.[5]

Women's presence in the work force is somewhat lower in the Latin American countries. In Venezuela 31 percent of women work; 28 percent of Mexican women and 27 percent of women in Brazil are in the labor force.[6] (Note that the number in Brazil is based on age ten and over. If the age base were raised, I think the proportion of women participating would also be higher.)

How Does This Compare With the Past?

Since 1960 there has been an increase in the number of working women in eight of the ten countries studied. The most dramatic gains were made in North America. In Canada the proportion of working women rose from 30 percent in 1960 to 52 percent in 1981. This represents an increase of 73 percent.[7] In absolute terms, there were more women working in the United States than in Canada in 1960 as well as in 1985. But the rate of growth was not as high in the United States as it was in Canada. In 1960, 35 percent of all women in the United States sixteen years and over went to work. The proportion of working women rose to 55 percent in 1985. This represents a 57 percent increase.[8]

There was an equally dramatic rise in the proportion of working women in Australia, from 29 percent in 1961 to 46 percent in 1981. This represents an increase of 59 percent.[9]

The proportion of women who work increased in Great Britain and Italy; however, the relative growth was more intense in Italy than in Great Britain. In 1961, 37 percent of all women in Great Britain, sixteen years and over, were in the work force; this rose to 47 percent in 1981. This represents a 27 percent increase.[10] Although the absolute level of working women is lower in Italy, their rate of growth is higher. In 1961, 23 percent of Italian women went to work. In 1981, 33 percent of women in Italy did so. This represents a growth rate of 44 percent. It should be noted that the 1961 census figure was based on females ten years and over, whereas the 1981 census figure was based on females fourteen years of age and over. Since the age bases are not the same, the comparison is approximate.[11]

Although the level of women's work-force participation is slightly lower in the three Latin American countries, there has been real change in that region. Again, the age upon which the census figures are based changed between 1960 and the 1980s. In Venezuela in 1961, 17 percent of all females ten years of age and over were in the work force. In 1984, 31 percent of all women aged fifteen and over went to work. Although the age bases are not the same, there was an increase of 82 percent.[12] In 1961, Mexico based its census reports on females eight years of age and over. In that year, 16 percent of all "women" were in the work force. In 1980, the census based its reports on females twelve years of age and over. The work-force participation of women rose to 28 percent in that year. This is a gain of 75 percent.[13] The census in Brazil reported on females ten years of age and over in both 1960 and 1980. The proportion of working women in Brazil rose from 17 percent in 1960 to 27 percent in 1980. This represents a 59 percent increase.[14]

In contrast, the proportion of women in the work force declined somewhat in Japan and West Germany. In 1960, 55 percent of women in Japan aged fifteen and over were in the work force, down from the peak of 57 percent in 1955. In 1985, women's participation in the labor force had declined to 49 percent. This represents a relative decline of 11 percent since 1960.[15]

A slight decline in women's work-force participation also occurred in West Germany. In 1961, 41 percent of all women fifteen years and over went to work. In 1980, the figure had declined to 39 percent. This represents a relative decline of 5 percent.[16]

Figure 1.2

WHAT PERCENT OF WOMEN ARE IN THE LABOR FORCE? TRENDS

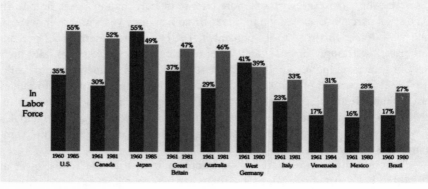

There are two reasons for the decline of working women in Japan and Germany: the aging of the population and the structural changes in the nature of women's occupations. The populations of these two countries are becoming older. Each country has a retirement age of sixty; there are therefore fewer available women of working age. In addition, in both countries more women in their early teens and early twenties are attending school and college than did so in the past. This means that relatively fewer very young women are in the work force compared to a generation ago. When the analysis is limited to women of working age, there is a gain in the number of working women in Germany.[17] In Japan there was a slight gain in the proportion of working women between the ages of twenty and fifty-five. The biggest decline occurred among teenagers and women over sixty-five years of age.[18]

There were also major structural changes in the nature of women's occupations in both countries. In West Germany there was a decline of women working in family businesses and a sharp increase in the proportion of women in paid employment (table 1.1).

There has also been a major structural change in the nature of women's occupations in Japan in the past thirty years. In 1957, when women's participation in the work force was near its peak, women were employed primarily in agriculture and forestry on family farms. By 1985, the number of women employed in agriculture had decreased dramatically, and the number of women

14

Table 1.1
Women's Occupations in West Germany, 1950–1982

	1950 %	1982 %
Self-employed	8	5
Helping in family business	32	7
Civil servants	1	4
Employees	19	53
Workers	40	31

Source: Statistisches Bundeamt, *Statistishe Jahrbuecher,* Wiesbaden, West Germany, *1950* and *1986.*

Table 1.2
Women's Occupations in Japan, 1955–1985

	1955 %	1985 %
Where Employed		
Agriculture and Forestry	44	10
Nonagricultural Section	56	90
Type of Employment		
Self-employed	16	13
Family employed	53	20
Employed	31	67

Source: Japan, Statistics Bureau, Management and Coordination Agency, Labour Force Survey.

working as paid employees of business organizations and the government had more than doubled (table 1.2).

But Not All Nonworking Women Are Housewives

We might assume that in the ten countries studied the women who don't work must be at home keeping house. Therefore, they must be the traditional consumers, the homemakers. But when we consider the occupational profiles of all women in these countries, we see that some women are neither keeping house nor going to work. The "others" include schoolgirls who are too young to be in the work force or to be married, and the retired or disabled women who

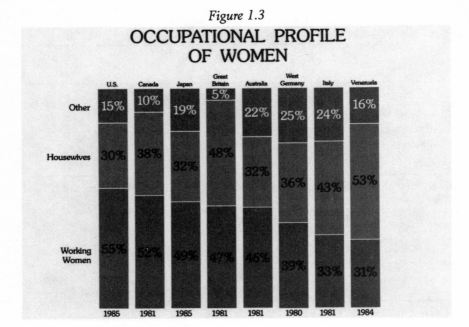

Figure 1.3

OCCUPATIONAL PROFILE OF WOMEN

are out of the mainstream. It is frustrating that complete occupational profiles are not available for all ten countries, but I will report on those for which I do have data.

The highest proportion of nonactive women or "others" is in West Germany, where 25 percent of women are out of the mainstream. The majority of them are past working age.[19] The third-highest level of "others" is found in Italy.[20] Germany and Italy are followed by Australia, where 22 percent of all women are neither at work nor at home keeping house.[21] In Japan 19 percent of the women are out of the mainstream, either retired, disabled, or still in school.[22] Sixteen percent of women in Venezuela are out of the mainstream; the majority of them are still in school.[23] Fifteen percent of women in the United States are neither keeping house nor in the work force.[24] A smaller proportion of women in Canada are labeled "others." Only 10 percent are either still in school or retired.[25] Great Britain has the lowest number of women who are out of the mainstream: 5 percent are neither at home keeping house nor working outside the home.[26]

We do not have comparable information for Mexico or Brazil. Therefore, we will be generalizing about working and nonworking women in those coun-

Figure 1.4

RATIO OF WORKING WOMEN TO HOUSEWIVES

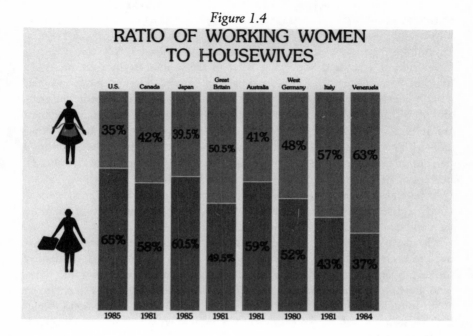

tries, although we realize that the "nonworking" designation no doubt includes women who are out of the mainstream.

The Ratio of Working Women to Housewives

If we confine our attention to active women, that is, those who are either full-time homemakers or in the work force, we get a truer picture of the ratio of working women to housewives. This ratio has shifted rapidly in the United States. In the early 1970s, slightly more women were keeping house than going to work. Currently in the United States, of active women 65 percent work and 35 percent are housewives. This is a ratio of almost two to one.

Japan is second to the United States in having a much higher proportion of women at work than at home keeping house. In Japan just over 60 percent work and just under 40 percent are housewives.

Australia follows, with 59 percent working and 41 percent full-time house-wives. In Canada, 58 percent of the active women work and 42 percent stay home and keep house. In West Germany, just over half of all active women

(52 percent) are working and just under half (48 percent) are full-time home-makers.

Although there are almost as many women working as keeping house in Great Britain, Italy, and Venezuela, more of the women in these countries are full-time homemakers than at work outside the home. The difference in Great Britain is extremely slight: among active women, 50.5 percent are housewives and 49.5 percent are working women. In Italy, 57 percent of all active women are full-time homemakers, compared to the 43 percent who are working women. The highest proportion of housewives occurs in Venezuela. Sixty-three percent of all active women in that country are full-time homemakers, and 37 percent of all active women participate in the labor force.

The reality of the quiet revolution has direct implications for marketers of goods and services aimed at women. Marketers can no longer assume that the women's market is defined by "any housewife 18 to 49."

To understand the nature of the changing consumer marketplace, marketers need to understand why some women go to work and others don't, to identify the demographic and attitudinal characteristics of women who work and those who are full-time homemakers, and to learn how the differences in their life styles influence how they buy and use products and how they respond to media. Most important, marketers need to determine whether this trend is a temporary aberration or a harbinger of the future.

two

Why Women Work

IN every country studied there are more women in the workplace today than a generation ago. A high proportion of these working women come from the traditional target group of housewives at home. Do women go to work because their husbands can't support them, or are they driven to work for other reasons?

There is no single definitive answer to the question. Nevertheless, we can identify several intertwining motivations for women's employment. Two are economic (necessity and desire for a second income) and two are attitudinal (emotional and psychological rewards).

Economic Reasons for Working

The fundamental reason why some women work is sheer economic necessity. These are women who must work if they or their families are to survive. This group includes unmarried women with no husbands or fathers to support them. Some women never marry and will always work for a living. Others have their marriages interrupted by death or divorce and are suddenly thrust into the working world. Still others are married to men earning incomes insufficient to support their families.

There is a second economic motivation, the second paycheck. Although many married women may not absolutely need the money, a second paycheck enables them to maintain or improve the family's standard of living. This reason for working tends to be far more common than that of sheer economic necessity.

Beyond the Paycheck

There are attractions beyond the paycheck that draw women into the work force. The emotional and psychological benefits that women receive from working are intertwined with economic reasons.

United States

Those skeptics who still believe that women's presence in the work force is surely a matter of economics might consider a question that was asked of women in the United States in 1972 and again in 1979 in a study conducted by the Newspaper Advertising Bureau: "Suppose that without working you could receive just as much money as your job pays you. Would you go on working or not?"[1] A surprisingly consistent three out of five working women in both years said that even if they were given the money, they would still rather go to work.

Confirmation that something beyond the paycheck drives women to work comes from a question that Roper interviewers asked of both men and women in the 1985 Virginia Slims American Women's Opinion Poll. The question, "Would you continue working if you were financially secure?" elicited identical answers from working people of both sexes. Exactly 66 percent of men and 66 percent of women say they would want to continue to work even if they didn't need the money.[2]

Europe

A similar question was asked of working women and men in the three European countries studied. They were asked, "If you had enough money to live as comfortably as you wished, would you nevertheless continue to work?" Italian men are most committed to working even if it is not financially necessary. Working men in Italy and the United Kingdom are more likely than their female counterparts to say they would prefer to continue working. However, German men are less likely than German women to want to stay on their jobs, if they have enough money to live comfortably without working. Just over three out of five of Italian and English working women say they would like to continue working. On the other hand, slightly fewer working women in Germany say they would like to continue their work, if they could afford to stop working.[3]

Australia

A similar picture was seen in Australia. Both working men and women were asked if they would stop working if they received the same salary that they earned at their jobs. Fifty-five percent of working women and an equal propor-

Table 2.1
Percentage of Men and Women
Who Prefer to Continue to Work

	Working Men	Working Women
Italy	71	61
United Kingdom	65	61
Germany	55	58

Source: Commission of the European Communities, "European Men and Women 1983."

tion of working men say they would continue to work. However, the desire of Australian men and women to continue working is slightly lower than the "continue to work" preferences expressed by men and women in the United States and the European countries.[4]

These figures raise obvious questions. Why do women want to go on working, even if they don't need the money? Clearly, there is something beyond the paycheck that attracts them to the workplace.

Broader Horizons

For many women, particularly those who say they are working for the second paycheck, the motivation to work is more a matter of what they are getting away from than what they are going to. The sense that the life of a housewife is a very narrow one seems to be a motivation that transcends national boundaries. Women appear to feel that "there must be something more to life than the kitchen sink." Even though many of the women who have entered the work force don't have highly stimulating or responsible jobs or professions, they share the sense that going to work is far more stimulating than being at home. The social stimulation and interaction in the workplace is a very important element in why they go to work.

Great Britain

In Great Britain, even working women who admit to holding an unstimulating job say there is much beyond the income that attracts them to work. According to these women, working gets them out of the house, they meet people, their interests are widened, they gain the respect of others, and they feel better about themselves because of that. A young middle-class mother said, "Going out to work means that you can talk to a lot of people. Life exists outside your home.

21

I became a more interesting person and gained confidence again. I felt I was becoming a cabbage." A young unmarried woman said, "It gives you a purpose to get up every morning. If you've no job, you just laze about. You don't have to do anything."[5]

The social benefits of work are described by a single woman: "I'm very outgoing. I like meeting lots of people and enjoy being around people all the time." On the other hand, an older woman said, "It keeps your mind active. Broadens your horizons beyond the children." One of her counterparts said, "I felt like a vegetable on my own at home with the children"[6]

Japan

Halfway around the world in Japan, working women express similar reasons for working. Economic reasons are intertwined with the psychic rewards of working. Many Japanese working women say it is necessary for them to earn a salary: the single ones need to support themselves or their families and working wives need money to supplement their husbands' incomes and to help pay for their children's schooling. In many cases economic need is the main reason they began to work. When money was no longer a primary factor for some, they wanted to continue to work.[7]

Japanese women want to work for other reasons as well: to have "some money of my own to spend" and that universal sense that there must be something more to life than housework. A woman reported, "When I hear full-time housewives talk, it seems the only thing they can do is complain about their husbands or brag about their children." Some Japanese women focus on the social stimulation in meeting other people: "I feel that I want to have some connection with overall society. I want to meet people other than just the members of my family. I want some kind of stimulation."[8]

Beyond the social values of a life with work, some Japanese working women feel that earning their own money gives them and their families a greater sense of their own worth: "When you work you receive a certain type of evaluation. A housewife is just considered a helper. When you receive money, though, it's a tangible return for the work you have done."

Australia

Working for money is also a primary reason why Australian women go to work, but, again, it is not the only reason. In contrast to men who were asked the same question, a substantially lower proportion of women say that money is the main reason why they work. Australian women also work for personal satisfaction as well as the social stimulation of meeting other people in the workplace. Some say they work because it gives them a break from the monotony of housework. Women are three times as likely as men to cite the social aspects of work as reasons for working. They are also more likely than men to say, "I like the extra money," and they are less likely to say they work because they are ambitious and want to do well.[10]

Two older working women in Australia, each of whom has grown children, testify to the emotional appeal of working. One said, "It starts off that you need the money so you go back to work. And then you find that you enjoy it because it gets you out of the house." The other woman is emphatic about her job: "I really love my job. I think I would be lost if I was retrenched. I think I would die of loneliness."[11]

Canada

Although some Canadian women say they work because it is necessary, financial independence seems to be far more important than financial necessity. The second paycheck enables them to buy things for the family that they might not be able to afford otherwise. This goes beyond financial necessity. Furthermore, the notion that "working makes me feel in control of my life" is more important than either financial reason.[12]

Clearly, economic motivation is less important to Canadian women than the psychic rewards. The women are most likely to say that they work because they enjoy the sense of achievement that work brings. They are also more likely to report that they are attracted to work by the social aspects of their jobs. They like the opportunity to meet and interact with people.[13]

Italy

Working women in Italy are also motivated by a desire for broader horizons. Work gives them the opportunity for more interaction with people. They also say that the economic independence they gain enables them to exercise financial freedom. They believe that going to work encourages them to remain young, active, and open to new ideas. The sense of leading a fuller life because they work also makes them feel that they are held in greater esteem by family members. Italian women say working leads to more cooperation from their husbands and children.

They also say that going to work helps them to get away from the narrow confines of life as a housewife. They report that working helps them put family problems in perspective and, therefore, helps them avoid concentrating on minor difficulties. As one of them said, it helps them avoid the "housewife's syndrome."[14]

West Germany

Working women in Germany are fairly positive about working. Almost three in ten say life without work would be unthinkable. On the other hand, almost half say, "If I had lots of money I would stop working." It is interesting that the question is asked in Germany from the negative point of view rather than the positive.[15] The Roper study in the United States and the European Economic Community (EEC) study posed the question in positive terms, of wanting to continue to work rather than wanting to stop. Nonetheless, working women in Germany are slightly less enthusiastic about work than women in other countries.

Venezuela

In Venezuela women work mainly for a second paycheck. They want to be able to augment their husbands' incomes to help maintain or improve their families' standard of living. Women in Venezuela are far more likely to work for a second paycheck than because of absolute economic necessity. Moreover, working women in Venezuela say that the psychic rewards are far more important than economic needs in motivating them to work. Two of the psychic rewards are personal satisfaction and heightened self-worth. A Venezuelan woman said, "What I really want to do [is] to be able to realize myself in a profession." To a moderate degree they work to get away from the monotony of housework, and working permits women to integrate themselves into the larger society.[16]

Mexico

The second paycheck is also a strong motivator for women in Mexico. It is more than twice as important to them as economic necessity. Among the non-economic reasons for working, Mexican working women report personal satisfaction and the heightened self-worth that comes from working. They also say they want the opportunity for personal fulfillment that comes from pursuing a career. Independence and getting away from the routines of housewifery are also moderately important to working women in Mexico.[17]

Brazil

Working women in Brazil express a variety of economic as well as emotional reasons for going to work. Their primary economic motivator is to earn money for their own expenses. This is another form of the second paycheck that enables them to augment their families' income. Close to this in importance is the feeling that a woman "must be economically independent." Similarly, many say that they work because they don't want to depend on their husbands for everything. Brazilian working women report financial independence and the second paycheck as reasons for working more often than straight economic necessity.[18]

A smaller number say, "I work because I earn practically the same amount as my husband." About one in four working women in Brazil gives this reason for going to work. It suggests economic partnership rather than income supplementation. The partnership notion is reflected in the claim that they work because it is better to divide household expenses with their husbands. On the emotional side, the partnership attitude is also reflected in the statement "I work because my husband gives me total support for going to work."

A great many working women in Brazil say matter of factly, "I work because I have always worked." This, of course, doesn't explain why they work now or why they have worked in the past. The major emotional reason they give for going to work is that "working gives me great personal satisfaction." Indeed, they cite personal satisfaction more frequently than any other reason for working. To a much smaller degree women say they work in order to get away from the confines of the home: "I work because I can't bear any more staying at home only taking care of the house and children."[19]

Achievement

A small number of women work for the same reasons that have always motivated ambitious men. Women go to work because work gives them a sense of achievement and for the stimulation of the work itself. These fortunate women find that work gives them strong psychic rewards as well as economic ones.

United States

Women's commitment to work is reflected in a number of ways. I noted earlier that Roper interviewers reported that 66 percent of all working women say they would prefer to continue to work even if they were financially secure. This attitude is held more intensely by working women with a college education and those in the upper-income levels. Close to three out of four would prefer to remain at their jobs in spite of all the pressures. Again, there is clearly something beyond the paycheck that draws women to work and is particularly attractive to executive women.[20]

Europe

Similarly, an average of 60 percent of the working women in the EEC countries say they would continue to work if given a choice. Not surprisingly, women in business and managerial occupations are more likely to want to remain in their careers than manual workers. Almost every woman in the "free professions"

(96 percent) says that she would prefer to practice in her profession even if the economic incentives were removed. This figure is substantially higher than the figure for their male counterparts. Only 65 percent of professional men say they would continue to practice if they had financial independence.[21]

Great Britain

In Great Britain, many women also have a strong desire to achieve. "The woman with a career enjoys her work as an end in itself, not merely as a means to an income. She believes that what she is doing is worthwhile both for herself and for others. She feels proud of herself and her achievements. She sees a career as a job which offers a future, one which she works hard at with a view to reaching a high position."[22] These women enjoy a sense of accomplishment that goes beyond the economic rewards and the social stimulation working women in general seem to enjoy. One said, "I feel proud I've achieved something, being able to run a home and a full-time job." Another expressed her enjoyment of the challenge of her career: "You're using your brain rather than just being with the children."[23]

Japan

Career women in Japan share a general attitude that they want to enjoy their lives, and they feel that work enriches them as people. One said, "Basically, I feel very strongly that I want to enjoy my life and that applies to my work and to other aspects of my life, too. I want to live a full life the best I can. That's how I feel about everything. I just don't want to do anything that I dislike doing." Another said, "I want a full life that I won't regret later."[24]

The difference between these women and those who are motivated by the combination of economics and broader horizons is that career women enjoy the work they do. In talking about their work they say, "It's fun," "It's interesting," "I like it," "It suits me," "Suits my personality," "I have never once thought of quitting." A young career-oriented woman summed up the emotional commitment to work: "My work is just so interesting. It's very strange but I've never once thought of leaving. I'm very happy that I can always find something new and interesting about my job. I think work is like a boyfriend—either it suits you or it doesn't. If a woman can find work that suits her, she's very lucky."[25]

Australia

Career-oriented women in Australia are also clearly committed to their work. Some 80 percent of them say they would not stop working if they received the same money they earned. What is it that motivates four out of five of these career women to continue working? They are most likely to say that the work they do gives them personal satisfaction; to a lesser extent they cite the social stimulation obtained from working.[26]

Canada

The major motivator for career women in Canada is the sense of achievement they enjoy from work. The opportunity to meet and socialize with people is also important to them, as is the sense that "working makes me feel I'm in control of my life." They also report that the financial independence that comes from working is important.[27]

Italy

Career women in Italy regard their work as a choice that stems from their need for personal fulfillment: "Working activity allows them to feel part of the social reality of the world they live in." Not surprisingly, these Italian career women feel very positive about the work they do. They find it interesting, and it stimulates personal development. Again, work helps them "to stay more alive and present culturally." It also helps them reach out to the larger world and opens them to social and human contacts. Italian career women also feel that their careers are a path to economic independence and will enable them to achieve a higher standard of living.[28]

Venezuela

Career-oriented women in Venezuela say that the second paycheck is a more important economic motivator than economic necessity. The psychic rewards of working are particularly important to these women: both the personal satisfaction and self-worth that come from working and the opportunity for self-development that comes from working in a profession.[29]

Mexico

Career women in Mexico share with all working women the relative emphasis on the second paycheck, but they are far less likely than other Mexican women to claim that economic necessity is their motivation for working. Indeed, they emphasize the psychic rewards of work. They say that pursuing a career gives them a feeling of personal satisfaction and self-worth. They appreciate the personal development that comes from practicing a career and developing professional skills.[30]

Brazil

Economic independence appears to be more important than economic necessity to career women in Brazil. They believe a woman must be economically independent, and working provides women with money for their own expenses. These women also believe that it is better to divide household expenses with their husbands.[31]

Brazilian career women are more motivated by the psychic benefits of working than by the economic ones. According to one woman "[I work] because I have a profession, a career." Many say matter of factly, "I have always worked and, therefore, I am in my career." They are pleased to report that their husbands give them total support to pursue careers. Work as a way to get away from the narrow confines of the home is of minor importance to them.[32]

Women in all parts of the world are motivated to work by a combination of economic and noneconomic factors. Some of those who work for reasons of economic necessity would find it liberating to be able to stop working. Others who work because they need the money find that being in the work force brings them unexpected psychic rewards. The very act of going to work brings them benefits beyond the paycheck.

For the most part, the psychic rewards are social stimulation, a sense of being part of the larger society, of leading a fuller life, and of being held in greater esteem by families and others. Also, for the most part, the work itself is neither stimulating nor rewarding. By contrast, career-oriented working women are motivated by a desire for professional achievement and self-fulfillment. These achieving women derive satisfaction and a sense of accomplishment from the work they do. They enjoy their work, and they enjoy their lives.

three

Will It Continue?

I AM often asked whether women's presence in the work force is a temporary fad or whether the trend will continue. I believe that there are two factors that suggest the quiet revolution is not a blip on the screen but an enduring light. One of these is the relationship of women's education to their presence in the work force; the other is their changing aspirations.

Education and Employment

There is a close correlation between women's education and their presence in the work force. The more education a woman has, the more likely she is to go to work. This refutes the notion that economic necessity is the only reason women work. Better-educated women come from more affluent households, and women in this group who are married tend to be married to the most achieving men. Conversely, women with the lowest levels of education are probably most in need of income and yet they are least likely to be in the work force. This pattern reappeared in country after country. One example will make the point. Of women with eight years or less of school, 21 percent are in the work force; with up to three years of high school, 40 percent; of high school graduates, 59 percent; of women with one to three years of college, 66 percent; of those with four years of college, 71 percent; and of those with five or more years of college, 77 percent.[1]

Because of the dramatic nature of the findings, I speculated on whether the level of a woman's educational achievements would correlate with the proportion of women in the labor force. I was aware that any international comparison of educational achievement would necessarily be very crude. Educational systems and terminology vary from country to country. Researchers at the Center for International Research of the U.S. Bureau of the Census, Department of Commerce, have attempted to correlate educational levels among various countries. They have created several categories of educational achievement to provide a basis for international comparison. I have limited my analysis to the top two categories: "completed secondary school" and "completed post-secondary plus." In the United States "completed secondary school" would be equivalent to graduation from high school, and "completed post-secondary plus" would be equivalent to a college degree plus advanced graduate study, if any.

Most demographic descriptions of education normally include people with some college education who have not obtained a college degree. In the present analysis such people would be included in the category "completed secondary school." Again, the quality of secondary education varies from country to country. In some countries secondary school graduates are qualified for employment in the public or private sectors. In other countries some secondary school graduates are not prepared to meet the standards of prospective employers.

Although there is not a direct correlation between women's educational achievements and their presence in the work force, the patterns described above are intriguing by inference. The three countries with the highest proportion of working women—the United States, Canada, and Japan—also have the highest proportions of women who have graduated from college.

Australia appears to have a disproportionate number of educated women in relation to their presence in the work force. In 1981, 46 percent of Australian women were in the labor force, while in 1984, 57 percent had completed their secondary or part of their secondary education.[2] Conversely, in Italy and the three Latin American countries, there are proportionately more women in the work force than have completed secondary and advanced education.

Overall, even though the correlation between women's educational achievements and their presence in the work force is not exact, the pattern suggests a definite relationship. In countries where women have achieved the highest levels of advanced education, they are most likely to be in the work force, and in countries where women have the lowest levels of education, they are less likely to go to work.

Women's Increasing Involvement in Higher Education

We have posed the question of whether women's participation in the work force will continue. If we accept the premise that the more education a woman has the more likely she is to go to work, more recent figures suggest an intensification of the quiet revolution. In recent years there has been an increase in the number of women seeking advanced education and entrance to professions that used to be the exclusive area of men. The specific fields of study vary from

Figure 3.1

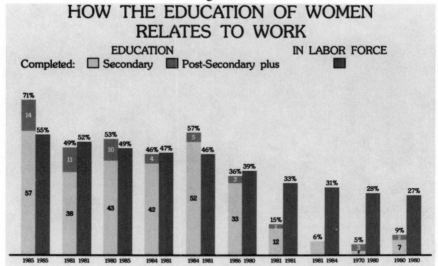

HOW THE EDUCATION OF WOMEN
RELATES TO WORK

country to country. In four of the five countries for which we have data the comparisons are based on data from 1965 and 1984 or 1985. For Canada, the comparison is based on data from 1971 and 1982.

Again, the pattern is consistent. In every country there has been a strong increase in the number of women earning advanced degrees in a variety of professional fields of study that have been almost exclusively the province of men.[3] A single example will suffice. Between 1965 and 1982 in the United States, the number of degrees women earned in medicine grew by over 700 percent, in accounting by over 2,000 percent, in law by 2,800 percent, and in engineering by 5,600 percent.[4]

In the United States today more than half of the students in colleges and universities are women. This is up substantially from a generation ago.[5] In the United States, Canada, Japan, and the United Kingdom, there were more women enrolled in colleges and universities in the 1980s than there were in the 1960s or the 1970s. The most dramatic change occurred in Canada. In twenty years, from 1965 to 1985, the number of women grew from 33 percent of enrollment in colleges and universities to 55 percent.[6] This is a larger gain than that made in the United States. During the same period women's enrollment in U.S. colleges and universities rose from 39 percent to 51 percent.

We do not have trend information for Venezuela and Brazil, but we do have some data. In 1970 in Venezuela, two out of five college students were female.

31

Figure 3.2

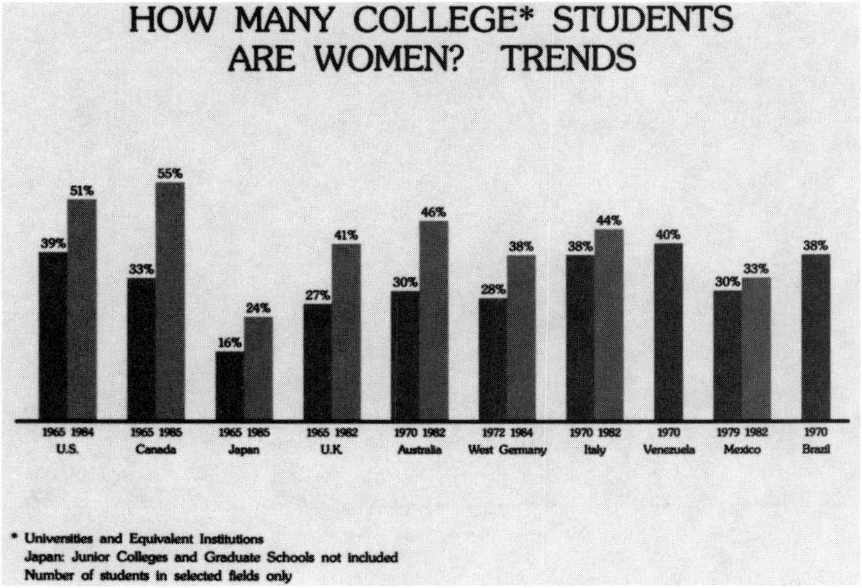
HOW MANY COLLEGE* STUDENTS ARE WOMEN? TRENDS
39%
51%
33%
55%
16%
24%
27%
41%
30%
46%
28%
38%
38%
44%
40%
30%
33%
38%
1965 1984
U.S.
1965 1985
Canada
1965 1985
Japan
1965 1982
U.K.
1970 1982
Australia
1972 1984
West Germany
1970 1982
Italy
1970
Venezuela
1979 1982
Mexico
1970
Brazil
* Universities and Equivalent Institutions
Japan: Junior Colleges and Graduate Schools not included
Number of students in selected fields only

In Brazil in 1970 the proportion was just under two out of five. This relatively high participation of Latin American women in higher education may be the reason for their relatively high participation in the work force. The absolute level of women university graduates is low in both countries, perhaps because relatively few people there go to college. In 1970, however, at least two out of five of those seeking higher education were women.[8]

Changing Aspirations

Women's increased involvement in higher education may be another facet of their desire to be involved in the larger world. Whereas the traditional notion was that a woman's occupational goal in life was to become a wife and mother, women, particularly younger women, now seek to combine marriage, career, and children.

United States

In Barbara Everitt Bryant's landmark study for the National Commission on the Observance of International Women's Year, she asked women of all ages what they thought was the ideal life style for a woman: to be mainly a homemaker; to stay home while children are young but combine work and home-making at other times in their lives; to combine job or career and children throughout; or, to focus on a job or a career.

The majority of women endorsed the sequential pattern: staying home when children are young and returning to work later. The younger the woman, the more likely she is to "want it all," although twice as many opted for the sequential pattern than wanted to do it all at once. The surprise was that among women over sixty-five years old, many of whom have no doubt lived in a traditional life style, only 41 percent chose the homemaker role. Half of the older women endorsed a combination of work and family life. An equal number chose the sequential pattern and the simultaneous pattern, that women should continue to work while raising their families.[9]

In the 1970s and 1980s, the Roper Organization conducted the American Women's Opinion Poll on behalf of Virginia Slims. The polls reflect the changes in women's attitudes and aspirations in a relatively brief time. In 1974, just over half of all women said that the ideal life for a woman was to combine marriage, career, and children. In 1985, two out of three women expressed this aspiration. Conversely, back in 1974, almost two out of five women endorsed the traditional role of nonworking wife and mother. By 1985, only one in four women aspired to the traditional role. A small percentage of women in each year would like to be married and have careers but not children. Another small percentage is committed to careers but rejects the idea of marriage and children.

If the career-oriented women are combined with those who want to "have it all," today seven in ten women prefer to be in the work force, with or without families. This aspiration is even more intense among young women between eighteen and twenty-nine and those with college educations. Four out of five college-educated women and young women aspire to careers with or without marriage and family, compared to seven in ten among all women.

Although the majority of women believe that the ideal life style is to combine marriage, family, and career, Roper interviewers asked them to hypothesize an "either-or" choice: either staying home and taking care of a house and family or working outside the home. In 1974, the respondents favored homemaking: three out of five women said they would prefer to stay at home and only one in three preferred a job. In 1985, a bare majority, 51 percent, voted for work; 45 percent said they would rather stay at home.

A clearer picture of women's aspirations emerges when we consider the employment status of women. Seven in ten of those who work full time say they would prefer to work than stay at home. Part-time workers favor work, but they are closer in their opinions for and against working or staying home. Fifty-four percent of them endorse going to work, and 46 percent vote to stay home and care for house and family. Another sign of women's changing aspirations are the

choices of women who are not currently working. Although more of them endorse the homemaker role than not, a surprising two out of five say they would
rather have a job than stay home and keep house.[10]

Australia

Only one in four Australian homemakers would prefer to spend her time as a
full-time homemaker. The others prefer a variety of patterns. The most popular
is part-time work along with family responsibilities. One in five yearns for a
full-time job, and one in eight would like to do paid work in her home—another way of juggling work and responsibility to the family.

Although not all housewives say they want to go to work, among those who
do only 12 percent would choose their current occupation of running a home
full-time, if given a choice. "This seems . . . to be a surprising and dramatic
finding: one that would suggest that women at home experience considerable
dissatisfaction with the full-time role of raising young children and running a
home. . . . They referred to the considerable loss of freedom and control over
their lives, the financial dependence on their husbands, the dramatic restric-
tions on their movements and on fulfilling their own ambitions and needs. The
story they tell is one of continuous compromise . . . to children, to spouse." One
frustrated young housewife described the narrowing horizons of her world:
"When you get married, people always expect you to have children. People
don't say 'are you prepared to give up your job and give up your social life with
your husband and have a family?' I don't think the majority of people realize
the implications of it."[11]

Canada

Approximately half of all women surveyed in Canada agree with the statement
that "a job outside the home keeps a woman feeling younger, happier, and more
with today's world." Not surprisingly, working women are far more likely to
agree with this assessment of the benefits of working. However, two out of five
full-time homemakers feel this way as well. Again, this is a clue that some
women who are currently living a traditional life have aspirations to enter or
reenter the work force.[12]

Great Britain

Although a certain proportion of full-time housewives in Great Britain say they
plan to go back to work "sometime," their aspirations are fairly limited. They
seem quite ambivalent about the pull between work and home. Some say that
if given a choice, they would revel in the life of a nonworking homemaker. A
few do express frustration with the somewhat limited horizons of their present
lives. A young homemaker said, "I feel I'm wasted now. I feel there is some-

thing else I should be doing instead of just being at home all day. I'm not contributing anything to the outside world really."

Others realize that the need for them at home changes as their children spend more and more time at school. Within this context they begin to see going to work as a way to expand their horizons: "It has come to the point where my children are grown up. My daughter is not home until five. It's a long day. It can get boring. They don't need you so much now."[13]

Some of them yearn for a niche of their own outside their roles as wives and mothers. One young mother said, "I wouldn't like to think I had done nothing in my life except clean floors and raise two children. I'd like to think I had reared them properly and they turned out to be well-balanced citizens. I owe them that. But apart from that, I'd like to think I've got something when they're grown and leave the nest, something that's mine." Another housewife yearns for "more": "I'm satisfied, but you want more. I'd like a job that filled in. I'd like Emma to have friends around, not just me and my mother. So I'll put her into nursery and get a little job. It will add money and interest."[14]

Some of the English housewives who want to work say, frankly, that money is their motivation. As one said, "My husband has provided everything. I suppose it would be nice to say that I've helped here as well. He's worked very hard. It would be nice to buy him something occasionally and the children." Another equated lack of money with helplessness: "Sometimes I feel helpless moneywise. I wish I could help out. I'd feel more useful."

A few of these women seek the social stimulation that comes with going to work: "Sometimes the home can get on top of you. You need your own independence. Something to look forward to and someone different to talk to." Others feel that work would give them a sense of personal growth: "Personal growth—it would keep your mind alive . . . make you more interesting, not stagnating." One saw work as a path to personal achievement: "It's something you can do and achieve yourself."[15]

Some housewives who say they have no desire to work did seem wistful for lost opportunities: "Just occasionally their words are tinged with regret." One woman said, "I haven't worked since I was eighteen. Not since the day I got married. My husband believes a woman's place is in the home. His mother was never there to look after him. I like my home, but I think I've missed out. I would have liked a career and stayed at work. After twenty-five years I feel I haven't achieved anything. I wouldn't have a family if I lived my life again."[16]

Japan

By contrast, the Japanese housewives who say they would like to work seem far less conflicted than the English ones in their view of work and full-time homemaking. Although money is certainly a consideration, Japanese women seem to see it as a symbol of value as well as a way for them to indulge themselves in interests or hobbies they would not expect their husbands to support. One young Japanese woman explained the symbolic meaning of earning money: "If I start to work I will get some result in monetary form. That is a significant factor. I think earning money makes you feel more fulfilled, more complete . . . a feeling you get from being part of society."[17]

Some of the Japanese housewives want to earn money so that they can indulge in their own interests and hobbies without imposing on their husbands: "I may be old fashioned, but I really don't believe that half of my husband's salary is mine. Any money that I earn myself is money that I can use without asking him, so I can use it as I see fit. I can use it for traveling or something else. Things that would be good experiences for me." Another explained her desire for some money of her own: "Any money that I earn from working will be my own. I can use it to buy anything that I like or to do anything that I want. I don't feel so comfortable about using my husband's money for things like that. If it's money that I've earned myself, I can just go right ahead."[18]

A number of them express a desire to participate in the larger world. They aspire to an identity of their own beyond that of wife and mother. They seek involvement: "There's no stimulation in just doing housework or child care. If you are at home all the time you end up clinging to the security of those four walls. Having something else is stimulating. I don't want to see just my husband and children. I want to meet all kinds of people and get involved." They seek broader horizons: "The time will come when my children won't need me anymore. I'm afraid of being left behind and isolated from society. People have more vitality if they have some sort of goal to work toward. When you don't work, your range of conversation is limited and you feel cut off from society at large." Some also seek self-realization: "I feel that I want to get involved in society. Get out there. It would be a good opportunity for me to learn about things in the everyday world. And besides, the working mothers I see look so alive. I feel that working would give me a chance to use the energy that has been bottled up in me."[19]

Europe

In the European countries, overall, a substantial proportion of women who do not currently work regret that they are not in paid employment. This is particularly true of women between twenty-five and thirty-nine and all those between forty and fifty-four. Those women who say they regret not working cite family responsibilities as the major reason. They also cite the difficulty of getting a job in the present economic climate. To a lesser degree, some report that their husbands prefer them to stay at home.[20]

Why Women Work

Italy

The housewives in Italy who say they would like to work or return to work outside the home consider work an opportunity for social interaction with other people and personal enrichment and development. They acknowledge that the money earned by working would enable them to improve the family's standard of living as well as giving them a certain amount of economic independence. They say that going to work stimulates a woman to take greater care of herself and her appearance. They feel that work would fill their days in a meaningful way and give them a greater sense of purpose.[21]

They think work makes women more dynamic and active; it stimulates them to develop their abilities at home as well as at work; and it gives them the opportunity of greater personal fulfillment. They believe that if they go to work they will be held in greater esteem in their own families, as well as by the people in their social circle. They see work in positive terms, believing it will have a beneficial effect on their children by encouraging them to become more responsible and more independent.

Some of the Italian housewives have worked in the past and had relatively satisfying work experiences. These women define themselves as "housewives but not by choice." They find their present situation as full-time homemakers frustrating. They consider housework generally unrewarding, repetitive, and alienating. They feel economically dependent on their husbands, unfulfilled, and without much occasion for social contact. Therefore, they have no opportunity to let themselves go, to be more active, more open and culturally alive.[22]

On the other hand, some of the housewives are satisfied with their present roles in life. They are happy to be able to follow their children's development, and enjoy having more time to pursue their personal interests and hobbies as well as social activities. They don't resent housework. Actually, they consider certain aspects of homemaking to be a source of gratification. They love their homes and appreciate keeping their houses up to their personal standards of cleanliness and order.[23]

Brazil

Housewives in Brazil who say they would like to go to work point out that the economic situation is critical, and that everything is more expensive today. Therefore, they think it will be necessary for them to work. They also appreciate the financial and personal independence that comes with working. To a lesser degree, they feel that the additional income will help improve the family's economic situation. They also say they want to work because they desire better things for their children. Some say they would like to go to work because of the personal satisfaction it will bring.[24]

37

Mexico

Housewives in Mexico who want to go to work say the second paycheck will help them improve their family's standard of living. They also say they want to work because of the difficult economic situation and the higher prices today. They perceive the emotional and psychic benefits of working in a more limited way. Some of them report that they would like to work because of the personal satisfaction they anticipate. They look forward to the social contacts and the financial and personal independence that comes with earning a paycheck.[25]

Venezuela

Housewives in Venezuela who want to work hope to improve their families' standard of living. They also cite the difficult economic situation. Others want the stimulation of meeting and dealing with other people, and, to a lesser extent, they look forward to the opportunity to practice a profession.[26]

Implications for the Future

The obvious question is, Will it continue? It is clear that college-educated women are most likely to seek careers and that younger women are far more likely than women over fifty to think of working as a natural part of their lives. But the aspirations expressed by nonworking homemakers suggest that some women currently living a traditional life want to break out of that pattern.

Will the trend continue? I leave it to the reader to judge. I believe that women's increasing participation in education is a strong indication that they will continue to seek participation in the work force. I also believe that the yearning of young wives to participate in the broader society will be reflected in their entry or reentry into the world of work. I believe that this trend is not a temporary aberration, but a forerunner of a redefinition of women's role in society. This, in turn, means that marketers will have to rethink their assumptions about the nature of the women's market.

four

Why Women Don't Work

NOT all women share the aspiration for work or a career. Approximately three out of five working women on three continents say they would continue to work even if they received the same amount of money they earned on their jobs.[1] Two in five working women, however, say they would stop working if they had the choice. Even though sizable proportions of full-time homemakers would like to go to work someday, sizable proportions of them have no desire to work outside the home. Despite the strong trend toward women's larger participation in the work force, particularly among younger and better-educated women, there is a segment of women who are not part of that trend.

There seem to be several reasons why women don't work or don't care to work. To varying degrees, these reasons reflect their perceptions that women's proper role is caring for the household and the children. Some report that their husbands do not allow them to work or can afford for them to stay at home. Others do not go to work for reasons of health or age. These women have taken themselves out of the mainstream.

Canada

In Canada, the major reason housewives don't work is that they enjoy caring for their children. A sizable proportion of housewives in that country hope to enter the work force sometime in the future, but for the present the children in their households keep them from seeking work. Interestingly, Canadian housewives who prefer to stay at home are less likely to report that children are the reason they don't wish to work.

Although motherhood is the dominant reason why Canadian housewives don't work, husbands are also a factor. Some women choose to remain at home because their husbands can afford to have them stay home or, to a lesser extent, because their husbands will not allow them to work. Husbands' attitudes are far more important to the housewives who have chosen not to work than to those who hope to do so.

The home is another reason why some nonworking housewives don't want to work. About one in ten says she enjoys being at home and is kept busy. Housewives who don't wish to work enjoy life at home more than those who do want to work. The idea that a woman's place is in the home is relatively rare among nonworking Canadian housewives, but it is slightly more common among those who don't want to work.

Another consideration is that a substantial number of Canadian housewives have been laid off. This is reported most frequently by those who plan to reenter the work force. Clearly this might be a temporary condition. On the other hand, those who have no intention of going to work are more likely to say they are too old or not well enough. To a lesser extent, both types of housewives say they lack sufficient education to enable them to find the kind of work they would like.

The young housewives who say, "I enjoy being a mother," also mention child-related problems that keep them out of the work force. Some are concerned about the cost of babysitters, others about their skills. Some don't want to leave their children with sitters at all and prefer to handle all parental duties themselves.[2]

Japan

Housewives in Japan who are not interested in working now or in the future say they are not attracted to the idea of work. They feel that working would entail too many sacrifices, and they don't see any personal advantage in doing so. Basically, these women are satisfied with their status as full-time homemakers. The perceived disadvantages are a reflection of their view of their role as a traditional mother and housewife.

Some see their own personal values bound up with and symbolized by housework: "Some of them felt that their value to the family was as a person doing housework and that by working they would be unable to do housework, which they viewed as their value to their family." Some say that if they went to work, they would not be able to do the housework properly and that their husbands and children would suffer as a result. Others say that if they went to work they wouldn't be able to care for their children properly.[3]

Although these women have no desire to work themselves, some recognize that other women enjoy working: "They expressed envy of women who did not work solely for the sake of money but enjoyed working or who lived for their jobs." Some also thought that working mothers who enjoy their work are good examples for their children: "Children really look at their mothers carefully. They can see that working is not easy. I envy women who can show that aspect of it to their children."

These Japanese housewives could think of no job about which they could feel so enthusiastic, and did not think it would be possible for them to find such work at this point in their lives. They were either resigned or thought they were happier in their present lives than they would be if they worked: "I didn't have any special skills. If I had, things might have been different. But there really wasn't any work I could do that I considered devoting my whole life to."[4]

Australia

As we saw earlier, a sizable proportion of Australian housewives would like to go to work sometime in the future. These women cite their children as the major reason they are not currently in the work force. Indeed children are central to the aspects of life they enjoy and the problems they anticipate if they should return to work. Unlike housewives who say they have no desire to work, these women are far more likely to say they are out of the work force because "the children need me at home full time." They are far more likely to say that being at home "gives me the opportunity to give myself to my family." They view child care as a major problem they would encounter if they began working full time.

On the other hand, the Australian housewives who prefer to stay at home focus more on the home and their personal interests than on the family and children. These women enjoy the flexibility and autonomy of their lives. Homemaking gives them the chance to do what they like when they want to, freedom from a fixed routine, and the feeling of "being my own boss." Life as a full-time homemaker gives them time to spend on their own interests and hobbies and time to work on the house and garden. Although they report "the opportunity to give myself to my family" as a reason for not working, this is less important to them than the general freedom they enjoy in their way of life.[5]

Great Britain

In Great Britain full-time homemakers who prefer to stay at home perceive their roles as housewives as very demanding, both physically and emotionally. Many of them had worked before and are delighted to be out of the work force: "It was terrific to know you could beat a man in his field. . . . It was self-satisfaction. I'm in a second marriage and maybe I have a different attitude. If a man can't afford a wife, he shouldn't take one. In my previous marriage I had to work. Now I don't." Another said, "The idea of going back to work in an office is anathema."[6]

Those with young children feel that their responsibilites as mothers come first, and this is their main justification for not going to work: "You can't take on the responsibility of another life and then just say, 'Well, too bad I'm missing this and that and the other and I want to go back to work.'" Some of them recall that they had working mothers, and they don't want to deprive their children of the security of having a mother at home all the time: "My mother was never there. Every day we came home from school and she wasn't there. I hated that. I'll never forget that. The ideal is to be at home with the children."[7]

As their children get older, they perceive their responsibilities differently, but they still feel needed at home: "As they come into teenage years, you're needed more. They have pressures. They need someone to talk to. Someone who is sane and stable. They're more independent but mentally they need you more for security and stability. As teenagers they need *you*. It's time consuming." Another said, "Even with children at school, they have days at home and different half terms. You have to visit the school. If you have a job, what comes first? And if I had a job and was being paid that would come first, and you would not visit the school or whatever. The children would suffer then. They take second place. You feel guilty." Another said, "I swapped my job for another—to bring up a child. My job, now that he is older, is to keep the house running. To do the various jobs in the house."[8]

Aside from meeting their perceived responsibilities, they appreciate the flexibility of the homemaker's schedule: "You have a little freedom, not having to rush up to town commuting. There's less pressure. You do things in your own time." Another said, "Now I have a little time to fit in things I like to do." A few of them describe the pleasure and satisfaction they get from their roles as full-time homemakers: "I get most satisfaction from my family and friends. Also, doing the things I want to do and haven't had time to do before." A woman said, "The fun side of it is enjoyable. I don't get down on the floor and play games, but I laugh a lot of the time."[9]

Some of the British housewives were uncomfortable about the term *housewife*. They feel that society projects a negative image of the full-time homemaker. At the same time, they are critical of women who work because they want to, and are quite negative about career women: "I feel slightly embarrassed because it's quite demanding being a housewife. It's a natural thing to be when you have children at home, but somehow you're made to think you're not really working." Another explained, "You feel as if people are going to write you off. I always hesitate when writing it [housewife] or whether to put 'home manager.'"

They see career women as hard, determined, and selfish: "She's selling herself to get to the top of her job. One housewife said, "I feel sorry for the ones that do work. They're missing out in their life. There is a certain hardness about them and their ability to discount their children. I think children should come first."[10]

Italy

Full-time homemakers in Italy who prefer to stay at home see in their situation a choice that allows them to fulfill their aspirations on both a social and emotional level. They believe that going to work outside the home would not allow them to follow their children's needs in a satisfying way. If they went to work, it would be incompatible with the needs of their families, and it could harm their relationship with their husbands. Moreover, if they worked, they would take on a double workload, for they assume they would continue their responsibilities in the house as well. They estimate that this would double their stress. They believe that if they worked, their time would be so constricted that they wouldn't have the flexibility to pursue their personal interests as well as their social lives.[11]

It is possible that these full-time homemakers feel negatively about work because of their limited job opportunities. They don't believe that they would find satisfying work if they should seek it. Therefore, when they consider the jobs they could obtain, they conclude that work outside the home would be just as repetitive and monotonous as housework. They see the role of the housewife as a part-time job that gives them the independence to function at their own pace. In turn, this gives them the "space" for the more creative and gratifying activities they believe any well-balanced woman with energy can create for herself.

Italian housewives who choose to stay at home acknowledge that women who work outside the home may enjoy greater esteem from members of their families and may also have more diversified social lives because of the contacts they make at work in addition to more economic independence. But the full-time homemakers don't believe that the benefits of working compensate for the difficulties of balancing work and family responsibilities, which would lead them to feel guilty toward their children and sometimes their husbands. They also think that working mothers must endure stress and a lack of freedom. They acknowledge that there are rare cases in which the position reached by a working woman gives her major satisfaction on a professional level and, therefore, possibly high economic benefits, but they don't personally aspire to this level of achievement.[12]

Brazil

The housewives in Brazil who don't work and don't wish to work are clearly oriented toward the traditional definition of the role of women: they believe a woman's place is in the home and only the mother should care for her children. In addition, many of them say they don't need to work, and they feel it is much more necessary for them to be at home to meet their home responsibilities than to work. They go on to say that their husbands and children don't want them to work. They point out that it would be difficult to find a replacement for themselves; they want to dedicate themselves to their children and their homes.

The only nontraditional reasons they give for not going to work are age (they are too old) or health. In addition, their comments lack the defensiveness of housewives in Great Britain and the guilt of Italian housewives. Brazilian homemakers have a clear sense of their own mission and are at peace with it.[13]

Mexico

Full-time homemakers in Mexico who don't work and don't plan to work focus less on their role when explaining why they don't work. Their major reason is that there is simply no replacement help available for the care of their families or homes. To a lesser extent, they say their husbands and children don't want them to work, they don't need to work, and it is necessary for them to be at home.

Besides these reasons, a substantial number have never worked before, and don't plan to do so now. They also cite their age and health as barriers to entering the work force. A small number have worked before and feel it's time for a rest.[14]

Venezuela

In Venezuela nonworking housewives who don't plan to enter the work force say they don't need to work. They feel it is far more important for them to be at home to cope with the needs of their families and husbands. To a lesser extent, they want to dedicate themselves to their children and their homes. They point out, realistically, that there is no one to replace them in meeting the needs of their households. Again, they articulate the traditional view that a woman's place is in the home. A proportion of them also cite their age or health as factors keeping them out of the work force. A small number have never worked before, and have no intention of starting now.[15]

Clearly, not all women are part of the quiet revolution. Approximately two out of three working women are committed to work even if they could afford to stay at home, and some housewives hope to enter or reenter the work force, but other housewives have no desire to go back to work. Some reject work because of limitations of education and health. Others simply don't want to work. These full-time homemakers subscribe to the traditional definitions of men and women. They believe that it is a man's place to support the family and a woman's place to stay at home and care for her husband and children.

II

Women, Work, and Family

Chapter Five, "Attitudes toward the Role of Women," examines the attitudes of women toward their roles as wives and mothers. In order to understand the dynamics of the women's market in different parts of the world, marketers need to consider how all women, both full-time homemakers and working women, feel about their roles. Traditionally, the role of wife and mother was a woman's only goal. Therefore, how women feel about children and marriage is essential to understanding women's perceptions of their roles in life. In order to identify cultural differences among women, Chapter Five examines the attitudes of women country by country. Where appropriate I will comment on the attitudes of working women and housewives. Later chapters will analyze how specific segments of women within a country feel about the role of women.

Chapter Six, "The Role of the Life Cycle," discusses how to keep a realistic perspective on the women's market in each country. Whether or not a woman is married and has children defines her place in the life cycle, determining her needs as a consumer. Clearly, married women, unmarried women, and those who have children have different life styles and therefore different patterns as consumers. The life-cycle framework adds a discriminating dimension to analyses of the consumer behavior of working women and housewives.

Chapter Seven, "The Dynamics of the Life Cycle," considers the life cycle as a dynamic process. Just as women's consumer needs change as they move from one stage to another, their participation in and attitudes toward work also change. There is a discontinuity in the working lives of many women. During the child-rearing years many women drop out of the work force or seek part-

---

time work. The work patterns of unmarried women and childless wives are different from those of young mothers.

Chapter Eight, "Work and Family," discusses how a wife's work affects her children and husband. Some child-oriented issues are whether the children of working mothers are well adjusted, or whether a woman should give up her job if it inconveniences her family. Some of the husband-related issues are whether working women feel pressure to stay at home, whether husbands believe that wives should go to work, how husbands would feel if their wives earned more than they did, and whether a husband or a wife should leave a job if the spouse is relocated.

The investigations lead to several conclusions and recommendations.

Action Implications

1. I recommend that marketers build the life-cycle framework into marketing analysis. Past studies of the marketplace can be reanalyzed from this perspective by creating a simple cross-tabulation of marital status and presence of children. This results in the four life-cycle groups: married with children, childless wives, unmarried with no children, and single mothers. This framework, in turn, should be extended to compare working women and housewives at each stage of the life cycle.

2. The precise size of each life-cycle segment can be defined from census data or government statistics. The data are available for most of the countries studied. However, these data were not available for West Germany or the three Latin American countries. In West Germany the life-cycle profile was obtained from a survey sample of the Trendmonitor conducted by Basisresearch. In Brazil, Mexico, and Venezuela, the consumer studies did not project to the total population, and it was therefore not possible to define the life-cycle profiles of women in those countries. Finally, the Italian census reports the marital status of women but not the number of children. The presence of children is reported on a household basis only. Therefore, it is not possible to define the life-cycle profile of Italian women.

I urge marketers in these countries to request that marital status and presence of children be included in future surveys of the population and the information be made available in a form that would enable marketers to cross-tabulate the life-cycle profiles of women by their occupational status.

five

Attitudes toward the Role of Women

I N order to understand the dynamics of the women's market in different parts of the world, we need to consider how all women, whether they are full-time homemakers or working women, feel about the basic role of women. Traditionally, the role of wife and mother was seen as a woman's destiny and her only career choice. Many men and women in all parts of the world still subscribe to this traditional view. The role of women has usually been defined in terms of marriage and children. The traditional assumption is that raising a family is a major reason for marrying and that children are essential to a happy marriage. Let us examine how women feel about children.

The Importance of Children

Latin America

Men and women in the three Latin American countries are strongly committed to children. Overwhelming proportions of men and women in Brazil, Mexico, and Venezuela endorse the concept that "having a child is an experience every couple should have."[1]

Australia

While just over half of the women (53 percent) agree that "all women should experience having a child," their endorsement of motherhood is far less intense than that of men and women in Latin America. A sizable proportion of Australian women disagree. Thirty percent of Australian women, both working women and housewives, reject the notion that all women should experience motherhood.[2]

Table 5.1
Having a Child Is an Experience
Every Couple Should Have

	Women %	Men %
Agree		
Brazil	92	93
Mexico	83	82
Venezuela	95	94

Source: "Target: Latin America," J. Walter Thompson Latin America, 1986.

Europe

In Europe men and women were asked whether they think that a woman has to have children in order to be fulfilled, or whether children are not necessary.

Italy

Italians of both genders are most likely to agree that a woman needs children in order to be fulfilled. But, Italian men are more enthusiastic than Italian women about this notion. Fifty-three percent of Italian men believe that a child is necessary to a woman's fulfillment; 40 percent disagree. Forty-nine percent of Italian women believe that children are not necessary to a woman's personal fulfillment; 46 percent say a woman needs children in order to be fulfilled.[3]

West Germany

Men and women in West Germany are more likely to believe children are not necessary to a woman's fulfillment. Thirty percent of women and 29 percent of men in Germany say that having a child is necessary for a woman to be fulfilled. On the other hand, exactly half of all women and 44 percent of the men say that children are not necessary for a woman's fulfillment.[4]

Great Britain

Men and women in Great Britain place an even lower priority on children. Only 14 percent of the women believe that a woman has to have children in order to be fulfilled; an overwhelming 84 percent say that children are not necessary for a woman's personal fulfillment. Twenty-four percent of men in Great Britain believe that having children is necessary to a woman's fulfillment; 67 percent say that children are not necessary.[5]

Attitudes toward the Role of Women

Canada

In Canada two out of three women (64 percent) believe that a woman can have a satisfactory life without children; just 17 percent say that a woman's life could not be satisfactory if she does not have children.[6]

The Relationship between Children and Marriage

In contrast to how men and women rate the importance of children for a woman's personal fulfillment or experience, a slightly different picture emerges when children are considered in the context of marriage. People in the three European countries are far more likely to say that having children is a very important element in a happy marriage than they are to believe that a woman needs children in order to be fulfilled.[7]

Italy

Italians are most consistent on the issue of children and marriage. The same percentage of Italian men (53 percent) who believe that having children is a very important element in a happy marriage also believe that women need children in order to be fulfilled. On the other hand, more Italian women think children are important to a marriage (56 percent) than think children are necessary for a woman's personal fulfillment.[8]

Great Britain

Although men and women in Great Britain are least likely to say that a woman needs children in order to be fulfilled personally, they believe strongly that children are important to a happy marriage. British men are more likely to stress the importance of children to a happy marriage than are men in Italy or Germany. Fifty-eight percent of British men feel this way. More than half of British women (52 percent) say that having children is a very important element in a happy marriage even though only 14 percent believe children are necessary for a woman's personal fulfillment.[9]

Germany

Forty-three percent of German women and 40 percent of German men say that having children is very important to the success of a marriage (table 5.2).[10]

Canada

Women in Canada are less likely than women in Europe to consider children essential to marriage. Forty-seven percent of Canadian women say that a mar-

Table 5.2
Attitudes of European Men and Women toward Children

	Women			Men		
	Italy %	*West Germany* %	*Great Britain* %	*Italy* %	*West Germany* %	*Great Britain* %
A woman needs children in order to be fulfilled	46	30	14	53	29	24
Having children is a very important element in a happy marriage	53	43	52	56	40	58

Source: Gallup Report on European Values, 1987.

riage can be complete without children; while just 36 percent think that a marriage would not be complete without children. Canadian women are particularly unlikely to consider continuing an unhappy marriage for the sake of children. Just under three out of four Canadian women say that if a marriage is unhappy a couple should not stay together because of the children.[11]

United States

In the United States large majorities of both men and women believe that a childless marriage can be happy. Eighty-one percent of women and 76 percent of men believe that a childless couple can have a happy marriage. Only 15 percent of women and 19 percent of men think that a marriage without children cannot be happy. Despite these figures, having children is a key reason why many get married. While the primary motivations for marriage in America are romantic, being in love, or wanting to be with a particular person, having children has ranked third among reasons for getting married. The concept that men and women are motivated to get married in order to have children has consistently ranked in third place in trend studies conducted since 1974.

Further evidence that American men and women believe that children are not essential to marriage comes from the priority that people place on parenthood as an element in a good marriage. Among thirteen items that might contribute to a good marriage, respondents ranked having children twelfth. Being in love is considered to be the number-one element in a good marriage by 91

Table 5.3
Men Prefer That Women Do Not Go to Work
and Dedicate Themselves to the Home

	Women %	*Men* %
Agree		
Brazil	75	72
Mexico	63	57
Venezuela	62	59

Source: "Target Latin America," J. Walter Thompson Latin America, 1986.

percent of women and 89 percent of men. By contrast, 46 percent of women and 45 percent of men believe that having children contributes to a good marriage.[12]

Italy

In Italy only 22 percent of women believe that children and motherhood is a fundamental experience for women. However, when they think of the elements that make for a happy marriage, they are three times as likely to say that reciprocal love (68 percent) and reciprocal esteem (64 percent) between a man and a woman make for a happy marriage. According to an analyst, "psychologically the core of the family no longer lies in the parental ties or in the relationships with children but actually in the relationship of the couple."[13]

The Roles of Men and Women

The traditional definition of marriage is that the husband works to support the family and the wife stays home and takes care of the children.

Latin America

Not surprisingly, this traditional view is most likely to be endorsed by consumers in the three Latin American countries. There, women are slightly more likely than men to think that men prefer women to stay home (table 5.3).[14]

However, when this issue is rephrased in financial terms, women are less likely to agree that maintaining the family economically is mainly the responsibility of the man (table 5.4).[15]

Japan

Endorsement of the traditional roles for men and for women is moderate. Women in Japan are almost evenly split on whether a man's place is at work

Table 5.4
Maintaining the Family Is Mainly
the Responsibility of the Man

	Women %	*Men* %
Agree		
Brazil	54	76
Mexico	50	62
Venezuela	46	59

Source: "Target Latin America," J. Walter Thompson Latin America, 1986.

and a woman's place is at home. Two out of five of all women, both working women and housewives, agree with the traditional view. On the other hand, almost as many (39 percent) disagree. One in five Japanese women takes no position on the question.[16]

West Germany

Forty-five percent of German women, both homemakers and working women, subscribe to the traditional view that "a wife should devote herself entirely to her husband and children because that is her job." Not surprisingly, full-time homemakers are more likely than working women to take this point of view. Nonetheless, fewer than half of the homemakers agree with this statement. Again, only one in three German women says that a man should have the last word in important decisions: higher proportions of homemakers than working women express this deferential attitude toward men. It should be noted, however, that only two in five homemakers feel this way, and one in three working women is willing to leave the last word to the men in their lives.[17]

United States

At the other end of the scale, in the United States, *traditional marriage* is defined as one in which the husband assumes the responsibility of providing for the family and the wife runs the house and takes care of the children. In 1974, half of all women and just under half of all men endorsed this point of view. In 1985, only 37 percent of all women and 43 percent of men agreed with the notion of a traditional marriage. Conversely, *partnership marriage* is defined as one in which the husband and wife share responsibilities: both husband and wife go to work and both husband and wife share responsibilities for housekeeping and child care. Men are more likely than women to endorse traditional

Table 5.5

Attitudes of American Men and Women toward
Traditional Marriage vs. Partnership Marriage

	Women		*Men*	
	1974	*1985*	*1974*	*1985*
	%	%	%	%
Endorse				
Traditional marriage	50	37	48	43
Partnership marriage	46	57	44	50

Source: The Roper Organization, Inc., The 1985 Virginia Slims American Women's Opinion Poll.

marriage, but there has been a real shift in opinion among both sexes. Even though sizable minorities of men and women still support the traditional view of marriage, more now favor a marriage in which both husband and wife earn money and share household responsibilities. Women are more enthusiastic than men about the partnership approach to marriage (table 5.5).[18]

Europe

In Europe in a 1983 survey, men and women were given three choices: *traditional marriage* where the husband works and the wife runs the home; *partnership marriage,* in which husband and wife have equal job, housework, and child-care responsibilities; and a *transitional marriage,* in which both work, but the wife has a less-demanding job and does more housework and child care.[19]

Italy

Women in Italy are most likely to endorse the partnership marriage, and Italian men equally support the traditional and partnership marriages.[20]

West Germany

Women in West Germany are least likely to endorse partnership marriage, and are more likely to favor the traditional marriage. German men favor the transitional marriage over the traditional or partnership marriage.[21]

United Kingdom

British women are more likely to choose the transitional form but British men are more in favor of partnership marriage than British women. The traditional marriage was the least-favored choice for both women and men (table 5.6).[22]

Table 5.6
Europe: Traditional vs. Partnership Marriage
Best Division of Roles in the Family

	Women			Men		
	Italy %	*United Kingdom* %	*West Germany* %	*Italy* %	*United Kingdom* %	*West Germany* %
Traditional	24	23	32	34	24	28
Transitional	27	39	28	30	32	41
Partnership	47	35	28	34	40	22

Source: Commission of the European Communities, "European Men and Women 1983."

Working women in the three European countries are far more likely than nonworking women to choose a partnership marriage, and nonworking women are more likely to choose the traditional marriage.[23] More working women in Italy choose the partnership marriage than British or German women. They are echoed in this by their nonworking counterparts. More nonworking women in Italy choose partnership marriage than British or German nonworking women.[24]

West Germany

The greatest contrast between working and nonworking women occurs in West Germany. Working women strongly favor partnership marriage over the traditional form, and nonworking women are twice as likely to vote for traditional marriage over partnership marriage. Only 28 percent of working and nonworking women favor a transitional marriage.[25]

United Kingdom

Working women in Great Britain are far less likely than their nonworking counterparts to endorse traditional marriage. Unlike employed women in the other two countries, however, they more often choose transitional marriage. Nonworking women in England are more evenly divided in their choices. Slightly more of them select partnership marriage and the transitional form than the traditional one (table 5.7).[26]

Canada

Canadian women are not very supportive of the traditional definition of the role of women. Only 22 percent of all Canadian women, both homemakers and

Table 5.7
Europe: Traditional vs. Partnership Marriage
Best Division of Roles in the Family

	Working Women			Nonworking Women		
	Italy %	United Kingdom %	West Germany %	Italy %	United Kingdom %	West Germany %
Traditional	10	9	5	31	31	41
Transitional	28	50	28	26	32	28
Partnership	60	37	53	41	34	20

Source: Commission of the European Communities, "European Men And Women 1983."

working women, believe that "a woman's place is in the home," compared to 59 percent who disagree with this point of view. On the other hand, although women in Canada reject the traditional role of women, they are emotionally committed to the care of their families. Two out of three say that a woman's most important task in life is to take care of her family. Only one in five disagrees. Three out of four say that being a housewife can be just as satisfying as working outside the home. Approximately one in ten disagrees. Canadian women do not subscribe to the traditional definition of women's role, but they support the traditional values of family and home. Consistent with this is the finding that 33 percent of Canadian women believe that a married man's first responsibility should be his job, and 54 percent disagree. Finally, 35 percent say that "the man should be the head of the family" and 51 percent disagree with this definition of a man's role.[27]

Australia
Three out of four Australian women, both homemakers and working women, believe that husbands and wives should share in earning a living, and fewer than one in four believes that "a woman's only responsibility is to her home and family." In spite of this dramatic endorsement of partnership marriage, however, they are less likely to expect their husbands to agree. Approximately two out of five say that husbands would be happier if women didn't work.[28]

A Redefinition of Marriage
The varying attitudes toward traditional and partnership marriage among women in different parts of the world raise the question of whether women think marriage is essential or necessary.

Canada

The most startling finding comes from Canada: Canadian women don't reject marriage per se, but they appear to believe that it is not absolutely necessary. Eighty-six percent agree with the statement that "a single woman can have a satisfying and enjoyable life."[29]

United States

American women are not as adamant as Canadian women on this point, but follow them closely. Seventy-two percent believe that a woman can have a complete and happy life if she remains single, while 23 percent disagree. American women seem to believe that men require marriage more than women do: only 57 percent think a man can have a complete and happy life if he remains single, and 35 percent think he cannot.

In spite of this high endorsement of life without marriage, when given a choice of the most satisfying and interesting life style, the majority of American women choose marriage, with or without careers, and with or without children. Ninety-four percent say that marriage in some combination with children or career is the most desirable life style. Slightly fewer of them (89 percent) would choose to have children with or without a career. Although traditional marriage may seem to be in decline in the United States, apparently the desire for marriage and children is still paramount among American women.[30]

The authors of the 1985 Virginia Slims American Women's Opinion Poll comment on the evolving sexual standards of American men and women:

> The responses of these men and women verify that there has been a major change in the prevailing morality. Almost all agree that the new morality will have an impact on the institution of marriage. For the most part the younger, better educated women see these changes as having a positive impact on marriage, while older and less well educated women believe that the country's morals will break down and the institution of marriage will be weakened. . . .
>
> The potential positive result of the changed morality is that it will make for better, more successful marriages, that people will make better choices of marriage partners, and that couples will have more honest relationships with each other. These attitudes are held most strongly by the youngest and best educated women, and they are least subscribed to by the oldest and least well educated.[31]

Italy

The report from Italy on "Italian Women Facing the '80s" says:

> There is a passage from a traditional model in which the woman revenged her dependence on the man by exercising an indirect domination of a non-explicit

power through "blackmail" and "deceit" to an equal one in which the woman is just as responsible as the man and in which the family's future is chosen and handled together.

They cite as evidence for this a high level of agreement with statements such as "today there is more dialogue between men and women" . . . "compared to before nowadays a man is a better companion for a woman" . . . "today's man joins in more in raising the children and in the housework" . . . "today's man is much less authoritarian than before."[32]

On the whole the evidence is that marriage is and will be an enduring institution, that there is a strong desire for a committed and continuing relationship with a spouse. There is an almost equally strong desire to have children, even in those cultures where children are not considered essential to either the personal fulfillment of the woman or the success of a marriage. To the extent that couples move away from the authoritarian pattern of marriage to a more egalitarian one, there is some indication that they may find more emotional fulfillment in a relationship based on "reciprocal love and reciprocal esteem."[33]

Identity

Whether women are full-time homemakers or working women, whether they believe in traditional or partnership marriage, there is mounting evidence that they want to be treated with respect, as individuals in their own right, and that they do not feel subservient or inferior to men.

Italy

Strong support for this emerging sense of self is found in Italy. Eighty-six percent of Italian women believe that even though a woman should dedicate herself to her children and family, she should not do so to the exclusion of her own desires and aspirations. Four in five Italian women say that "it is important for a woman to have her own friendships, activities, and interests independent of those of her husband." Eighty-five percent believe that the word *obey* should never be used in relationships between a man and a woman.[34]

Canada

The importance of personal dignity and self-worth is also emphasized by Canadian women. Three out of four Canadian women, both full-time homemakers and those in the work force, said, "I feel my family has a great deal of respect for the kind of work I do." Only 6 percent said they didn't feel this way.[35]

United States

In the United States, the majority of women, both full-time homemakers and working women, feel that women are regarded with more respect today than ten years ago. Three out of four feel that women are respected more today than a decade ago, just one in five thinks she is held in the same respect, and only 16 percent say they are respected less than they were ten years ago.[36]

Latin America

Another expression of a sense of self is the feeling that a woman has the right to spend time on herself in addition to her home and family. This attitude is endorsed quite strongly among men and women in the three Latin American countries. In Brazil, 84 percent of the women and 78 percent of the men endorse this idea; in Mexico, 55 percent of the women and 56 percent of the men do so; and in Venezuela, 64 percent of the women and 58 percent of the men do so.[37]

Australia

In Australia, 77 percent of women, both full-time homemakers and working women, also believe that a woman has the right to spend time on herself in addition to her home and family. This attitude reflects a fundamental change in the values of Australian women: "The focus of 'family before self' is giving way to 'self and family' with the emergence of a more confident and assertive female ego."[38] Australian women are now clearer in their own minds about their responsibilities. Evidence of this is their response to the statement, "I am confused about what is expected of me." Only one in four Australian women is confused about her role in today's society. Three out of four exhibit no confusion.[39]

Italy

Italian women reveal their assertion of self in the way they respond to questions on the treatment of sons and daughters. Ninety-six percent of Italian women say that it is right to provide daughters with a higher education because today women also have to be able to rely on themselves and on their own work. Ninety percent believe that sons and daughters should have an equal amount of formal education. Only 9 percent subscribe to the traditional view that it is appropriate to educate sons more than daughters.

Another side of the coin is the extent to which Italian women feel sons and daughters should be trained to take on household responsibilities. Eighty-seven percent say they believe that it is right to educate sons as well as daughters to do housework. Only 10 percent take the traditional view that only daughters should be taught how to keep house.[40]

Canada

Eighty-six percent of Canadian women think that girls should be permitted as much independence as boys, and 83 percent said it is equally important for a daughter and a son to have a career. Only 12 percent said a career is more important for a son. Not surprisingly, the vast majority (89 percent) believe that "in today's society it is important that a woman be able to support herself and any children she might have."[41]

The concept of identity or selfhood has been defined as "going beyond derived status." Traditionally, women were identified in terms of their roles as daughters, wives, or mothers. There is now a great deal of evidence that women want to be recognized as individuals in their own right, aside from their personal or family roles. This particular issue was measured in the Canadian study with striking results. Ninety-five percent of women in Canada, both full-time home-makers and working women, agree with the statement "I like to be recognized for what I do and not for being someone's wife, mother or girlfriend."[42] This is dramatic endorsement of the importance of a strong sense of identity to women.

six

The Role of the Life Cycle

NEITHER working women nor housewives are cut from the same cloth. Women's roles as consumers change as they move in and out of different stages of life whether they work or keep house full time.

One way to assess the consumer potential of women in any country is to consider their place within the life cycle. Are they married? Do they have young children? These two basic demographic facts define the way they live and affect their needs as consumers, the way they buy and use products, the way they spend their time, and the way they spend their money.

Women and Marriage

Although marketers tend to generalize about women consumers as being married, the reality is that not all women are wives. Let us look at the rates of marriage, in ascending order. Among the ten countries studied, women in Venezuela are least likely to be married: approximately half of all women in Venezuela are wives. (It should be noted that this is based on 1974 census data.) Just over half (54 percent) of the women in Mexico are married. (This is based on 1970 census data. Mexico bases its reports on women twelve years of age and over.) In the United States only 55 percent of all women sixteen years and over are currently married. The unmarried, of course, include those who have not yet married, whom we designate as "single," as well as those whose marriages were terminated by divorce or death.

West Germany is similar to the United States in its relatively high level of unmarried women and low level of those who are currently married. Only 57 percent of women in West Germany are married. The pattern in Brazil is iden-

Figure 6.1

WOMEN AND MARRIAGE

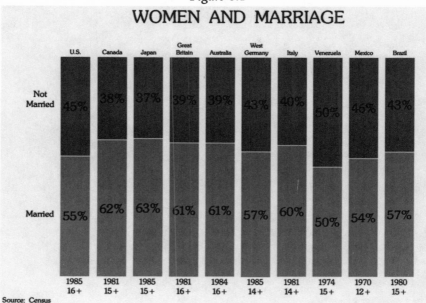

Source: Census

tical to that in West Germany. Exactly 57 percent of women in Brazil are married.

In Italy there are three married women to every two who are not currently
married. In Great Britain, exactly 61 percent of the women are married. Similarly, exactly 61 percent of women in Australia are wives. Sixty-two percent of
Canadian women are married. Thirty-eight percent are single. In Japan there
are two married women for every one who is not married.[1]

Women and Children

The second basic demographic fact is the presence of children. How many
women have children under the age of eighteen in their homes? Again, I will
discuss them in ascending order.

Women in Great Britain and Japan are least likely to have children. Only
one in three (35 percent) in each of those countries has at least one child under
the age of eighteen; 65 percent have no children at all in their homes.

Women in the United States and West Germany are similar. In each country, 36 percent have at least one child under the age of eighteen, and 64 percent

Figure 6.2

WOMEN AND CHILDREN

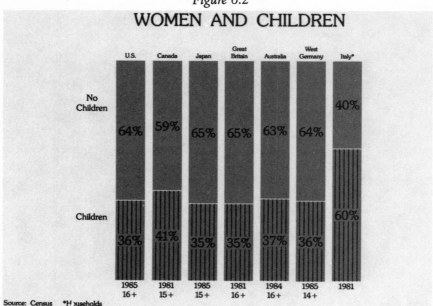

Source: Census *Households

have no children in their homes. Thirty-seven percent of women in Australia have at least one child, and 63 percent have no children in their households.

Women in Canada are somewhat more likely to have children: 41 percent of Canadian women have at least one child under the age of eighteen at home. And motherhood predominates in Italy. Sixty percent of Italian households have at least one child, 40 percent of the households are childless. (Note that Italian data relating to presence of children are based on households rather than individual women. Therefore, the proportion of women with children is approximate.)[2]

Women and the Life Cycle

When we combine the two basic demographic facts of marriage and parenthood, we create four life-cycle groups:

Married women with children;

Married women with no children at home;

Unmarried women with no children at home; and

Unmarried women with at least one child at home.

The Role of the Life Cycle

Married Women with Children

The traditional perspective of women consumers is that they are wives and mothers, living in a full-family group, complete with husbands and at least one child. What is the reality? Married women with children in their homes represent a minority in West Germany, the United States, and Great Britain, where 25 percent, 27 percent, and 29 percent, respectively, of the women are married with children at home. In Australia, 33 percent of the women are married and have at least one child in their households.

A similar pattern appears in Japan and Canada. Approximately one in three women in those two countries is married with at least one child at home. Only 34 percent of Japanese women live in this manner; 34 percent of women in Canada have both husbands and children in their homes.[3]

Married Women with No Children

There are more childless married women in West Germany (32 percent), Great Britain (32 percent), and the United States (28 percent) than married women with children under the age of eighteen. In Canada more married women have children than not, but a sizable proportion of women in that country (28 percent) are married and childless. A similar pattern occurs in Australia. More married women have children in their homes than are childless. Nevertheless, 28 percent of Australian women are married with no children. In Japan there are more married women with children than without, but a sizable proportion (30 percent) of Japanese women are married without children in their households.[4]

Unmarried Women with No Children

The largest life-cycle group in the United States consists of women with neither husbands nor children in their homes. Thirty-six percent of American women live in this way, compared to 27 percent who are married and have children. In West Germany 32 percent of the women have neither husband nor child at home; only 25 percent are married women with children in their households.

Women in Great Britain are also more likely to be living outside the full-family life style. Thirty-three percent of women in Great Britain have neither spouse nor child in their homes, as contrasted with 29 percent who are married and have at least one child under the age of eighteen at home.

In Australia the largest single life-cycle group is of women who are not married and have no children. Thirty-five percent of Australian women live in this way, compared to 33 percent who have both husbands and children in their household.

In Japan there is just one percent difference between women with neither husbands nor children in their homes (35 percent) and married women with

Figure 6.3

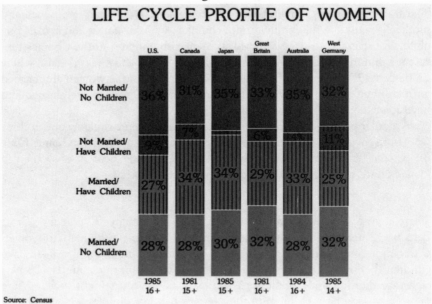

LIFE CYCLE PROFILE OF WOMEN

	U.S.	Canada	Japan	Great Britain	Australia	West Germany
Not Married/ No Children	36%	31%	35%	33%	35%	32%
Not Married/ Have Children	9%	7%		6%	4%	11%
Married/ Have Children	27%	34%	34%	29%	33%	25%
Married/ No Children	28%	28%	30%	32%	28%	32%
	1985 16+	1981 15+	1985 15+	1981 16+	1984 16+	1985 14+

Source: Census

children at home (34 percent). Canada has slightly fewer women with neither husband nor child at home (31 percent), than women living in a full-family group (34 percent), with husbands and children.[5]

Unmarried Women with Children

The number of single mothers who are bringing up children without benefit of fathers has increased in recent years, but these women still form the smallest group. The highest proportion of single mothers is found in West Germany, where 11 percent of the women are not married but have at least one child at home. In the United States, 9 percent of the women are single mothers; in Canada, 7 percent; in Great Britain, 6 percent.

The lowest percentages are found in Australia and Japan: 4 percent of Australian women are single mothers; and only 2 percent of Japanese women.[6]

It has been customary to think of the women's market in terms of the traditional image of the woman living in a full-family group complete with husband and at least one child at each side holding onto her apron strings. Clearly this image speaks for very few. If we omit women living in the traditional life style, we still have 73 percent of all women in the United States. Throughout the countries

studied, women living in the traditional manner constitute no more than a quar-
ter to a third of a country's population.

Marriage and the Working Woman

Contrary to the assumption that most working women are probably unmarried,
the proportions of working wives are very similar to the proportions of married
women in the total population. We have data on the marital status of working
women in eight of the ten countries studied. In six of those countries the marital
patterns of working women are very similar to those of all women: the countries
are the United States, Canada, Australia, Japan, West Germany, and Italy.

Fifty-five percent of all women in the United States are married and exactly
55 percent of working women are married. Sixty-two percent of Canadian
women are married, compared to 63 percent of working women who are married. In Australia, 61 percent of all women are married and 60 percent of the
working women are married. In Japan, 63 percent of all women are married,
and 67 percent of working women are married. In West Germany, 57 percent
of all women are married, and 59 percent of working women are married. The
proportion of working wives (59 percent) in Italy is almost identical to the
proportion of all Italian women who are married (60 percent).

In two countries there are marked differences between these groups of
women. In Great Britain, 61 percent of all women are married, but a dramatic
78 percent of working women are married. There are 17 percent more married
women in the work force than among the total population. The pattern in Brazil
is the reverse. Fifty-seven percent of Brazilian women are married women, but
only 36 percent of working women are married.[7]

Who Brings Home the Bacon?

An important question from a marketing point of view is, To what extent do
working wives contribute to the earnings of their households? The answer, in
turn, has direct implications for the buying power of the two-paycheck household. Therefore, we ask the idiomatic question "Who brings home the bacon?"
or who supports the household? Data are available from eight of the ten countries.

In the United States there are almost twice as many working wives as wives
living in the traditional life style. Thirty percent of American women are working wives; 16 percent live in the traditional pattern of breadwinner-husband
and homemaker-wife. In 9 percent of the households, neither the wife nor the
husband is employed.

There are also more working wives than traditional wives among married women in Japan. Thirty-two percent of Japanese women are working wives; 27 percent are full-time housewives supported by their husbands. Four percent of Japanese women are married with neither the husband nor the wife going to work.

Similarly, in Great Britain there are more working wives than married women who are supported by their husbands. Twenty-eight percent of women in Great Britain are married working women, compared to 22 percent of married women who live in the traditional pattern of breadwinner-husband and homemaker-wife. Ten percent of women are married to retired men and neither husband nor wife works.

A high proportion of married women in West Germany (14 percent) live in households where neither the husband nor the wife works. The traditional pattern is followed slightly more in West Germany. Twenty-two percent of women are full-time homemakers supported by their husbands, 20 percent are part of two-paycheck marriages.

In Canada 35 percent of women are full-time homemakers and 26 percent are working wives.

In Brazil 39 percent of all women are traditional housewives, and 19 percent are wives who bring in a second paycheck. In Venezuela 33 percent of all women are full-time homemakers supported by their husbands; 12 percent of all women are part of a two-income home. In that country, 3 percent of all women do not go to work and are married to men who are also out of the work force. In Mexico, 42 percent of all women live in the traditional husband-breadwinner and homemaker-wife marriage and only 9 percent participate in a two-paycheck marriage. Just one percent of women in that country are working wives married to men who are retired or out of the work force.

Working Women and the Life Cycle

In four of the countries studied, data for life-cycle profiles of working women confirm or challenge assumptions about working women. A common assumption is that working women might be childless wives, women who have no family obligations to keep them at home. As a matter of fact, in all four countries there are more married women with children among working women than among the female population as a whole.

In the United States there are fewer women who are married and childless among working women (25 percent) than among the total female population (28 percent). On the other hand, in Great Britain there is a higher percentage of childless wives among working women (39 percent) than among the total female population (32 percent).

Closely related to these figures are those for unmarried women with no children. In the United States the proportion of this group among working women (35 percent) is almost identical to the proportion of this segment among all women (36 percent). In Great Britain, 33 percent of all women have neither husbands nor children in their households, but only 15 percent of working women are unmarried with no children.

In West Germany 31 percent of working women are unmarried and childless; 32 percent of the total female population are unmarried with no children. In Japan 31 percent of working women are childless and unmarried, and 35 percent of the total female population are in this group.

The smallest group in all the countries studied is that for the single mother: This ranges among working women from a low of 3 percent in Japan to a high of 10 percent in the United States and West Germany.[8] For the most part, the presence of single mothers in the work force is in proportion to their presence in the population.

The marketing application of the life-cycle concept necessarily takes a cross-sectional snapshot of the situations of women at a single moment in time. But another dimension of the life cycle is beginning to emerge, a realization that the life cycle is a dynamic process that has implications for women's changing participation in the work force.

seven

The Dynamics of the Life Cycle

J UST as women's consumer needs change as they move in and out of different stages in life, their attitude toward work also changes. Let us look at the different groups women fall into.

Unmarried/No Children: Young Singles

At the earliest stage of the life cycle, women are unmarried and dependent on their parents. They usually live at home and might move out to attend school. After school they sometimes return to their parents' home, or live on their own as single, young working women.

Married/No Children: Young Couples

These days marriage does not always occur. Or marriage is postponed to a later date. When women do marry, their living context changes. The life-style patterns of young wives are dramatically different from those of young single women.

Married/Young Children

If and when children are born into that marriage, the couple becomes a full mily, and its life-style context changes once again. This, in turn, affects every aspect of their lives.

Married/Older Children

The next stage of the life cycle is that children do grow up. As they emerge from dependent infancy to babyhood to their teens, children might still live

under the family roof, but they no longer require their mothers' full-time attention.

Children/No Husband: Single Mothers

Regrettably, sometimes the marriage dissolves because of death or divorce. So,
the full-family group could become a single-parent household, and, of course,
the life-style patterns of single mothers are very different from those of wives
living in households with husbands and children.

Married/No Children: Empty Nesters

Ultimately, as children grow up and leave the nest, the full-family group becomes an empty-nest household of husband and wife with no children at home.

Not Married/No Children: Widows/Divorcees/Never Married

Since husbands tend to predecease their wives, if the marriage dissolves
through death or divorce, the woman is once again alone, with neither husband
nor child in her household.

Work plays a different role at each stage of women's lives. Traditionally, women
might have worked during the years between school and marriage and then
stayed home to pursue the permanent career of wife and mother. Some women
who were not supported by husbands, either because they had never married
or because the marriage had been dissolved through death or divorce, had to
support themselves. Other than that, outside employment often did not play a
part in a woman's life once she had married and taken on family responsibilities.

As women's aspirations change, their options are no longer limited to an
"either/or" choice between work and homemaking, but instead allow a continuous interaction between the two. One result of this is that working women
and nonworking women are not completely separate and distinct groups. Most
full-time homemakers have worked at some time in their lives. Therefore, their
move from work to home responsibilities is a continuum. For example, four out
of five nonworking women in Canada have worked outside the home in the
past. Three-fifths of those formerly employed housewives have worked within
the last five years. When they did work, three out of four had full-time jobs.[1]

Almost seven in ten of the nonworking women interviewed for the study on
"European Men and Women 1983" conducted for the Commission of European Communities have worked in the past. As a matter of fact, among women
between the ages of twenty-five and forty, 90 percent have worked before, and
more than eight in ten of those aged forty and over were formerly working

women. Two out of five of these women who worked in the past have been out of the work force for six or more years.

Work and the Life Cycle

By tracking the working and nonworking situation of women through different stages in life, the dynamics of the relationship of the life cycle and work become clear. In Australia, for example, married women without children and women with adult children are most likely to work.[2] Seventy-seven percent of young married women without children go to work, but only 22 percent of those who are raising small children are in the work force. As children get older, their mothers are more likely to work. Forty-six percent of women with older children go to work. When children leave home, their mothers also return to the work force. Fifty-one percent of the empty nesters are also working women. Finally, 14 percent of the oldest group work.[3]

It is clear that the very low work-force participation of wives in young families is because of children. According to one report, "The age of her children is the best predictor of whether or not a mother works . . . for instance 51% of the women with children aged twelve to sixteen years now work, but only 17% of women with children under two years are in the work force. However, we find it astonishing that one woman in four (24%) with kindergarten age children works."[4]

The relationship between the stage in the life cycle of women and their presence in the work force is also documented in West Germany. There has been a major change in the age and marital status of working women since the 1950s. In 1950, only 21.5 percent of married women in that country were working. In 1982, 45.4 percent of married women went to work: "In the early 1950s single women made up two-thirds of the female work force. This ratio has now been reversed. In 1982 two-thirds of working women were married." In Germany there has been a major decrease in the proportion of working women among the very young, fifteen to twenty years of age. This appears to be because younger women are staying in school longer to attain the education that will give them the qualifications for a higher-level working life.[5]

The greatest increases in the number of working women in Germany have occurred among women between the ages of twenty-five and forty-five: "Compared with several years ago, women are working longer after getting married and go back to work more frequently in middle age. The typical situation for women today is as follows: The dominant type of working woman is no longer very young but a married woman who has had special training for her job. The total increase in working women is, therefore, mainly due to changed patterns among married women."[6]

The Discontinuity of Women's Working Lives

The dynamics of work and the life cycle are reflected in the German report:

A characteristic of working women is the discontinuity of women's working lives, especially of married women. A relatively large number of married women stop working when they marry or when children are born. This discontinuity results in women working only at certain times and becoming housewives. This creates a constant state of flux between women's stopping work and returning to work later. The big increase in women with children working and the increase in these women working in the age groups between twenty-five and forty-five is a characteristic development. There has been an increase in the percentage of married women who return to work after a period of staying at home. The length of time they stay at home has become shorter. It is taken as a matter of course especially for younger married women to take on this dual role of working and being a mother.[7]

Researchers in Australia confirmed the pattern: "There is not the same routine and continuity about women's lives. They leave school and become members of the work force until they have their first child when they tend to leave the work force and become full-time mothers. Once their children are older, many rejoin the work force."[8]

Work and the Single Girl

In Great Britain young, unmarried women with relatively modest jobs live at home with their parents and tend to be satisfied with their lives and optimistic. They are not preoccupied with thoughts of marriage, although most would be happy at some time to marry and some would like to own their own homes.

Some of the young single women with more career-oriented jobs are proud to be independent and able to handle all aspects of their lives successfully and efficiently. They revel in their self-sufficiency, and those who are homeowners feel a strong sense of achievement. One young woman said, "I've gotten more satisfaction out of life since I've had my own home. I look around and think I've done pretty well for myself. I'm quite pleased with the way I manage my life." Another concurred. She said, "It used to be getting a car that mattered. Now, it's getting your own home that matters."[9] Clearly, these young working women don't feel it's necessary to be married in order to enjoy the pleasures of domesticity: "You feel like doing things to your home. I'd like to spend more money on the home. When you decorate a room, you get satisfaction and when you put your first carpet down and put double glazing in, you keep looking at it."[10]

These young career women seem content and fulfilled. They don't put a high priority on marriage and having children. Indeed, motherhood has no appeal at all to some of them. One young woman said, "I see children as a prison." Another explained, "I can't see myself having children. It would interfere with my life too much." Should they have families in the future, some envision continuing to work: "If I was going to get married, I'd still work. I have no desire to have children, but if I had them, I'd enjoy them. But I'd like to be able to afford a nanny because if I had to be with my children twenty-four hours a day, it would drive me crazy."[11]

Some young unmarried women in Japan said they would probably stop working when they married, depending on the kind of men they married. One anticipated the pressure of trying to meet the demands of her home and work responsibilities: "If I was married and working, I think working would be very hard on me. I might stop working because I couldn't handle two roles at once." The same young woman, however, expressed the hope that she would be able to reenter the work force once her family responsibilities were behind her: "It would be better if there were more opportunities to do something for women whose children are grown and want to start working again."[12]

On the other hand, some unmarried working women in Japan do not intend to stop working if and when they should marry. These young women are more committed to the work they do: "I've been introduced to men with a view to marriage five or six times. They agreed in general they like a woman who works but many of them wanted their own wife to stay at home. Maybe I just happen not to have met the man I want to give everything up for. But I liked working, so I didn't get married." Another one said, "I won't marry a man who will tell me to stop working." On the other hand, although these ambitious young women want to continue their careers after marriage, they also anticipate that they would enjoy the domestic side of life: "I don't want to be a woman who can only do work. I want to be able to cook, clean and do the laundry."[13]

Working Wives without Children

Some of the young childless working wives are not anxious to start raising families. These young wives are happy with their present lives and quite optimistic about the future. Apparently, they don't want to change the status quo. One of them said, "I've never wanted to have a family and stay at home. I think that's one of the most boring things in the world." Another reported, "I don't want to have children for hundreds of reasons. My husband does—but I can't see any good points in having them at the moment." [14]

When Children Arrive: To Work or Not to Work?

If and when these young wives do have children, they will face the decision about whether or not to continue working. If the past is any guide, most of them will drop out of the work force, at least for a time, to become full-time mothers and homemakers. But not all of them will live happily ever after. For many, the marriage will not last and this means returning to work. Single mothers are more likely to work than those who have husbands as well as children. [15]

A divorced mother in Great Britain said, "I was at home for two years before my divorce when I had to go to work. I only worked part-time and I found it hard getting someone to look after them, but I was happier going out to work even though it was a dead end job. I enjoy craft work but not housework. Most of my friends work. I couldn't like being at home shut in all day not seeing anyone." [16] A German study reported: "Whether mothers go out to work also depends on the number of children they have. The more children, the less likely the mothers are going to work. For this reason the fall in the birth rate since the mid-60s will probably result in an increase in the number of mothers working. The age of the children is also a decisive factor. More mothers go out to work as their children grow older. Looking after very young children is obviously a factor that limits the desire to go out to work." [17]

Many young housewives with small children at home do aspire to work sometime in the future. This aspiration to work, in turn, is a direct reflection of their perceptions of the role of women. Many of these younger housewives, particularly those who are well educated, yearn for an expanded identity outside the traditional role of wife and mother. It isn't that they don't value their families, because they do, but they want to participate in the larger world as well. Their reasons for wanting to do this are a combination of frustration from being at home with small children all day, a desire for financial independence, and a longing for broader horizons.

Accommodating Family and Work

Women's concerns with their families are paramount. During this time, some will seek accommodation between their family responsibilities and their desire to work. In the United States, a study asked women what they thought was the ideal life for women. More than three out of four younger women would like a combination of work and family life. Two-thirds of those who choose work and family prefer a sequential pattern of work and family life: to take a few years out when the children are small and then return to the work force when they are older. Only one in three of these young women hopes to "have it all": to marry, have children, and continue to work throughout her lifetime.[18]

Many young European housewives who are currently out of the work force aspire to something far more modest. To accommodate the conflicting demands of work and family, many choose part-time work, at least while their children are young.

Part-Time Work

One way that women adjust to the dual demands of family and work is to seek part-time employment rather than attempt full-time work while their children are young. As a matter of fact, the European Community Study documents that one of the major differences in the employment patterns of men and women is the tendency of women to work part time. Almost all employed men (95 percent) are full-time workers. Conversely, 61 percent of working women are employed full time and 39 percent have part-time jobs. "Rare among men, part-time working is common among women." In addition, "the youngest and most educated are found least often in part-time jobs. The proportion of working men in part-time jobs is almost as low regardless of age and education."[19]

Women clearly prefer part-time work more frequently than men do. This is shown by the answers to two questions. Those working full time are asked, "Would you prefer to work part-time for less money?" Even though the level is low, 22 percent of women and 11 percent of men who now work full time would like to work part time.[20]

Confirmation of the importance of the part-time work option for women again comes from Europe. According to a survey, "Compared with men, women seeking work seem to be older, more educated, more often married, and more often with children in their care. Finally, they appear to come from higher income groups than the men in this group. Yet, again, women seeking work show a greater preference for part-time employment than men in the same situation."[21] When part-time workers were asked if they would prefer to work full time, 78 percent of the women who now work part time reject the idea; only 55 percent of men share this attitude.

The report says:

In both cases and for both sexes, the majority prefer to stay as they are. Nevertheless, more women than men in full-time employment are attracted by the idea of part-time work. Among part-time workers more women reject the possibility of working full-time. Considering only people in full-time employment, the *propensity for women to wish to work part-time varies according to elements in the life cycle.*[22]

The Dynamics of the Life Cycle

The preference for part-time work is the same for both sexes among young people, under twenty-five, and people fifty-five and older. Again, single people or those with no responsibilities for child care express similar preference about part-time work whether they are men or women.

But when it comes to people of intermediate age, married and with children to take care of—especially children under eight—then the greatest divergences of opinions between men and women appear. Faced with the double problem of full-time job and family responsibilities, it is women rather than men who are led to consider the more flexible option of part-time working.[23]

Temporary Work

An alternate solution to part-time work is temporary work. This appears to be the path taken in West Germany: "The problem of combining the role of house-wife, motherhood and going to work is reflected in the high proportion of temporary work among married women with children." The number of women working temporarily in the total female work force grew from 8 percent in 1960 to 33 percent in 1982.[24]

The report continues:

The temporary work rate depends mainly on the number of children and marital status. The highest percentage of temporary work (55%) is among married women with children. But income also apparently plays a major role. The figure for single, widowed, and divorced mothers who on average have lower incomes than married mothers is below average at 27%. In other words the percentage of women working full-time among all working women is higher in this group than among married women.[25]

The Yearning for Flexible Working Arrangements

In Australia, even among full-time homemakers as well as those in the work force, two out of three say they would prefer to work and most of these would prefer part-time employment (31 percent); some would prefer paid work from home (12 percent). This desire for varied working arrangements is a reflection of the yearning for accommodation between their work and home lives: "work plays a much more important part in women's lives than might have been thought. The majority of women would prefer to work given a choice and are less likely than men to say they work just for the income."[26]

The Other Option: To Stay Home

Not every woman wants to combine the roles of worker and mother; this is the working woman who would like to stay home and be a full-time homemaker. In Italy mothers who have always worked and never been full-time housewives

are quite negative about their jobs. They feel it is a disadvantage to be a working mother. They are conflicted about working. They have feelings of guilt
toward their children. They wish they could spend more time with them—to
supervise them properly and to experience the joys of motherhood. They feel
the stress of the double burden of home responsibilities and work responsibilities. Because of this burden they feel they have very little time for themselves.

These women also have few career opportunities. They see their work as a
necessity and, at times, find it very constricting. They see the housewife's situation as a privileged position to which they would like to aspire. They feel that
only by remaining at home can they find the time to follow their personal interests and inclinations.[27]

Women in Great Britain aren't as positive. One working woman in Great
Britain wasn't sure whether she would enjoy staying at home: "I'm looking
forward to giving up working but I can't say that once I do it, I'll be happy. It
would be fine for a month and then I'd want to go back. I admire people who've
got a husband, children, and a responsible job and I'd like to be one of them."
For the most part, older housewives in most of the countries studied did not
aspire to enter or reenter the work force. These are traditional housewives, with
traditional beliefs about men and women. These women are at peace with their
roles in life and have no desire to change.[28]

The Empty Nest

For still other women, the empty-nest stage of their lives gives them an opportunity to spread their wings and "reach for something more." A mature working
woman in Great Britain said, "Once the children leave school, you look for
something more as they get older. When they're younger, your whole life is
dedicated to them. When they go to school and get more independent you can
take on more responsibility so that when they leave you're ready to start something new, to build a career and do something apart from the home. You've got
to start by forty otherwise it is very difficult to make a specialist career."[29]

A widow who had neither husband nor child to care for at this point in her
life explained how her attitude toward work changed when she moved from one
stage of her life to another: "The children were at school before I went back to
work and only part-time for pin money. When I was widowed, I continued
part-time and then went full-time and now I count it as a career."[30]

The stages in the life cycle are paralleled by a range of values. Young housewives and working women

> shared a very different perception of the role of women in society compared
> both to older women who don't intend to work and to men. The older women
> appear to believe that a woman's primary responsibility is and remains through-

out her life to her children. Other women, however, tended to see their role as more varied. They were more likely to describe childraising as a phase that is all important when children are young but forms only one aspect of their lives once children are older. . . .[31]

The future will see a continuing growth in the importance attributed to work in women's lives. The realization and acceptance that a woman's life, unlike that of men, has distinct phases where responsibilities to work and to children change in emphasis may help women to overcome the sense of conflict that many currently experience. [32]

We have seen that as women move through the life cycle the changing emphasis of their responsibilities to work and to family are reflected in changing priorities at each stage. What impact does their work have on their children and their husbands?

eight

Work and Family

Children and Working Mothers

What is the reality of the lives of mothers who work? How does their work affect the lives of their children? How does having children affect the lives of working mothers? There are strong differences from country to country in women's beliefs on the effect that a mother's work has on her children.

Japan

In Japan, for example, twice as many women, both full-time homemakers and working women, believe that it is not good for children when mothers go to work as say that having a working mother is better for children. Not surprisingly, full-time homemakers are more critical than women who are in the workplace of the impact of mothers' working on children. It should also be noted that two out of five Japanese women did not express any opinion on this question.[1]

Canada

By contrast, more than half of Canadian women, both full-time homemakers and those who work, believe that the children of working mothers are as well adjusted as children whose mothers stay at home. Not surprisingly, homemakers are slightly less likely to feel this way, although just about half of them agree. Working women, particularly those who are career oriented, are most likely to believe that the children of working mothers are well adjusted. Canadian women are also more likely to feel that a woman should not give up her job when it inconveniences her family. There is a real split of opinion over this issue between homemakers and women in the work force.[2]

Australia

One solution to the potential conflict between mothers going to work and the care their children require is the idea that mothers should not work when children are young or should seek part-time work they can do while their children are in school. In Australia, three out of five women endorse the idea that women should work only while their children are in school. Not surprisingly, full-time homemakers are more likely than women in the work force to feel this way.[3]

Latin America

A similar viewpoint was expressed in Latin America. We have responses on this issue from Mexico and Venezuela but not from Brazil. Just under half of Mexican women (48 percent) and over half of women in Venezuela (51 percent) agree that a woman with children under twelve should work only if it is absolutely necessary. Slightly higher proportions of men in each of those countries endorse this position (50 percent of the men in Mexico and 54 percent in Venezuela).[4]

Is Sequential Work the Solution?

Another way of coping with the potential conflict of children and work is the sequential pattern identified by Barbara Everitt Bryant.[5] According to her research, the ideal situation for a woman is to remain at home when her children are small and to go to work when they are older. The sequential pattern is endorsed by more than half of the men and women in the three Latin American countries. Brazilian women (60 percent) are more enthusiastic about the idea than women in Mexico (51 percent) and Venezuela (53 percent). Conversely, the men in the latter two countries are more likely to agree with it than are the women in those countries (55 percent of the men in Mexico and 57 percent in Venezuela).[6]

Australia

A study in Australia raised the question whether career-minded women should be mothers at all. Overall, more than half of all women, both those who work and those who don't, believe that there is no reason why career-oriented women should not have children. Just under half of the men feel this way. Not surprisingly, working women were far more likely than nonworking women to defend the right of career women to be mothers.[7]

United States

The Roper Virginia Slims study faces the issue directly by asking, Are children worse off when their mother works? The report comments:

> Although children and their working mothers may spend less time together their parents do not think the children suffer for it. More than eighty percent of working women with young children and fathers with working wives (83%) say that their children are just as well off as if the mothers did not work. . . . But the quality of the relationship between adults as well as between adults and children cannot be measured by toting up the hours spent together. Because of their work outside the home women may spend less time with their children but they also say that they give as much to their children as non-working mothers because of the way they spend time with the children.
>
> Furthermore, they reject the idea that they would be better mothers if they did not work. A job for them is essential to a fuller, more satisfying life and they believe that leading such a life makes their relations with their children much richer. They feel similarly about the relationships with their husbands. A majority of working women (58%) reject the notion that they would be better wives if they did not work. Of those who are married, eighty-two percent are especially critical of that idea. They believe that the satisfaction they get in working outside the home makes them better wives and mothers when they are home.[8]

Roper asks two direct questions about the potential conflict or adjustment required in combining work and family. One of these is, "Is there less time for the children?" According to the Virginia Slims report, "a wife and mother who assumes professional responsibilities must make compromises." According to both men and women, those who tend to lose out the most are the children. By virtually the same margin women (43 percent) and men (46 percent) say that children get slighted the most when a woman works.

The Virginia Slims report goes on:

> When analyzed by demographic groups, absolute majorities of homemakers (51%), the over-fifties generation (51%), blacks and non-high school graduates (52%) each agree. Employed women are less inclined (37%) than non-working women (49%) to think that children get slighted. The feeling that children get slighted correlates closely with certain age, education, and income groups. Young, college educated, more affluent women are the least likely to say that children get less time because of the mother's work obligations. Furthermore,

these women are generally the most inclined to believe that in their array of responsibilities neither marriage nor children gets slighted. Among women who are older, earn less than $15,000 annually or have less education, the opposite is true.

In her three-part role as worker, wife, and mother which role gets slighted most? Practically no one thinks that women in these situations neglect their outside jobs. It is life at home—as wife and mother—that gets less attention.[9]

Guilt and the Working Mother

Do working women feel guilty for not spending more time with their families? Women in Canada apparently are not very troubled by this potential conflict. Just over one in five working women in that country admits a sense of guilt. It should be noted that half as many housewives also admit to feeling guilty even though their time is not occupied by work outside the home.[10]

The Pressure to Stay at Home

Japan

Twice as many Japanese women disagree with this idea as believe they are pressured to stay at home. One in four Japanese women has no opinion on the subject. Career women are particularly likely to reject the notion that working women feel pressure to stay at home.[11]

Canada

Women in Canada do not seem to be too troubled by marital opposition to work. Thirty-one percent of all women there, both full-time homemakers and working women, say their families would prefer they didn't work, compared to just under half (47 percent) who disagree with this statement. Just about one in five working women reports family opposition to her going to work, and two out of three say that they do not have the problem.[12]

Should a Wife Go to Work?

An interesting insight into this comes from the European Communities study. Just half of all wives in Germany believe that the wife should go to work. Two in three married women in Great Britain endorse a wife's presence in the work force. And three out of four wives in Italy believe that married women should go to work. Husbands are far less likely than wives to agree that it is desirable for wives to work in each of the three countries.[13]

Table 8.1
Husbands and Wives on the Desirability of the Wife Working

	Wives %	Husbands %	Percentage Difference %
Agree			
Italy	76	43	33
Great Britain	65	37	28
Germany	50	44	6

Source: Commission of the European Communities, "European Men and Women 1983."

West Germany

The lowest level of marital disagreement on this issue is found in Germany. Only half of the wives in that country say they believe in working, and 44 percent of the husbands endorse the idea of married women going to work.[14]

Italy

The most dramatic contrast is found in Italy. In that country, 76 percent of the wives think it is desirable to work, but only 43 percent of the husbands agree.[15]

Great Britain

There is also a strong difference of opinion between husbands and wives in Great Britain. Sixty-five percent of wives think it is a good idea to work, but only 37 percent of husbands agree that they should do so (table 8.1).[11]

An amusing footnote to this issue is revealed by two questions that were asked of both husbands and wives.

> Apart from what women themselves think, the issue of women working creates some conflict among couples. The essentials of this can be ascertained from three further questions. In turn these reveal what the wife supposes her husband's attitude to be, what husbands actually think, and what husbands suppose their wives think. This almost takes on the dimensions of a party game in which every married person having given his or her own attitude then proceeds to give his or her opinion about the attitudes of the marriage partner. So, we have not only what wives think and what husbands think they think, but what husbands think and what wives think they think.[17]

Wives in all three countries believe their husbands are more approving of married women going to work than they really are. The greatest difference of opinion on this issue occurs between husbands and wives in Great Britain.

Table 8.2

Husbands and Wives on Desirability of the Wife Working

	Wife's Preference According to		Husband's Preference According to	
	Themselves %	*Their Husbands* %	*Their Wives* %	*Themselves* %
Agree				
Italy	76	61	47	43
Great Britain	65	54	51	37
Germany	50	58	46	44

Source: Commission of the European Communities, "European Men and Women 1983."

With the exception of Germany, wives are more likely to want to go to work than their husbands think they do. In Germany, 58 percent of husbands believe their wives would like to work, but the reality is that only 50 percent of German wives say they would like to work (table 8.2).[18]

There are reasons for the discrepancies.

> The wishes of married people about the wife working are basically linked to two criteria, the employment situation in the family and age. For both sexes, but more strongly among women, a preference for the wife being at work diminishes distinctly with increasing age. This preference is distinctly stronger among two paycheck couples and distinctly lower when neither wife nor husband are in the work force . . . it should be noted that it is among the least educated and the lowest income groups that the largest disagreement among men and women occurs. Even in low income groups the majority of women wish or would wish to be working (59%) while only 28% of men are for the idea of their wives working.[19]

What If a Wife Earns More Than Her Husband?

Husbands and wives clearly have different perceptions of the extent to which women want to work. We can explore this issue further by asking whether the wife's work in a two-income family is as important as the husband's. Attitudes toward the issue vary greatly.

Table 8.3
What If a Woman Earns More Than Her Husband?

	Women %	Men %
Perfectly Comfortable		
1980	59	63
1985	68	74

Source: The Roper Organization, Inc., The 1985 Virginia Slims American Women's Opinion Poll.

Japan

For example, in Japan three out of five women, both homemakers and working women, believe that women would be discomforted if they earned a higher salary than their husbands.[20]

Australia

On the other hand, just over one in four Australian women feels that way. Traditional housewives in Australia are most likely to be concerned about the sense of discomfort, but only 23 percent of working women believe that they would be uncomfortable if they earned more than their husbands.[21]

United States

In the United States majorities of both men and women say they would be perfectly comfortable if a wife earned more than her husband. There has been an increase in this attitude in the last five years. Moreover, the men are more comfortable with this notion than the women (table 8.3)![22]

Men's Work versus Women's Work

Australia

Although American men take the lead on this issue, the majority of Australian men also believe that "compared to men, a woman's career is as important to her." Sixty-eight percent of Australian women believe a career is as important to a woman as it is to a man, and 61 percent of Australian men feel this way. Not surprisingly, working women are far more likely than traditional housewives to take this position.[23]

Europe

The European Communities study posed the question in starker terms with this proposition: "Some say that in a period of high unemployment, a man has a greater right to work than a woman." A large majority of both European men and women tend to agree that men should have a priority over women in their right to have a paid job. However, young people of both sexes and better-educated women are less inclined to support this concept.

In most countries men are somewhat more in agreement with the idea than are women. The pattern holds for Germany and Italy, where women are less likely to feel that men have a prior right to jobs. The reverse is true in Great Britain. British men are less likely than women to agree that they have a prior right to work in a period of high unemployment.[24]

According to the European Communities report:

> Men's prior right to work is recognized to varying extents in almost all countries of the community. Only in Denmark is there a majority against the idea that women take second place to men. Within some countries the opinions of women sometimes diverge fairly strongly from those of men. This is the case in Italy . . . and Germany where the men support masculine priority much more strongly than women do. Whereas in the United Kingdom the opposite tendency can be seen. The male prerogative as expressed in men's prior right to a job appears to be generalizable to the political scene. In this way at least one can understand the fact that the more a country agrees with the idea [men's prior right to a job] as far as work is concerned, the more it is opposed to women's equal right of access to a political career. The strong negative correlation between these two opinions shows, if it were needed, the close links between the two domains of work and politics as far as women's rights are concerned.[25]

The Double Standard

United States

In spite of the extent to which American men seem to approve of their wives going to work and their claim that they would be perfectly comfortable if their wives earned more than they did, there appears to be a double standard toward wives' and husbands' careers. The questions as to whether a woman should quit her job if her husband is relocated and whether a man should quit his job if his wife is relocated, the answers are dramatically different. For the most part, both men (62 percent) and women (72 percent) are more likely to endorse women giving up their jobs in favor of their husbands' careers than vice versa.

Again, women are more likely than men to believe that a woman should give up her job in favor of her husband's.[26]

According to the Roper report, "the overall response to this question is proof of a double standard. Men's jobs take precedence over women's and women still bow to their husbands' career decisions. More than anything else, practical considerations may be at work here. Men's wages and salaries are generally higher than women's and when forced to choose, the decision about moving is likely to favor the stronger wage earner. Remember, too, the majority of women (58%) still consider their work as 'just a job,' while the majority of men think of their work as a career."[27]

Canada

In contrast, women in Canada are more likely to believe that a man should be willing to move to advance his spouse's career. Fifty-one percent of all women, both full-time homemakers and working women, feel this way.[28]

Aside from the potential husband-wife conflict, there is the question of how working women interact with men in the workplace. This subject was dealt with only in Canada. Canadian women, at least, reject the idea that women should be subservient to men in taking positions of authority or in the way they handle themselves in a work situation.[29] In response to the statement "it goes against nature to place women in positions of authority over men," only 19 percent of total women in Canada agree with this concept, and 67 percent reject it. Their response to another stereotype—if a woman works she should not try to get ahead in the same way a man does—is similar: only 14 percent of women agree and 79 percent disagree.[30]

In some countries, a number of stereotypes of working women were examined.

Are Women Who Work Selfish?

Only 12 percent of Australian women agree with this. An overwhelming 87 percent of Australian women reject the notion that working women are selfish.[31] In Japan, just 18 percent of all women, both homemakers and working women, agree that working women are selfish. On the other hand, more than three times as many Japanese women disagree.[32]

Do Working Women Deprive Young People of Jobs?

Just one in four Australian women believes this. Three out of four reject the notion.[33] Just under one in four Japanese women (23 percent) agrees that working women deprive young people of jobs; more than twice as many (55 percent) disagree.[34]

Are Working Women Too Ambitious?

Men and women in the three Latin American countries considered the issue of whether women who work are too ambitious. Men are slightly more likely than women to have this impression of working women. For the most part, however, there is more disagreement than agreement on the question. People in Venezuela are least likely to believe that working women are too ambitious: 79 percent of women and 70 percent of men disagree with the idea the women who work are too ambitious. Consumers in Mexico are also not very likely to hold this view: 58 percent of women and 56 percent of men disagree with the idea. Men and women in Brazil are somewhat more likely to agree that working women are too ambitious, but more still disagree (59 percent of women and 52 percent of men).[35]

Does Personal Satisfaction Play a Role in Women's Participation in the Work Force?

The majority of both sexes in Mexico (77 percent of women and men) and Venezuela (86 percent of women and 80 percent of men) believe that "besides earning money, working is a source of personal satisfaction for women."[36]

Do Women Go to Work Simply to Free Themselves of the Drudgery of Housework?

There is a difference of opinion on this issue between men and women in Mexico and in Venezuela. For the most part Mexican men and women are evenly split, with approximately the same percentage of both groups agreeing and disagreeing (38 percent). Both men and women in Venezuela are far more likely to disagree with this statement: 51 percent of women and 47 percent of men disagree.[37]

Are Working Women Extravagant?

Finally, for the most part, men and women in Latin America tend to believe that women who work spend more money than those who don't work. Women in Venezuela are the exception. They are more likely to disagree with the notion that working women spend more money. In Brazil, 57 percent of women and

55 percent of men agree that women who work spend more money; in Mexico, 43 percent of women and 45 percent of men agree; and in Venezuela, 36 percent of women and 46 percent of men agree.[38]

From a marketing point of view, if working women do, in fact, spend more money than nonworking women, they are particularly attractive as potential customers.

Are Working Women Happier?

Regardless of their feelings about income, an overwhelming majority of women in Canada believe that a job outside the home keeps a woman feeling younger, happier, and more adaptive to today's world. More than seven in ten Canadian women feel this way, and only one in eight disagrees. Not surprisingly, working women endorse this point to an overwhelming extent. Nevertheless, housewives are also far more likely to agree than disagree that a job outside the home keeps a woman feeling younger, happier, and more in contact with today's world.[39]

III

The New Demographics

Chapter Nine, "Meet the New Demographics," presents another way of segmenting the women's market that goes beyond their occupations and their situation in the life cycle. This approach divides housewives into those who don't want to work and those who say they would like to work someday. The "plan-to-work" intention is a reflection of the aspirations to be "something more than just a wife and mother." Working women, in turn, are divided into those who see their work as "just a job" and those who are career oriented. These categories reflect the relative ambition and work involvement of the two segments of working women. Chapter Nine documents the proportions of the New Demographic segments in each of the countries studied and describes the demographic characteristics of each segment.

Chapter Ten, "Understanding the New Demographics," reports on the values and attitudes of the New Demographic segments within countries. The attitudes of women in each country toward the basic role of women were discussed in Chapter Five, which revealed the variations from country to country in how women feel about children and marriage. Chapter Ten reviews the same issues from the New Demographic perspective. Although the four New Demographic segments in each country tend to reflect a spectrum of values, from traditional to contemporary, the total attitudinal context in some countries is so different from that of others that the most traditional women in some countries are more supportive of changing values than the most nontraditional women in other countries.

Chapter Eleven, "How the New Demographics Feel about Work," discusses the attitudes of the four New Demographic segments of women toward work. The reasons why young housewives aspire to work and why some housewives don't want to work are documented by the attitudes of stay-at-home and plan-to-work housewives. The differing work orientations of just-a-job working women and career women are also clear evidence that working women are not a monolithic group.

Action Implications

1. I recommend that marketers add the New Demographic perspective to their analyses of the marketplace. Since these are new questions, not included in past marketing studies, I recommend that they be added to ongoing and future studies and that the analytic framework suggested in Parts I and II be expanded to include the New Demographics. This creates a sixteen-cell analytic model, which combines the four life-cycle groups and the four New Demographic segments.

2. This framework will enable marketers to evaluate the market potential of the New Demographic and life-cycle segments. An objective appraisal of their marketing behavior can tell whether they buy or use products differently or whether their media behavior is distinctive. An equally objective appraisal of their incidence or volume of product use can identify the potential each group represents for a product category or brand.

3. This perspective should be incorporated in copy tests or other studies using small samples, so that the responses and attitudes of each segment can be factored into the marketing decision process. If some of the segments are underrepresented in such small sample studies, it may be necessary to set quotas or weight the cells in order to represent each constituency in its true proportion.

4. I suggest that it is possible to go from quantitative evidence of marketing behavior to qualitative exploration of the reasons for that behavior. This is a reverse of the classic research sequence of proceeding from qualitative exploration to quantification. I recommend using the New Demographic questions as screening questions for qualitative studies of attitudes and reasons for market behavior.

   Re-analysis of existing data and of the information available in a number of information bases around the world makes it possible for marketers to know the size of each group, exactly which products and brands it buys and how much, and how to reach them through media. Therefore the results are actionable.

5. The New Demographic questions are currently incorporated in a number of data bases around the world. In the United States they are included in the two basic sources of market and media data, Simmons

Market Research Bureau and Mediamark Research Inc. The New Demographic perspective on attitudinal and opinion research issues are tracked by the Roper Organization in their reports, and in the Gallup Poll conducted by the Gallup Organization.

In the United Kingdom, the questions are built into the Target Group Index, which is an annual market and media study conducted by the British Market Research Bureau. They are also included in the Gallup Poll conducted by Social Surveys Limited, which studies opinions and attitudes.

In West Germany, the questions are incorporated in the Trendmonitor Omnibus Surveys of attitudes and behavior conducted by Basisresearch. In Japan the JMRB National Survey conducted by the Japan Market Research Bureau, Inc., also incorporates the New Demographic questions.

nine

Meet the New Demographics

THE themes of work and family and attitudes toward work and family help us understand why some women don't want to work, why some women work reluctantly because they need the money, and while still others who are supported by their husbands join the work force. The conceptual approach to the women's market that I term the *New Demographics* is based on a pair of questions on the attitudes of housewives and working women toward work that were originated by the Yankelovich Monitor some years ago.[1] The New Demographic questions capture the essence of the changing attitudes and self-perceptions of women.

How Housewives Feel about Going to Work

Housewives were asked if they ever planned to go to work: near term, in the next five years, sometime in the future, or not at all. Housewives who say they do not ever plan to work are termed stay-at-home housewives, and those who answer yes to any of the other questions are termed plan-to-work housewives. An expression of a desire to work is not necessarily a prediction that a woman will do so, but it is a sensitive indicator of different attitudes and predispositions that, in turn, translate into differences in the marketplace. It is also a reflection of the aspirations expressed by many young housewives to go beyond their traditional roles as wives and mothers and participate in the larger society.

In most countries, more housewives say they prefer to stay at home than aspire to enter the work force. Almost three out of four housewives in Great Britain (73 percent) opt to stay at home, whereas just over one in four (27 percent) says she plans to go to work.[2] Housewives in West Germany and

Figure 9.1

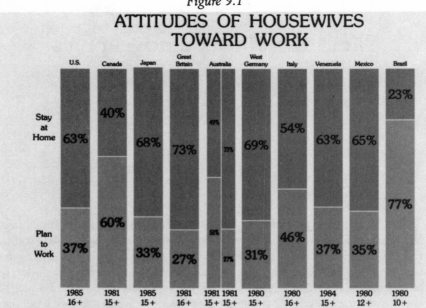

ATTITUDES OF HOUSEWIVES
TOWARD WORK

Japan are also far more likely to say they would prefer to stay at home than go to work (69 percent and 68 percent, respectively).[3] Approximately two out of three housewives in Mexico and Venezuela prefer to stay at home (65 and 63 percent, respectively).[4] Almost two out of every three housewives (63 percent) in the United States say they would prefer to stay at home.[5] Although more housewives in Italy say they want to stay at home (54 percent), a sizable proportion of Italian homemakers yearn to enter the work force (46 percent).[6]

The pattern is sharply reversed in Brazil, where only 23 percent of the target housewives interviewed say they prefer to stay at home. Seventy-seven percent express a desire to work.[7] Housewives in Canada are far more likely to want to go to work than stay at home. Some 60 percent of Canadian housewives say they plan to go to work.[8]

We have two sources of data about the New Demographics in Australia. Just over half of the housewives in Sydney and Melbourne (51 percent) say they plan to go to work.[9] On the other hand, if we consider housewives in the five mainland capital cities, almost three opt to stay at home (73 percent) for every one who says she plans to go to work (27 percent) (see figure 9.1).[10]

How Working Women Feel about
Their Work

Working women were asked whether they consider the work they do "just a job" or a career. This question does not relate to their occupations but rather to their attitudes toward their work. Responses to this question provide a discriminating reflection of different values and life styles, which, in turn, translate into real differences in the way they buy and use products.

The highest level of career perception occurs in Venezuela. Fifty-seven percent of working women in that country are career oriented and 43 percent say their work is "just a job."[11] Working women in Canada are also highly career oriented. Fifty-six percent say their work is a career, and 44 percent think it is "just a job."[12] Australian women in Sydney and Melbourne are somewhat similar to their Canadian counterparts. Just over half of working women (53 percent) in those cities are career oriented. Just under half (48 percent) say that the work they do is "just a job."[13] On the other hand, when we consider working women in the five mainland cities, just over a third (36 percent) consider themselves career women, and 64 percent think their work is "just a job."[14]

In the United States, more women who work consider their work "just a job" than perceive their work as a career. Nonetheless, two out of five designate themselves as career oriented.[15] Great Britain, Brazil, and Mexico have fairly similar proportions of career-oriented women. Just under two out of five working women in each of these countries see their work as a career.[16]

In Japan, there are two working women who feel their work is "just a job" for every one who considers her work a career.[17] In Italy seven of ten working women think their work is "just a job," compared to only three in ten who are career oriented.[18] The lowest level of career orientation occurs in West Germany, where only one working woman considers her work a career for every three who say that it is "just a job" (see figure 9.2).[19]

The size of the New Demographic segments is determined by projecting the attitudes of housewives and working women toward work to the actual ratio of housewives and working women in the population of each country. If we consider career orientation among working women and the desire to work among housewives as evidence of ambition and aspiration, the highest proportion of plan-to-work housewives and career-oriented working women occurs in Brazil. This is due primarily to a very high proportion of plan-to-work intentions among housewives. This suggests strong potential for change in Brazil.[20]

It is also striking that both Canada and Sydney and Melbourne in Australia

Figure 9.2

ATTITUDES OF WORKING WOMEN TOWARD WORK

have very high proportions of career-oriented working women and plan-to-work housewives.[21] This suggests that the quiet revolution is boiling up in each of these countries but has not reached its full expression as yet. Women in Venezuela rank next in this level of ambition and aspiration.[22]

The United States has the highest ratio of working women to housewives. However, the combined proportions of career women and plan-to-work housewives is 40 percent.[23]

Although there are relatively fewer working women in Italy than in the United States, there are almost identical proportions of "outward bound" women in Italy (39 percent). This is due to the strong presence of plan-to-work housewives who yearn to enter the work force.

There are similar proportions of "outward bound" women in Mexico, Japan, Great Britain, and the five mainland cities of Australia, but the emphasis differs. Plan-to-work housewives in Mexico are the source of the aspiration potential in that country.[24] In Japan, Great Britain, and the five mainland cities of Australia, there are relatively more career-oriented working women than plan-to-work housewives.

Women in West Germany are the least likely to express this combination of

Figure 9.3

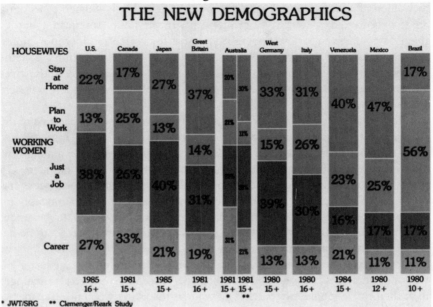

aspiration and ambition. There are slightly more plan-to-work housewives than career-oriented working women in West Germany (see figure 9.3).[22]

The Demography of the New Demographics

In the United States we have over ten years' worth of evidence that the four New Demographic segments differ from one another demographically and attitudinally, and the way they behave in the marketplace. Two key demographic characteristics that differentiate them are age and education; two other factors also play a role, children and income. An examination of the demographic profiles of these segments in the nine international countries parallels the observations we have made about the New Demographics in the United States.

Age

Stay-at-home housewives are the oldest segment of women in every country we studied. This is true even though the samples in each country are not precisely parallel in age. For example, some samples begin with women eighteen and over, others with women fourteen or fifteen and over, and in the Latin American countries with women age twenty and over. Some countries project their studies to women of all ages. Others cut off samples to reflect only women of working ages: sixty-five, sixty-four, sixty, or fifty-nine. In the Latin American countries the oldest women interviewed were as young as forty-nine and fifty-four. None-theless, in spite of the age differences of the samples, the in-country patterns are remarkably similar. In each of the ten countries stay-at-home housewives are consistently the oldest segment of women, and plan-to-work housewives are consistently the youngest.

Despite these findings, there are some differences in the age patterns of the two segments of working women from country to country. In the United States, there are twice as many women between eighteen and twenty-five among just-a-job young working women than among those who are career oriented. On the other hand, career women are more likely to be between twenty-five and fifty years of age. Canada resembles the United States in that just-a-job working women are somewhat more likely than career-oriented women to be under twenty-five years old. Career-oriented women are slightly more likely to be be-tween twenty-five and thirty-five years of age.

Career women in Great Britain are significantly younger than just-a-job working women. Career-oriented women in West Germany are also younger than their just-a-job counterparts. The youngest working women in Japan, be-tween the ages of twenty and twenty-five, are likely to be job oriented. Career-oriented working women are more likely to be between twenty-five and thirty-five years old, and slightly more likely to be in the thirty-five to fifty age group.

Australia has an equal proportion of job and career-oriented women under the age of twenty-five. Just-a-job women are slightly more likely to be between twenty-five and thirty-five years old. Conversely, career women are more likely to be between the ages of thirty-five and fifty.

Young working women in Brazil are more likely to be job oriented, and those between thirty and forty-five are more career oriented. The opposite is true in Mexico, where career women are far more likely to be between twenty and thirty years of age than are women who think their work is "just a job." On the other hand, slightly more Mexican career women are likely to be under thirty. And a substantial number of career women are likely to be between thirty and forty-five years old.

Education

Education is the second key demographic characteristic. Two statements can be made of women in the countries studied: Stay-at-home housewives are the least well educated of any group of women in any of the countries. Career women are the most highly educated group of women in each of the countries.

There is no question that plan-to-work housewives are far better educated than their stay-at-home counterparts. There is some variation, however, from country to country in the levels of education of plan-to-work housewives and just-a-job working women: in some cases education levels are similar, in some cases plan-to-work housewives are better educated than just-a-job working women, and in other cases just-a-job working women are slightly better educated than plan-to-work housewives.

Children

In the United States it has become clear that the main reason why plan-to-work housewives are temporarily out of the work force is because they are most likely to have young children. Seven out of ten plan-to-work housewives are mothers of at least one child under the age of eighteen at home, whereas only one in four stay-at-home housewives has any children at home. Working women are somewhere between the two. Just under half of just-a-job working women have children in their households and 45 percent of career women are mothers of at least one child under eighteen.

In Great Britain and West Germany, plan-to-work housewives are also more likely than their stay-at-home neighbors to have children in their households. The differences between the proportion of plan-to-work housewives and stay-at-home housewives who have children at home are less dramatic in Great Britain and West Germany than in the United States. Although more than seven in ten of the plan-to-work housewives in the two European countries have children at home, approximately two in five of their stay-at-home neighbors are also mothers. Again, 41 percent of just-a-job working women in Great Britain and 42 percent in West Germany have children.

Women among the target consumer samples in the three Latin American countries are most likely to be parents. As a matter of fact, there is very little difference between plan-to-work and stay-at-home housewives in relation to children. In Brazil, in both groups, 96 percent are parents. In Mexico, 92 percent of stay-at-home housewives and 91 percent of plan-to-work housewives have children at home. There is a slight difference between them in Venezuela. Slightly more stay-at-home housewives (91 percent) than plan-to-work housewives (86 percent) have children at home.

Stay-at-home housewives in Canada are most likely to be mothers of at least one child under eighteen years of age (93 percent); 81 percent of the plan-to-work housewives are mothers of young children. A similar pattern occurs in Australia, where 90 percent of stay-at-home housewives have children at home and 82 percent of the plan-to-work housewives have young children.

In all countries except Brazil, career women are least likely to have children, but this does not mean that they are not parents. Although children are least likely to be found in the homes of career-oriented women, the level of motherhood among these women is remarkably high. In the United States 45 percent of career women have at least one child under the age of eighteen. The lowest proportion of career mothers occurs in Great Britain (30 percent). In West Germany just 35 percent of career-oriented women have children in their homes. In all other countries, the proportion of career mothers ranges from 49 percent in Australia to 60 percent in Canada, and in the high eightieth and ninetieth percentiles in the three Latin American countries. It is simply a myth that career women are not likely to have children.

Income

Another pattern that emerged in the countries studied is that career women are clearly the most affluent segment of all women. The countries are not consistent in the relative income levels of the other three segments of women.

There is a clear progression in the United States. The two groups of housewives are less affluent than the two groups of working women. Stay-at-home housewives are the least affluent segment of all women. The plan-to-work housewives are slightly more affluent than their stay-at-home neighbors. Just-a-job working women enjoy substantially higher levels of household income than their plan-to-work counterparts. Career women are the most affluent of all.

A similar pattern occurs in Great Britain. The difference in income levels between the two groups of housewives is not great, but the stay-at-homes are at the lowest income level. The household incomes of just-a-job working women are significantly higher than those of either segment of housewives. Career women are the most affluent of all women. A comparable pattern exists in West Germany.

Another pattern occurs in Canada, Australia, Venezuela, and Mexico. In each country career women are consistently the most affluent segment of women. And the just-a-job working women enjoy higher levels of household income than either type of housewife. But stay-at-home housewives are slightly more affluent than their plan-to-work neighbors.

A third pattern emerged in Japan and Brazil. In those countries, even though career women are consistently the most affluent of all segments of women, stay-at-home housewives are second to career women in levels of household income. The plan-to-work housewives have lower levels of household income than just-a-job working women. Stay-at-home housewives are more affluent than either plan-to-work housewives or just-a-job working women. In Brazil, the difference in household income between the stay-at-home housewife and the just-a-job working woman is not great.

Japan is the one country in which the income levels are quite different. Stay-at-home housewives are substantially more affluent than either plan-to-work housewives or just-a-job working women. Although career women hold their lead over all other groups, there is a less dramatic difference between their levels of income and those of the stay-at-homes compared to any other country.

I have described the relative size of the New Demographic segments in each country, and the ways in which they differ from each other in terms of age, education, income, and presence of children. In the following chapters of this part, I will examine the more fundamental questions of how they differ in their attitudes and value systems, and how they feel about their lives.

ten

Understanding the New Demographics

I F one had to generalize about the differences among the New Demographic segments overall, it would be safe to say that in addition to being the oldest and least educated of any segment of women in the countries studied, stay-at-home housewives have the most traditional outlook. They are most likely to believe that women's place is in the home, that men should work to support wife and family, and that women's primary responsibilities are to care for their husbands and children. These women have no desire to work and have no conflict about their roles in life. They take the most traditional viewpoint on almost every issue considered here.

At the other extreme, career-oriented working women in all countries are the best educated and most affluent of any segment of women. They tend to be the most supportive of nontraditional values. They are most likely to endorse partnership marriage over the traditional form. Although many have children or want to have children, they are most likely to feel that a husband and children do not set the boundaries of a woman's life. They are most likely to believe that women have the right to aspire to fulfillment in areas outside the family. They are most likely to endorse the notion that a woman should seek an identity beyond that derived from being somebody's wife and somebody's mother.

Plan-to-work housewives are the youngest segment of women in all countries and tend to have very young children. Even in those countries where they and stay-at-home housewives are equally likely to be mothers, the former express yearnings to enter the larger world sometime in the future. They are particularly concerned about their children, and that is why they are currently out of the work force. Of course, their stated intentions are no guarantee that they will, in fact, return to work. Nonetheless, their attitudes toward themselves and their roles in life are far more outward bound than those of the stay-at-home housewife. They are responsive to nontraditional values and to the notion that a woman has a right to seek personal fulfillment beyond the basic role of a wife and mother.

Just-a-job working women are, perhaps, the least secure of any group of women. Many of them say they work purely for economic reasons. In some cases, they report that although they went to work because they needed the money, they find the social stimulation in the workplace an attractive byproduct of their working. Approximately three in five would prefer to continue to work even if they could afford to stay home. There is something beyond the paycheck that attracts them to the workplace. Nonetheless, this is a somewhat conflicted group. For every three just-a-job women who say they would continue to work even if they could afford not to, two of them would return home and become full-time homemakers. In part, their conflicts arise from the stress of carrying the double responsibilities of family and work and, in part, from the frustration of the work itself. They see themselves in unrewarding, dead-end jobs. But even here there appears to be a difference in attitude according to age. Younger just-a-job working women tend to feel more positive about the work they do than some older women, who express disillusionment.

This overview of the differences among the four New Demographic segments should be considered within the cultural context of each country. The total attitudinal context in some countries is so different from that of others that the most traditional women in some countries are far more supportive of contemporary or changing values than the most nontraditional women in other countries.

In many countries there is more agreement than disagreement among the New Demographic groups on some issues. It is always a temptation in this sort of analysis to stress the differences, but here I will comment on the ways in which the four segments of women tend to agree and the ways in which they diverge.

Feelings about Children

Latin America

People in the three Latin American countries are intensely committed to the importance of children in their lives. From 83 to 95 percent of women in each of the three countries believe that having a child is an experience every couple should have. This is true for all four New Demographic segments. There is very little variation in the way that the New Demographic groups in the Latin American countries feel about children.

Venezuela

For example, women in Venezuela are particularly committed to children. In that country, there are only minor differences between the way housewives and working women respond to the issue. Ninety-six percent of both segments of housewives agree on the importance of children, whereas 92 percent of just-a-job women and 93 percent of career women agree. Statistically, this means that there is really no difference at all in how the four New Demographic segments in Venezuela feel about children.[1]

Brazil

There is a slightly lower level of endorsement of the importance of children in Brazil, but still 92 percent of all women say that having a child is an experience that should not be missed. The only real variation in the response came from career women, who lag slightly behind the others in agreeing with this. Nonetheless, 85 percent of career women, compared to 94 percent of stay-at-home housewives, agree that having a child is an experience every couple should have.[2]

Mexico

Mexican women are overwhelmingly in favor of having children. But their commitment to children is slightly below that of their counterparts in the other two Latin American countries. Eighty-three percent of Mexican women stress the importance of children. Again, there is a minor variation between career women and the other three segments of women. Seventy-five percent of career women believe that "having a child is an experience every couple should have," in contrast with the other three segments, which hover between 83 and 82 percent in their agreement with this statement.[3]

Australia

On the other hand, although just over half of women in Australia believe that all women should experience having a child, there is more divergence among the New Demographic segments in relation to children than there was in Latin America. Sixty-seven percent of stay-at-home housewives in Australia believe that all women should experience having a child, whereas just under half of the two segments of working women agree. Forty-nine percent of the just-a-job working women and 48 percent of career women stress the importance of children.[4]

Although Australian women don't put as much emphasis on the importance of children as do women in some other countries, they are deeply committed to family values. Eighty-nine percent of them are concerned about devoting enough time to their families. Interestingly, plan-to-work housewives and just-a-job working women are somewhat more concerned about devoting time to their families than are stay-at-home housewives or career women. This is one of the few attitudinal issues in which the New Demographic spectrum does not follow a predictable pattern.[5]

West Germany

Another instance in which the New Demographic spectrum does not follow a predictable pattern is in West Germany. In that country, 58 percent of all women believe that "a family is only a real family with children"; 10 percent disagree. Stay-at-home housewives and just-a-job working women are most supportive of the importance of children to the family, while career women and plan-to-work housewives are less likely than their counterparts in other countries to insist that a family is only a real family with children. Nonetheless, the majority among all four segments support the importance of children to the family group.[6]

Canada

I noted earlier that two out of three Canadian women believe that a woman can have a happy, satisfying life without children and that only 17 percent insist that children are necessary. The majority of all New Demographic segments believe that children are not essential for a woman to have a happy, satisfying life. Just-a-job working women are most likely to feel this way. Seven in ten women who say their work is "just a job" agree that life can be satisyfing without children; only 12 percent disagree. As might be expected, stay-at-home housewives are more likely than the others to say that life cannot be complete without children. Nonetheless, 55 percent of these women say that a woman's life can be satisfying without children, compared to 27 percent who think that children are essential to a happy life.[7]

Only one in three women in Canada believes that a marriage is incomplete without children. Thirty-six percent of Canadian women, both housewives and working women, feel this way. On the other hand, just under half of Canadian women think that a marriage does not require children in order to be complete. Just over half of the stay-at-home housewives in Canada believe that a marriage would not be complete without children. Fifty-two percent of them take this point of view; 31 percent disagree. Conversely, half or more than half of the other three groups of women say that a marriage can be complete without children. The most extreme position is expressed by career women: only one in four Canadian career women says a marriage isn't complete without children;

more than half (56 percent) say that a marriage can be perfectly complete with-out children.[8]

Although most Canadian women don't think children are necessary for a complete marriage, 60 percent do believe that a woman's greatest reward and satisfaction in life should be her children. Here there is strong divergence among the New Demographic segments. Three out of four stay-at-home house-wives (76 percent) endorse this view, whereas only 44 percent of career women agree. Plan-to-work housewives and just-a-job working women are between the two extremes.[9]

Since only one in three Canadian women regards children as essential to a marriage, it is not surprising that three out of four believe that a couple should not stay in an unhappy marriage because of the children. Substantial majorities of all segments of women take this position, but stay-at-home housewives are least likely to endorse breaking up an unhappy marriage. Fifty-eight percent of these women say that a couple should not stay together because of their chil-dren. Conversely, 83 percent of career women believe that the presence of chil-dren does not justify continuing an unhappy marriage.[10]

United States

In the United States four out of five women believe it is perfectly possible for a husband and wife to have a complete and happy marriage if they have no chil-dren. The majority of all New Demographic groups feel this way as well. As might be expected, career women are slightly more likely to endorse a childless marriage (85 percent); the two groups of housewives are slightly less likely to do so. Nonetheless, close to four out of five of each type of housewife believe that a marriage could be complete and happy without children.[11]

Ironically, housewives and just-a-job working wives are slightly more likely than their unmarried counterparts to agree that a childless marriage could be happy. Unmarried career women are slightly more likely than career wives to believe a childless marriage could be happy. It should be noted that the levels of agreement with this point of view are extremely high among all segments of women regardless of marital status.[12]

Feelings about the Role of Women

Latin America

Women in the three Latin American countries are most likely to endorse tradi-tional marriage. The levels of their endorsement vary: women in Brazil are the most supportive; Mexican women are second; and women in Venezuela are least likely to take the traditional view of marriage.

Table 10.1
Maintaining the Family Economically
Is the Main Responsibility of the Man

	Total Women %	Stay at Home %	Plan to Work %	Just a Job %	Career %
Agree					
Brazil	54	70	54	54	39
Mexico	50	55	49	46	33
Venezuela	46	54	53	40	23

Source: "Target Latin America," J. Walter Thompson Latin America, 1986.

Within these parameters there is a clear and consistent pattern. Stay-at-home housewives in all three countries are most likely to believe that maintaining the family economically is the main responsibility of the man. Career women in the three countries are least likely to agree with this view of marriage. In all three countries, the two middle groups, plan-to-work housewives and just-a-job working women, hold milder views on the subject. There is a clear pattern of attitudes toward traditional marriage among the New Demographic groups (see table 10.1).[13]

Australia
Fewer than one in four Australian women believes that a woman's only responsibility is to her home and family. Predictably, stay-at-home housewives are most likely to feel this way. But even among this traditional group, more than half reject this perspective. It is striking to note that among the other three segments, anywhere from 76 to 86 percent do not agree that her home and family is a woman's only responsibility. Just-a-job working women are slightly less adamant about this issue than the housewives who plan to go to work (see table 10.2).[14]

Just as Australian women are not likely to believe that a woman's only responsibility is to her home and family, they are very likely to believe that a "husband and wife should share in earning a living." Three out of four Australian women endorse the partnership approach to marriage; only 14 percent disagree. As might be expected, their attitudes are consistent with their place in the New Demographic spectrum. Just under seven in ten stay-at-home housewives endorse partnership marriage and just under one in five rejects it. Again, just under nine out of ten career women favor partnership marriage and only 3 percent do not (see table 10.3).[15]

109

Table 10.2
A Woman's Only Responsibility
Is to Her Home and Family

	Total Women %	Stay at Home %	Plan to Work %	Just a Job %	Career %
Australia					
Agree	23	43	17	22	13
Disagree	76	56	82	76	86

Source: "Target Australia: Women, the Quiet Revolution," J. Walter Thompson Australia, 1984.

Table 10.3
Husband and Wife Should Share in Earning a Living

	Total Women %	Stay at Home %	Plan to Work %	Just a Job %	Career %
Australia					
Agree	76	68	75	78	89
Disagree	14	18	14	15	3

Source: "Target Australia: Women, the Quiet Revolution," J. Walter Thompson Australia, 1984.

Japan

Japanese women are also less likely than women in Latin America to endorse traditional roles. In that country, only 40 percent of all women believe that "man's place is at work and that woman's place is in the home." Almost an equal number disagree. Nonetheless, there is the same range of response among the four New Demographic groups in Japan. Stay-at-home housewives take the most traditional view of man's place and woman's place, whereas career-oriented women are least likely to agree with this perception of man's place and woman's place (see table 10.4).[16]

United States

The Virginia Slims Women's Opinion Poll in the United States asked men and women to select the most satisfying and interesting life style. They were asked to choose between "partnership marriage," in which husband and wife share responsibilities for work, housekeeping, and child care, and "traditional marriage," with husbands assuming responsibility for providing for the family and the wife running the house and taking care of the children. We saw earlier that

Table 10.4
Man's Place Is at Work
and Woman's Place Is at Home

	Total Women %	Stay at Home %	Plan to Work %	Just a Job %	Career %
Japan					
Agree	40	54	42	39	30
Disagree	39	28	36	38	49

Source: "The Moving Target in Japan," J. Walter Thompson Japan, 1986.

Table 10.5
Best Division of Roles in the Family

	Total Women %	Stay at Home %	Plan to Work %	Just a Job %	Career %
United States					
Traditional Marriage	37	64	32	30	16
Partnership Marriage	57	32	62	63	76

Source: The Roper Organization, Inc., The 1985 Virginia Slims American Women's Opinion Poll.

more women, overall, selected the partnership marriage than the traditional one. But when we examine the responses of the New Demographic segments to this question, a dramatic picture emerges. Stay-at-home housewives come forth strongly on the side of traditional marriage. Exactly twice as many of them select the traditional form as the most satisfying and interesting life style. Conversely, plan-to-work housewives take the opposite point of view. Almost twice as many vote for partnership marriage as the traditional marriage. Not surprisingly, both working women groups are strongly committed to partnership marriage. For every one career woman who endorses a traditional marriage, five vote for a partnership with their husbands (see table 10.5).[17]

Feelings about Work and Children

Latin America

The majority of women in the three Latin American countries believe that the ideal situation for a woman is to remain at home when her children are small

Table 10.6

The Ideal Situation for a Woman Is to Remain at Home When Children Are
Small and Go to Work When They Are Older

	Total Women %	Stay at Home %	Plan to Work %	Just a Job %	Career %
Agree					
Brazil	77	81	83	74	60
Mexico	64	67	68	54	45
Venezuela	65	75	66	59	44

Source: "Target Latin America," J. Walter Thompson Latin America, 1986.

Table 10.7

A Woman with Children under Twelve Years of Age
Should Work Only If Necessary

	Total Women %	Stay at Home %	Plan to Work %	Just a Job %	Career %
Agree					
Mexico	62	66	62	59	44
Venezuela	63	74	63	58	43

Source: "Target Latin America," J. Walter Thompson Latin America, 1986.

and go to work when they are older. Plan-to-work housewives in Brazil and
Mexico are slightly more likely than any other segment of women in their countries to endorse this pattern. They are followed closely by stay-at-home housewives. Just-a-job women are slightly less likely to endorse this notion, and career women least likely of all to do so. A minor difference in Venezuela is that
the stay-at-home housewives are more likely than their plan-to-work neighbors
to support the idea (see table 10.6).[18]

Another facet of the delicate balance between children and work is the view
that a woman with children under twelve years of age should work only if it is
absolutely necessary. This question was asked in Mexico and Venezuela.
Slightly more than three out of five women in each country feel this way. In
each case, the responses of the New Demographics follow the familiar pattern
of highest endorsement by stay-at-homes and lowest by career women (see table
10.7).[19]

Table 10.8
Should Mothers of Children under Eighteen Work Outside Only If Absolutely Necessary Or If They Choose To?

	Total Women %	Stay at Home %	Plan to Work %	Just a Job %	Career %
United States					
Only If Financially Necessary	38	57	37	32	23
If They Choose	53	34	54	59	70

Source: The Roper Organization, Inc., The 1985 Virginia Slims American Women's Opinion Poll.

Canada

Just under three out of five Canadian women (57 percent) believe that a mother of young children should work only if her family needs the money. The four New Demographic segments differ dramatically on this issue. More than twice as many stay-at-home housewives (78 percent) as career women (35 percent) feel this way, while plan-to-work wives and just-a-job working women are in the middle. Fifty-seven percent each of the two middle groups agree with this notion.[20]

United States

Men and women were asked whether women who have children under the age of eighteen should have a job outside the home only if it is absolutely necessary financially or whether they should have a job outside the home if they choose to, regardless of the ages of their children. Overall, American women are more likely to believe that mothers have a right to work outside the home if they choose (53 percent). As might be expected, stay-at-home housewives are the only segment of women who were more likely to believe that mothers of young children should work only if it is financially necessary (57 percent). Across the New Demographic spectrum, the other three segments are more inclined to agree that the decision to work outside the home should be freely made (see table 10.8).[21]

Canada

More than half of Canadian women (54 percent) believe that children of working mothers are as well adjusted as children whose mothers stay at home. Not surprisingly, career women are most likely to feel this way (65 percent), and

Table 10.9
It Is Better for Children That Their Mothers Work

	Total Women %	Stay at Home %	Plan to Work %	Just a Job %	Career %
Japan					
Agree	20	13	13	24	24
Disagree	39	52	51	33	30

Source: "The Moving Target in Japan," J. Walter Thompson Japan, 1986.

stay-at-home housewives are least likely to agree (48 percent). The plan-to-work wives and just-a-job working women fall between (50 and 56 percent, respectively). Their patterns of response are in step with their place in the New Demographic spectrum.[22]

Japan

Only one in five Japanese women believes that it is better for children that their mothers work. There is clear disagreement between the two segments of housewives and the two segments of working women on the question. It should be noted, however, that even though almost twice as many working women as housewives believe that it is better for children if their mothers work, the level of agreement is relatively low. More of each segment of working women disagree than agree, but their opposition is not nearly as intense as that of the housewives (see table 10.9).[23]

Canada

Although more than half of Canadian women think that the children of working mothers are well adjusted, 40 percent believe that a woman should give up her job when it inconveniences her family. There is sharp disagreement among the New Demographic segments on the issue. Half of the stay-at-home housewives believe that a woman should give up her job for her family, but only 22 percent of career women think so. Only 42 percent of plan-to-work wives and 36 percent of just-a-job working women also think a woman should give up her job under those conditions.[24]

Australia

In Australia women were asked, "Should career-minded women be mothers?" Implicit in this question is the notion that career women can't possibly do justice to their children. More than half of Australian women (56 percent) believe

114

that career-minded women should be mothers. Not surprisingly, career women hold this belief most strongly (70 percent), whereas stay-at-home housewives are least likely to agree: only 45 percent in that group agree that career women should be mothers. Sixty-two percent of plan-to-work mothers and 64 percent of just-a-job wives agree.[25]

United States

According to the 1985 Virginia Slims American Women's Opinion Poll, the majority of working mothers, in both categories, do not feel that they would be better mothers if they didn't go to work. Sixty-one percent of working mothers feel this way. Conversely, better than three out of four believe that they make enough time for their children even though they work. By a ratio of one to three they agree with the statement, "I may spend less time with my children because I work, but I feel I give them as much as non-working mothers because of the way I spend my time with them."

Working women are fairly evenly split on the notion that "when I'm home I try to make up to my family for being away at work and as a result I really haven't any time for myself." It should be noted that for each of these issues, there is fairly close agreement between the two segments of working women but career women are more likely to endorse the positive aspects of being a working mother.[26]

Feelings about Work and Husbands

Latin America

One expression of the traditional attitude toward the relationship between men and women is the feeling that husbands prefer that women not work and dedicate themselves to the care of the home. Women in the three Latin American countries are inclined to endorse this view. Women in Brazil are most likely to agree.

Within each country the patterns of response of the New Demographic groups reflect their place in the spectrum. Stay-at-home housewives are most likely to agree with the traditional perspective and career women are least likely to do so. Plan-to-work housewives and just-a-job women are in the middle (see table 10.10).[27]

Australia

Women in Australia are less likely than Latin American women to endorse the traditional view. In Australia, 42 percent of all active women, housewives and

Table 10.10

Men/Husbands Prefer That Women Do Not Go to Work and Dedicate Themselves to the Care of the Home

	Total Women %	Stay at Home %	Plan to Work %	Just a Job %	Career %
Agree					
Brazil	75	81	78	72	64
Mexico	63	69	62	54	42
Venezuela	62	70	65	54	48

Source: "Target Latin America," J. Walter Thompson Latin America, 1986.

working women, agree that husbands would be happier if women didn't work; 45 percent disagree. Stay-at-home housewives are the only segment of women that support this traditional perspective: 59 percent agree and 31 percent disagree that husbands would be happier if women didn't work. Just-a-job working women are somewhat conflicted over this. Slightly more of them (43 percent) think that husbands would be happier if women didn't work than think husbands would not mind (37 percent). As might be expected, career women reject this concept most strongly (63 percent). It is interesting that plan-to-work housewives are more likely to disagree (54 percent) than agree (42 percent) that their husbands would be happier if women didn't work.[28]

Japan

Women in Japan also considered the assumption that husbands would be happier if women didn't work. Just over one in four of all active women in Japan believes this (26 percent), but more disagree (37 percent). The New Demographic segments show the predictable pattern of response to the question. It should be noted that although stay-at-home housewives are most likely to endorse the traditional perspective and career women least likely to do so, only one in three of stay-at-home housewives believes that husbands would be happier if their wives didn't work (see table 10.11).[29]

Women in Japan were also asked whether they thought that working women feel pressure to stay at home. Only one in four women believes that working women feel such pressure, compared to two in four who believe they do not. The responses of the four New Demographic segments to this notion are fairly similar. Just-a-job working women are slightly more likely than the others to believe that working women feel pressure to stay home. Career women are most likely to believe that women do not feel pressure to leave the work force (see table 10.12).[30]

Table 10.11
Husbands Would Be Happier If Women Didn't Work

	Total Women %	Stay at Home %	Plan to Work %	Just a Job %	Career %
Japan					
Agree	26	35	26	25	22
Disagree	37	27	39	37	42

Source: "The Moving Target in Japan," J. Walter Thompson Japan, 1986.

Table 10.12
Working Women Feel Pressure to Stay at Home

	Total Women %	Stay at Home %	Plan to Work %	Just a Job %	Career %
Japan					
Agree	24	21	23	26	23
Disagree	50	46	54	50	57

Source: "The Moving Target in Japan," J. Walter Thompson Japan, 1986.

Table 10.13
Working Women Feel Pressure to Stay at Home

	Just a Job %	Career %
Australia		
Yes	14	5
Sometimes	26	33
No	59	63

Source: "Target Australia: Women, the Quiet Revolution," J. Walter Thompson Australia, 1984.

Australia

The question whether working women feel pressure to stay at home was also raised in Australia. Although the majority of both groups of working women say they do not feel pressure, just-a-job working women are somewhat more likely than career women to report that they do feel some pressure to stay at home (see table 10.13).[31]

United States

Working wives in the United States tend to feel positive about the impact of their work on their marriages. When asked to respond to the statement "I feel I would be a better wife if I didn't work," 88 percent of married career women and 78 percent of just-a-job working wives disagree.[32] Indeed, these women feel that their work has a positive effect on their marriages. Seventy-nine percent of career wives and 59 percent of just-a-job working wives believe that they are more interesting to their husbands because they work. Nor do they believe that going to work means that they neglect their spouses. Eighty percent of just-a-job working wives and 79 percent of career wives say that they make enough time to spend with their husbands even though they work.[33]

Earlier I discussed a number of assumptions about working women. In every case the levels of response to various assumptions and stereotypes in some countries are different from those in others, but the pattern of response within the countries generally follows the spectrum of the New Demographics with stay-at-home housewives taking the most negative view and career women the most positive.

Work as a Source of Personal Satisfaction

People in Mexico and Venezuela, for example, considered the assumption that "besides earning money, working is a source of personal satisfaction for women." Women in both countries agree with this perception with great enthusiasm. Eighty-six percent of women in Venezuela and 77 percent of women in Mexico believe that working is a source of personal satisfaction. The range of response among the New Demographics is fairly narrow. In Mexico the spectrum ranges from a low of 75 percent agreement among stay-at-home housewives to a high of 88 percent among career women, and in Venezuela from 85 percent among stay-at-homes to 92 percent among career women.[34]

Women Go to Work to Avoid Housework

Just over half of women in Venezuela disagree with the more controversial notion that "freeing yourself of household jobs is one of the main advantages of working outside the home." Although each of the segments is more likely to disagree than agree that women go to work to avoid housework, their responses range from 44 percent of stay-at-home housewives who disagree to 66 percent of career women who disagree.[35]

Women in Mexico are evenly split on whether working women go to work to avoid housework. Stay-at-home housewives are more likely to believe that they do than that they do not (42 percent to 32 percent). The other three segments of women are more likely to believe that working women do not go to work to avoid housework. As might be expected, career women are far less likely than any other segment of women to agree that the main advantage of working outside the home is to free oneself of housework.[36]

Working Women Are Selfish

Women in both Australia and Japan considered the proposition that working women are selfish. The responses of Japanese women are somewhat milder than those of women in Australia.

Fifty-eight percent of Japanese women reject this view of working women, compared to 18 percent who agree with it. The range of response is very close among the four New Demographic segments. In each case, they are far more likely to reject than to agree with the idea that working women are selfish. Career women and plan-to-work housewives, however, reject the notion more intensely than either stay-at-homes or just-a-job working women. The range of response is again narrow, with 54 percent of stay-at-homes disagreeing with the proposition, compared to 63 percent of career women.[37]

On the other hand, an overwhelming 80 percent of Australian women insist that working women are not selfish. Although stay-at-home housewives feel less strongly than the other groups, better than two out of three (67 percent) disagree that working women are selfish. At the other end of the spectrum, 93 percent of career women reject the proposition.[38]

Working Women Deprive
Young People of Jobs

More than twice as many Japanese women disagree than agree with the idea that working women deprive young people of jobs. The responses of the New Demographics to this issue are fairly close. Slightly fewer stay-at-home housewives and just-a-job working women disagree with the idea that working women deprive young people of jobs (52 percent and 53 percent, respectively). Plan-to-work housewives are the most indignant at the idea. Fifty-nine percent of them disagree with it, whereas 58 percent of career women disagree that working women deprive young people of jobs.[39]

Women in Australia have stronger opinions, both pro and con, on the subject. More of them both agree and disagree with this notion than do the women in Japan. Nonetheless, Australian women are strongly opposed to the idea that working women deprive young people of jobs. There is greater variation among the New Demographic segments in Australia than in Japan. Although all groups are more likely to disagree than agree with the notion, more stay-at-home housewives than any other segment think that perhaps working women do deprive young people of jobs (40 percent), and slightly over half of them disagree with the idea (52 percent). On the other hand, the other three segments of women feel very strongly that working women do not take jobs away from young people. Sixty-six percent of the plan-to-work wives and just-a-job wives and 78 percent of career women disagree.[40]

Women Who Work Are Too Ambitious

The proposition that women who work are too ambitious is rejected by women in the three Latin American countries.

Women in Venezuela are particularly strong in their feelings about this issue. The range of response follows the predictable New Demographic pattern: 73 percent of stay-at-homes disagree that women who work are too ambitious, and 89 percent of career women disagree.[41]

Stay-at-home housewives in Brazil are evenly split on the issue. The remaining segments feel that working women are not too ambitious. Career women are particularly strong in their opinions on this question.[42]

The range of response is narrower in Mexico, with a minor variation. Fifty-six percent of stay-at-home housewives disagree that women who work are too ambitious, and 60 percent of career women disagree. Plan-to-work housewives, just-a-job working women, and career women are just one or two points apart. They don't follow the usual pattern. Sixty-one percent of plan-to-work housewives disagree that working women are too ambitious, and 62 percent of just-a-job working women feel that way.[43]

Women Who Work Spend More Money

Finally, Latin American women considered the notion that women who work spend more money. There are some differences among the women in the three countries in their responses to this proposition and sharp differences between career women and housewives.

More women in Brazil agree than disagree that women who work spend more money (57 percent versus 40 percent). The vote among career women is close in Brazil: 55 percent disagree and 43 percent agree.[44]

The vote on this issue is closer in Mexico. More women there also believe that women who work spend more money (43 percent agree and 32 percent disagree). Career women insist that women who work do not spend more money. Fifty-one percent of career women disagree with the proposition; only 19 percent endorse it.[45]

Opinion in Venezuela speaks to the other view. Although 36 percent of women in that country believe that women who work spend more money, 42 percent disagree. Disagreement is particularly strong among both career women (59 percent) and just-a-job working women (56 percent).[46]

Just as the four New Demographic segments diverge sharply in terms of age, education, and income, their social values and attitudes as well as their perceptions of working women reveal equally sharp differences. It is clear that we cannot ignore the cultural context in which these women live. We have seen that in many cases, the cultural values of women in some countries are so different from those of women in others that it would be overly simplistic to generalize about the New Demographics. Nevertheless, with very few exceptions, within each country women have a broad range of social beliefs that parallel the spectrum of the New Demographics.

Although the hard facts of the demographics of each of these groups are valuable in defining the nature of the marketplace, the attitudes and social values of each segment are equally valuable in helping marketers understand the nature of the consumers with whom they want to communicate. This insight into their social values should provide valuable guidelines to any advertiser who wishes to communicate with women in the changing consumer marketplaces of the world.

eleven
The New Demographics and Work

WOMEN in each New Demographic group share characteristics that cut across national boundaries, as well as attitudes that link them to their own culture. Here I will examine each segment separately.

Stay-at-Home Housewives

Given the consistent endorsement of traditional values among stay-at-home housewives in the countries studied, it is not surprising that these women have no interest in seeking work outside the home.

Great Britain

Stay-at-home housewives in Great Britain believe that the only good reason for women to go to work is if they need the money. According to a report from Great Britain, some believe that many women today "work out of greed. We live in a materialistic society, one that is far more demanding and acquisitive than in past generations. In turn, far more is expected of women today. With numerous labor-saving devices for her use, a woman can in theory manage home, family, and job all at once. But stay-at-home housewives believe that it is not possible to do it all successfully."[1]

Just as they reject working because of greed, they also feel that if they did go to work they would feel guilty about neglecting their children. They believe that staying at home gives them freedom from time restraints and fixed schedules, and they find their life styles fulfilling because they can not only take care of their husbands and children but also have time to pursue their own personal interests.

They are particularly sensitive to the negative connotations of the term *housewife.* "While housewives feel that their role is valuable, many think that society sees it as low status." Some of them believe that too much pressure is put on women to work today. They actually feel a need to justify not going to work. "You're made to feel inadequate. You should be doing something else."[2]

They disapprove of mothers of young children who work. "You can't take on the responsibility of another life and then just say 'well, too bad, I'm missing this, that, and the other. I want to go back to work.'"[3] Some of these stay-at-home housewives had working mothers and they are reacting to a sense of personal deprivation of women staying home while their children are small, and returning to work when the children no longer need them at home.

They do accept that women should work or can work at some stage of their lives. They endorse the sequential pattern that "ideally women should be able to leave the work force to raise a family and return if and when it suits them with updating or retraining as necessary." Just as they are defensive about the term *housewife,* they are very negative about the term *career woman.* Stay-at-home housewives "see career women as 'hard, determined, and selfish.'" Even though they admire the achievements of some career women, they do not envy them and feel somewhat defensive toward them. As one housewife said, if she met a career woman, "we'd have nothing in common. I'd have nothing to interest her. She'd not be interested in me (buying a sliced loaf). She'd be too concerned with the next business meeting and her own image."[4]

Japan

Stay-at-home housewives in Japan seem to be much less concerned with their own images or the images of career women. They are very comfortable with their roles as full-time homemakers, and have no desire to work. They think working requires too many sacrifices. They believe that a wife who works would not be able to do her housework properly. Therefore, she would not be able to take care of her children properly. In addition, she would lose her personal time and freedom to enjoy her interests. Moreover, these housewives believe that their husbands and children don't want them to work. They believe that their place in life is to respond to their husbands' and children's wishes by caring for the home.[5]

Their perception of women who work is that they have the advantage of earning a salary, meeting more people on the job, and setting a good example for their children. Although Japanese stay-at-home housewives recognize that working women do, of course, earn money, they themselves feel that they would not want to work just for the money. Some point out that going to work would entail additional expenses such as clothing and travel. One said, "I don't think that any amount I could earn would really contribute that much to improving my family's standard of living."[6]

They recognize that women in the workplace meet people and enjoy a social stimulation that they do not get at home, but these stay-at-home housewives have developed social activities that bring them in touch with other women.

It is interesting that although these women feel that if they went to work themselves, they would be neglecting their children, some think that working mothers who are not working solely for money but also for enjoyment set a good example for their children. Nevertheless, Japanese stay-at-home housewives don't aspire to that achievement. Many feel they are not qualified to have satisfying careers.

Some worked before they were married, but left their jobs as soon as they decided to get married, and those who have never worked do not appear to have any interest in working. According to a Japanese report, "they appeared never to have thought that working might be enjoyable or satisfying and regarded working as something entirely foreign to them."[7]

In short, Japanese stay-at-home housewives have very traditional aspirations, and feel at peace with the choice they have made: "I live in comfort every day. I like being a housewife and I really don't want to do anything else. Some women work one or two days a week, but I couldn't do something like that." Again, "I feel every day that there is no better place for me than at home."[8]

Canada

Stay-at-home housewives in Canada cite their children and husbands as their main reasons for not wanting to work. They typically say, "I enjoy being a mother." They also say that their husbands can afford for them to stay at home, or that their husbands would not permit them to work. Finally, other Canadian stay-at-homes say they are too old to enter the work force or they are not well enough to do so.[9]

Australia

A sizable proportion of housewives in Australia say they would choose their present roles as full-time homemakers over any other combination of paid or unpaid employment. Their major reason is that running a home is a full-time job. In addition, they typically may say that "the children need me at home full-time" or that "I have been out of the work force too long."[10]

Stay-at-home housewives say they enjoy "being my own boss" or "not having to follow a fixed routine." Above all, they enjoy the "freedom to do what I like when I like." The "opportunity to give myself to my family" follows the first two reasons. For these women, being at home means time to spend on their interests and hobbies, and time to work on the house and garden. They place almost as much emphasis on their homes and gardens as on their families. Twenty-four percent say that "the opportunity to give myself to my family" and 21 percent say that "time to work on my house and garden" are benefits of being out of the work force. When they are asked to project the problems they might anticipate if they should go to work full time, the stay-at-homes say they would face problems of age, health, and stamina.[11] The advantages cited here are subjective, but many cite a disadvantage that is not: financial dependence. "The financial dependence associated with being a housewife . . . emerges as a real concern to [these] women."[12]

Italy

Stay-at-home housewives in Italy see their life style as a choice "which allows them to fulfill their aspirations on a social and emotional level." They appear to believe that if they should work outside of the home, it would conflict with their personal desires and the needs of their families. They say that if they worked, they would not be able to take care of their children satisfactorily. Since work would be incompatible with the needs of their families, it could harm their relationships with their husbands. They anticipate that if they went to work, they would take on double responsibilities and, therefore, find themselves under stress.[13]

Finally, they believe that the pressure of meeting the needs of a job and caring for their husbands and families would erode their own personal time and prevent them from pursuing the interests, hobbies, and social life they currently find rewarding. Their negative feelings about work outside the home may be a reflection of the fact that "compared to the jobs to which they could realistically aspire which appear to them to be just as repetitive and monotonous as domestic work, the role of the housewife becomes a part-time job which they can run with complete autonomy and which finally gives them space for the more creative and gratifying activities which any woman with good interior balance and sufficient vital energy can create for herself."[14]

They acknowledge that women who work outside the home probably enjoy greater respect from their families and may have more stimulating social contacts in addition to the economic independence that comes with working. Nevertheless, they believe that the potential advantages of work are not enough to compensate for the potential conflict they would feel if they should choose to work. They feel if they worked they would suffer from feelings of guilt, especially toward their children and sometimes toward their husbands. They don't believe that the limited financial rewards to which they might aspire would warrant the stress and lack of freedom that would result.[15]

Brazil

Stay-at-home housewives in Brazil have no desire to work. Their major reason for choosing to stay at home is that they believe that a woman's place is in the home and that children are best cared for by their mothers. Moreover, they say they don't need to work, that it is more important for them to be at home, and that their husbands and children would not want them to work. The other major reasons why some Brazilian housewives choose not to work are age or health concerns.[16]

Mexico

In Mexico stay-at-home housewives choose not to work because there would be no one to replace them at home in fulfilling their responsibilities for their husbands and children. A number of them said, "I've never worked before and I'm not going to do it now." They also cite age and health concerns as reasons for staying out of the work force.[17]

Venezuela

In Venezuela stay-at-home housewives choose to stay home because they don't need to work. They believe it is more important for them to be at home caring for their husbands and children. They want to devote themselves to their children and their households. They also say that they have problems with age and health, which in turn prevent them from entering the work force. To a lesser extent, they say that if they did go to work, they would not be able to find help to replace them at home.[18]

Plan-to-Work Housewives

Plan-to-work housewives are a group in transition. They reject the traditional definition of "women's place," and aspire to participate in the outside world. Their children are the main reason that they are presently occupied as full-time homemakers.

Canada

Although stay-at-home housewives and plan-to-work housewives in Canada have similar reasons for being out of the work force, their emphasis varies enormously. Plan-to-work housewives are far more likely to mention their roles as mothers as the single most compelling consideration that keeps them from going to work. The major reason why plan-to-work housewives are currently out of the work force is their enjoyment of motherhood. The second reason is being laid off from a job.[19]

Australia

Plan-to-work housewives in Australia are far more concerned about their children than about their homes and gardens. Thirty-nine percent of them say the "opportunity to give myself to my family" is the main advantage of being a full-time housewife; only 12 percent say that time to work on the house and garden is a reason to stay at home. Although plan-to-work housewives do agree that freedom from a fixed routine and freedom to do what they like are important, they are far more likely than stay-at-home housewives to say that the "opportunity to give myself to my family" is an important advantage in being a full-time homemaker.

Plan-to-work housewives "are currently at home almost exclusively because of their young children. They do not believe that running a home is as rewarding as a full-time job. The vast majority who would rather not be at home full-time cite the lack of opportunity or lack of availability of suitable jobs to explain why they aren't working . . . this suggests that these young women are dissatisfied with their current arrangement and would prefer a dual role of mother and worker."[20]

Just-a-Job Working Women

Just-a-job working women, for the most part, reject the limitations of the housewife's role. They feel that work connects them with the larger society and provides social stimulation and a greater sense of self-worth. However, they are not stimulated by an involvement with the work that they do.

Great Britain

In Great Britain, most of the working women who think their work is "just a job" say that they have more self-respect than they would have if they were full-time housewives. They also think they are better organized, and more valued and valuable: "I don't think of myself as a housewife. The word makes people sound middle aged." Again, "You're taken for granted at home doing the same jobs all the time. You feel you're part of the community when you are working." Finally, "I think my husband would lose respect for me if I wasn't working. If I did stay home, I think he would get bored and look elsewhere."[21]

In contrast, some of the older women who see their work as "just a job," particularly those with aging husbands and mundane jobs, are dissatisfied with their lives. Few have high regard for themselves. They feel dull and domesticated compared to women who have satisfying careers. They express a sense of missed opportunity and thwarted ambition: "I would like to have had the opportunity of a career. Career women have ability and foresight. They avoid the marriage and baby trap."[22]

Their children are a paramount consideration for the young mothers who work. Most of them work only part time so that they can be with their children after school hours. Some of the women who work full time are conflicted about leaving their children at a nursery school or a play school: "We needed the income to buy a house. It was the wrong thing to do for such long hours. She didn't like me leaving her at play school. I should have had a part-time job."

On the other hand, some of these working mothers feel that both they and their children have gained from the experience: The children "are far more confident, whereas I couldn't walk out of the room before without the little one screaming and I think it has made me a better person. When you're stuck in all day, you get staid." Again, "I don't get bored or as bad tempered [as I did before I worked], otherwise it's easy to start shouting at your children as soon as you meet them at the school gate."[23]

Money is the major reason why these just-a-job working women go to work. They do not find the work itself particularly stimulating or rewarding. Nevertheless, they find being in the workplace brings them benefits beyond the paycheck. The social stimulation and sense of purpose that come with work give them a greater sense of self-worth: "Going out to work means you can talk to a lot of people. Life exists outside your home. I became a more interesting person and gained confidence again. I felt I was becoming a cabbage." Again, "It gives you a purpose to get up every morning. If you've no job, you just laze about. You don't have to do anything."[24]

One woman articulated the sense of identity that comes with work: "Working you have your own independence. You're a person in your own right, not an extension of your husband." An older woman said, "Today's women are equal to their husbands. I don't think he keeps me. My mother-in-law is quite happy to think that her husband kept her. She would never go out on her own . . . she's never lived her own life which I couldn't tolerate. I couldn't stand a man telling me what to do and where I could go."[25]

British working women share negative feelings about career women with their housewife neighbors. They cannot accept the possibility that a woman can have a serious career and do justice to her family: "their whole life is a career. Work comes first and nothing gets in the way of your work. You can't have a career and a family." Again, "It's a total commitment even to the exclusion of your home life and marriage."

Just-a-job working women in Great Britain are somewhere between the housewife who hopes to go to work to get away from the confines of her life style and the career woman. Their comments about full-time housewives reflect this: "she's a slave," or "it's a never-ending job," or "I get bored." On the other hand, they feel that a career woman's life is more hectic than their own, with little time for home and family. They believe that career women are selfish and determined: "they don't see why you want to stay at home with children."[26]

Japan

Just-a-job working women in Japan are motivated to work primarily because they need the money to support themselves or to supplement their husband's incomes. But they find there are benefits to be gained from working. They feel that work gives them a connection with the broader world, that by working they are more alert and focused. They believe that the money they earn is accepted by society as a symbol of their own worth. The real difference between these women and career women is that the former don't find their work either attractive or challenging. They think it would be difficult to find a job that would interest them.[27]

They also dislike the limitations of being a full-time housewife: "I'm glad I'm working. I'm amazed that [housewives] can keep on saying the same things day after day." Again, "I'd be so bored if I was at home."[28]

Many of these women see the paycheck as recognition of their own worth: "With strangers you always have to be alert so, generally speaking, you will be evaluated impartially." Again, "When you work you receive a certain type of evaluation. A housewife is just considered a helper. When you receive money, it's a tangible return for the work you have done."[29]

The main disadvantage Japanese working women see in going to work is the loss of free time for shopping or sports. Some of them say they don't have enough time for their children, and some initially feel guilty because of this. But their children adjust to having their mothers working: "I've stopped feeling that my children should be pitied. Deep down I do feel that I should be spending more time with them, but I don't show that feeling openly. I've noticed that the children have changed gradually. They've become much more considerate of me."[30]

Another woman found that her work schedule prevented her from eating with her husband, and she missed the chance for communication with him, but she didn't feel guilty about eating out often. Some of these women have husbands and children who cooperate in running the household and others yearn for cooperation: "On his day off my husband helps with everything from cleaning to laundry. On working days whichever one of us gets home first prepares the meal." Again, "I don't feel any particular guilt towards my husband. He's the type of man who prefers a working woman."[31]

Italy

In Italy, working women who consider their work "just a job" have varying attitudes toward work depending on their situations in the life cycle. Young women without children and those who returned to work recently after having been full-time homemakers for a number of years share a perception of the advantages that come from working outside the home. They feel that it gives them an opportunity for social interaction with other people. They appreciate the economic independence and the ability to improve their standard of living. They believe that working keeps them young and active and open to new ideas. In addition, work puts family problems in a better perspective and helps them avoid the "housewife's syndrome." They believe that by going to work they lead a fuller life and receive greater respect from members of their families.[32]

On the other hand, working mothers who have always worked and who never had the opportunity to be full-time homemakers are more aware of the disadvantages of working. They have a sense of guilt toward their children, and they wish they had the time to supervise them and enjoy them more. They suffer from the stress of the double responsibility of home and work. They say that because of these pressures they have little time for themselves. They are realistic in believing that their present jobs give them few opportunities for achieving a career. Therefore, although they have the benefits of the salaries they earn, they see real obstacles in attempting to reach a position that would give them a sense of self-fulfillment.

For these women their jobs are a necessity and, in fact, a constriction. Therefore, they yearn for the freedom that they perceive the housewife to have. Many of these women hope to stay at home to follow their own interests and inclinations as soon as they reach the minimum age for a pension.[33]

Career Women

The major difference between just-a-job working women and career women is that career women gain personal satisfaction and a sense of achievement from the work that they do. Consequently, they are far more committed to their careers.

Australia

The reasons why just-a-job working women and career women in Australia work are pretty much the same, but there is a difference in emphasis. Both groups say they work primarily for the income, and both groups also say that independence and enjoyment are important reasons for going to work. The difference is that career-oriented working women are slightly less likely to stress income and far more likely to stress the enjoyment and independence that come from work.[34]

Another Australian study reveals that even though both groups of women give similar reasons for working, their priorities are different. Women for whom work is just a job are far more likely than career women to say they need the money. Although both groups say that work gives them personal satisfaction and social stimulation, personal satisfaction is far more important to career women than any other single reason for going to work.[35]

A reflection of the importance that work plays in their lives and the importance of the noneconomic benefits is demonstrated in their response to the question of whether they would stop working if they received the same money they earned on the job. Three out of five just-a-job working women said they would stop, but two in five said they would continue to work. Eight in ten career women say they would continue to work. Only 19 percent of career women say they would give up their careers if they received the same amount of money.[36]

An interesting sidelight on the just-a-job working women is that although three in five would stop if they could receive the same amount of money they earn now, only 48 percent said they would stop working if their spouses received a pay rise equivalent to their salaries. This is evidence that even though they are not attracted to work as such, they do want the independence provided by earning their own money.[37]

Canada

The stronger motivations of career women are also observed in Canada. Eighty percent of career women there say they like to work because of the sense of achievement it brings. In addition, 59 percent of career women feel that "working makes me feel that I am in control of my life."

Career women are more likely to emphasize financial independence and a sense of control (58 percent).[38] Only 35 percent of career women think of their job as a way to afford things for their families that they wouldn't otherwise be able to buy, and only 32 percent say, "Frankly, I work because we need the income."[39]

United States

In the United States there is a similar contrast in attitudes between career women and those who think the work they do is "just a job." In answer to the question, "If you were financially secure and did not need the income from your job, do you think you would continue to work or not?" 82 percent of career women say they would prefer to stay on the job, compared to 56 percent of just-a-job working women.[40]

Perhaps a clue to why more career women would continue to work even if they didn't need the money is the personal satisfaction they derive from their work. Sixty-five percent of career women, compared to 19 percent of just-a-job working women, say they get great personal satisfaction from their work. At the other extreme, only 3 percent of career women get little or no personal satisfaction.[41]

Venezuela

A similar difference in emphasis is observed in Venezuela. Both segments of working women say the additional income is a very important reason for their going to work. But job-oriented women are slightly more likely to say they work because it is financially necessary. They are more likely than career women to stress financial independence, although this is at a fairly low level. Sixteen percent of job-oriented women, compared to 10 percent of career women, give this as a reason for working. Second to income, career women are twice as likely to say that working gives them personal satisfaction and a sense of self-worth. They are far more likely to stress the personal satisfaction that comes from pursuing a career or a profession.[42]

Mexico

A similar pattern occurs in Mexico, with minor differences. Both segments are equally likely to say they work to supplement their husbands' incomes so they don't lack anything at home, but job-oriented women are more likely to say they are working for additional income and more than twice as likely to say they are working because it is financially necessary. Mexican career women strongly emphasize the personal satisfaction and emotional benefits of working. They feel that going to work enhances their sense of self-worth, and they appreciate the personal development that comes from an opportunity to pursue a career or profession.[43]

Brazil

Working women in Brazil place far more emphasis on the personal independence that comes from earning an income. Both job and career women cite as a major reason for working having the money for personal expenses. Second to this is the belief that a woman must be economically independent. This is important to both segments, but career women are slightly more likely to stress this point of view.

Another view unique to Brazil is that these women work because it is better to divide the household expenses with their husbands. Again, this is important to both segments but slightly more emphasized by career women. The other side of this coin is that they work "because I don't want to depend on my husband for everything." When expressed in these terms it is slightly more important to just-a-job working women. Career women are somewhat more likely than just-a-job women to say they work because they earn practically the same as their husbands.[44]

Brazilian working women mention a number of noneconomic reasons for working. One of these is that working gives them great personal satisfaction. Although this is slightly more important to career women, it is also very important to women who say their work is "just a job." This is quite different from the attitude observed among job-oriented women in other countries. In Brazil, 90 percent of women who say their work is "just a job" say that they work for personal satisfaction, and 95 percent of career women feel that way.[45]

The greatest difference between the two groups is in the relative stress on the work itself. Ninety-one percent of career women say, "I work because I have a profession or a career." Just over half (53 percent) of job-oriented women agree with the statement. Just under three out of four women in each segment say they work because their husbands give them total support for this. Again, this contrasts with the responses of working women in other countries. Finally, some say they work in order to get out of the house. Thirty percent of job-oriented women say, "I work because I can't bear staying home only taking care of the house and children"; only 19 percent of career women feel this way.[46]

West Germany

In Germany, career-oriented women are far more committed to working than women who say their work is "just a job." Eighty percent of German career women say that life without working would be unthinkable. Forty-six percent of career women say they are completely satisfied with their lives and would not change a thing.[47] Indeed, only 13 percent of German career women would stop working if they had enough money. Career-oriented women are also far more likely to be very satisfied with the work they do. Forty-six percent of career women say they are very satisfied with their work, and 50 percent of career women say they are "somewhat satisfied" with their work.[48]

Great Britain

Career women in Great Britain share with career women in other countries pleasure in their work and a sense of personal fulfillment from their professional achievements. Their place in the life cycle colors their general attitude toward their own lives and work.

133

Some career mothers dropped out of the work force while their children were small, chose to work from home, or took part-time jobs. Others worked throughout and express regret that they weren't able to be with their children when they were very small: "I felt guilty going out to work while she was young. We were short of money for the mortgage. I needed to work . . . I felt awful leaving her with someone else to do my job."[49]

Another career woman said that her work means more to her than the money she earns: "Even if I didn't have to go to work I would have to have something. But I don't consider that I ill-treated my children. I only used to go in the mornings. I once asked the boys if they resented it and they said they'd not considered it. Most of their friends' mums worked, so I thought why should I have felt guilty."[50]

The major difference between career women and just-a-job working women in Great Britain is the enjoyment and recognition that career women find in their work: "You're using your brain rather than just being with the children." Again, "Your talents are spotted and you have a chance of rising in the job." The work becomes a part of their personal identities: "What would you do without your work? How would you survive without your work?"[51]

The recurring theme of work and family is expressed somewhat differently by some career women. Several of them took time out while their children were small and then returned to work: "If you had an interesting job, quite a good job before you had your children, I feel that you owe it to yourself to be able to achieve that sort of goal again, once your children are off hand. It's self-respect, really." Again, "I definitely feel I am a career woman. I just couldn't bear being at home. It drove me absolutely crackers being at home for five years. All I used to think about was when this awful time would be over and I would be independent again and have my own job."[52]

Many career women report that their husbands are cooperative in sharing domestic responsibilities, particularly child care: "It made a lot of difference to my husband having the children for one day a week while I worked. He can understand how I said it drove me up the wall. It drives him up the wall."

On the other hand, some of them think that their husbands have mixed feelings about their achievements. "Apart from the fact that it adds to the responsibilities and commitments, living with a woman who is ambitious or successful may introduce an element of competition into their lives which they find hard to cope with." Career women are aware of this: "Both of us were in professions and in a way he was very pleased that I worked. But also very resentful in many ways because I was also climbing up. He liked the extra money coming in. He was happy that I was satisfied with my job, but there was a certain

resentment. I think it was his upbringing and being a Scot. He was very traditional minded."[53]

On the other hand, they say that even if they were not pursuing careers,
they would want something more from life than domesticity. They love their
families and their homes give them pleasure, but that is not enough. They admire those women who are content to be full-time homemakers, but they see
the homemaker role as a restricted one: "I'd be bored out of my mind. I think
I'd become an alcoholic or end up in a mental home."[54]

British career women offer a range of attitudes about whether a woman
should work when her children are small. As one career woman said, "I firmly
believe you should be at home when they are small." On the other hand, several
of them pointed out that a woman with a satisfactory job is "a much better
parent for having had that job."

More affluent career women have nursemaids at home, but others feel
"that's just palming your family off onto the au pair." On the other hand, "for
some women it's better for the children than being [with] a frustrated mum."[55]

Japan

Career-oriented women in Japan express a sense of exuberance about their lives
and about their work. They seem to aspire to personal growth, to learn more
and expand their horizons, and work helps them do that: "Basically, I feel very
strongly that I want to enjoy my life. That applies to my work and to other
aspects of my life, too. I want to live a full life, the best I can. That's how I feel
about everything. I just don't want to do anything that I dislike doing." Again,
"I want to live a life that I won't regret later."[56]

In Japan, there are few opportunities for a satisfying career for women.
Instead of settling for jobs that they don't find stimulating, some career-oriented
women make special efforts to improve their situations. They may change jobs
a number of times in hopes of finding a more satisfactory position. Others may
take special courses to learn new skills.

These women reject the housewife role as too limiting and too narrow. An
unmarried woman said, "In general I think full-time housewives are limited in
their interests. I don't think they have a broad point of view." A career wife said,
"I stayed at home for a while after my child was born but I felt that I just wasn't
suited to be a full-time housewife. I just couldn't stand it."[57]

Japanese career women find work a path to personal growth: "My work
broadens my horizons. I'm always learning something new and I find myself
growing as a human being." Again, "My work gets more interesting the more I
do. It gives me a feeling of satisfaction when I finish and I always discover

something new. I like hearing that my work has improved, too. It gives me confidence in myself." Although they are obviously deeply committed to their work, they also enjoy their leisure time as well: "Once I finish work, I want to concentrate on other things." Again, "Outside of work I like to have a good time. If I'm off work, I'm off."[58]

Some Japanese career women can find no disadvantages in their work. As one said, "I work because I like to, so I don't see any disadvantages to it." A few others mentioned that the time demands of work mean that they have no time to enjoy hobbies or not enough time to spend with their children. Some feel they are imposing on their husbands because they can't prepare elaborate meals every day. One woman feels she is not doing justice to her husband because she doesn't prepare meals from scratch every day but prepares meals on the weekend for the coming week and then puts them in the freezer. Most of the married women, however, say they don't feel guilty because they don't have time to do housework thoroughly. One said that it is only natural for a husband and wife to share the housework (including shopping and child care). Another said she works only a limited number of hours and, therefore, it doesn't affect her household. Another said that her husband cooperates with the house-work.[59]

Although some are concerned about not having enough time to spend with their children, they apparently do not feel guilty because they are working. They take the position that, in fact, it is better for them to work because it helps them develop their sense of independence: "Of course, I don't have that much time to spend with my children and I can't hover over them when they do their homework. I can barely manage to cook for them when I get home from work. I do feel that they suffer, but my work comes first. I tell my children, frankly, that I do feel under pressure because of my work and I've raised them to be able to take care of themselves." Another said, "If both parents are working, children just can't go wrong. If they went wrong it must be due to their own fault. There is absolutely nothing strange about a woman working after mar-riage."[60]

The differentiation of four New Demographic segments of women is docu-mented by their clearly differentiated spectrum of values in relation to marriage, children, and the basic role of women. Their attitudes toward work provide further confirmation that there are distinctly different segments of women.

Stay-at-home housewives cling to the traditional role of wife and mother as their destiny and occupation in life. Plan-to-work housewives are devoted to their children but aspire to work as a way of expanding their horizons. Just-a-job working women are motivated to work by money but find psychic rewards in the social interaction at work and an enhanced sense of self-worth. Career women also work for money and psychic rewards. But they find satisfaction in the work they do and their work gives them a sense of achievement and personal fulfillment.

In the following chapters we will examine how their demographic and attitudinal differences are expressed in their behavior in the marketplace.

IV

Changing Markets: The Traditional Women's Products

The products that are normally marketed to women are those relating to home-making tasks such as cleaning and laundry, the preparation and serving of food, and the eternal chore of shopping for all of these products. The other products normally marketed to women are those relating to personal adornment: fashion, fragrance, cosmetics, and jewelry. This section examines these product categories from the perspective of the New Demographics: the attitudes of women toward these activities and their market behavior in relation to household products, food, and fashion.

Chapter Twelve, "Women and Homemaking," reports on the extent to which women believe that the partnership approach to marriage should extend to the homemaking sphere and the extent to which husbands actually participate in household chores. The whole area of shopping for groceries will also be examined, from the perspective of who does the shopping and the extent to which these consumers take a consumerist point of view when they shop. Their attitudes toward advertised brands, their response to generics, and the strategies they employ to get the value for their money are also discussed.

Chapter Thirteen, "Women and Food," examines the patterns of eating at home and away from home, concern with diet and nutrition, the particular elements of diet that are of major concern, and the extent to which health concerns affect the foods that people buy and avoid. The use of coffee, tea, and soft drinks as well as alcoholic beverages will be examined. Although cigarettes are not a food, they fall into the "indulgence" category. Women's feelings about cigarettes are therefore included here.

Chapter Fourteen, "Women and Fashion," examines the way that women approach fashion and the extent to which their position in the New Demographic spectrum affects their feelings about clothes and purchase behavior.

Chapter Fifteen, "Women and Grooming," continues the study of how the New Demographic segments respond to cosmetics and to fragrance and the implications of their attitudes toward personal grooming for the marketing of such products.

Not all countries reported on the consumer activities of women in every product category. In the following I have included data from those countries that deal with specific product categories and areas of behavior. By its nature, this cannot be a definitive report on how the segments of women in all countries approach particular types of products. It could serve as a framework, however, for examining the market behavior of segments of women for specific categories in specific countries.

Action Implications

The overview of the way women in different parts of the world respond to products normally marketed to women indicates that the astute marketer should keep in touch with the wants and needs of the customer. The precise procedure for this was explained in Part III.

1. Husbands participate in the shopping chores; therefore, they may be involved in brand choice in a way that has not been considered to date. To the extent that husbands share in household responsibilities, their perspective should be considered in terms of defining both the target group for the category or the brand and the context within which it is presented. Even though there is more lip service than reality in husbands sharing household responsibilities, the attitude of sharing could be tapped into for communications in contrast to the conventional approach, which concentrates only on the housewife.

2. The consumerist concerns of women in some parts of the world are also a clue to the importance of credibility and clarity in making product claims. This has implications for labeling and nutrition information, for example. Consumer response to generics is also a warning that brand

names need to be nurtured and protected. Marketing practices should be examined from the perspective of whether or not they are eroding the quality of the brand image and whether they might be reducing brands to the level of commodities vulnerable to generic and no-name competition.

3. The varying attitudes of women toward fashion and personal grooming suggest that there are many motivations for the purchase and use of these products that go beyond the traditional assumption that the only reason women try to be attractive is to capture or keep a man. The responses of the New Demographic groups suggest that these different segments of women represent varying opportunities or niches for the astute marketer.

4. I suggest that the marketer who applies the New Demographic framework recommended in Part III carefully analyze the relative value of each New Demographic and life-cycle group to the particular product or category. A "value index" can be constructed that would consider both the size of the segment in the population and the extent to which that segment is above or below the norm in purchase or volume of use. This enables the marketer to create a value index that can serve as a guideline to strategy decisions. It would also serve as an important screen through which to determine the optimum media plans for reaching the different segments in the market. And, of course, as communications are developed, the responses of the various segments to the product and the presentation of the product will serve as guidelines to achieving the most effective communication to the most desirable customers.

twelve

Women and Homemaking

THE conventional wisdom in marketing circles has been that the woman is the prime target for products related to the home. These include home cleaning products, laundry products, and, of course, food products and appliances related to the preparation of meals. Homemaking also encompasses the selection and care of clothing for members of the family and household furnishings such as table linens, dishes, cookware, and bedding. The assumption is that the products are purchased by the female head of household and that all aspects of the care and feeding of the family and the maintenance of the home are the woman's direct responsibility.

Traditionally, it was assumed that woman's only role in life was to serve her husband and children and that her reward for being a good housewife was her family's appreciation or approval. We have seen that in some countries there is a move away from the traditional definition of the male and female roles to a partnership approach to marriage. How does this express itself in the homemaking sphere? To what extent do women and their husbands believe that husbands should share in homemaking responsibilities? To what extent do women expect it? And what is the reality? Do husbands share in homemaking chores? If so, how much do they do?

The answers to these questions have direct application to how we define the target groups for the marketing of food and household products. If the woman is not the only purchaser of these products, this will have profound implications for marketing strategies.

Once we have defined the targets, we need to understand the context within which women approach the various activities that relate to housekeeping in order to market food and household products effectively. How do they feel about housework? How do they feel about the role of the housewife? Understanding how they feel about homemaking is essential to how we market home-related products and talk to women and men in advertising. Understanding the way women feel about homemaking chores would ensure that communication about home-related products would be consonant with contemporary attitudes.

Feelings about Keeping House

Latin America

Men and women in Latin America are in fairly close agreement that working at home is monotonous, boring, and unrewarding. Brazilian women (72 percent) and men (71 percent) are much more likely to feel this way than men and women in Mexico and Venezuela. In Mexico, 43 percent of the women and 46 percent of the men agree with this view of housework, and in Venezuela, 46 percent of the women and 37 percent of the men agree.[1]

The New Demographic segments are also in fairly close agreement on this issue. Plan-to-work housewives are most negative about housework. Just-a-job working women are slightly more likely than career women to find housework boring and monotonous. Stay-at-home housewives in Mexico and Venezuela are more likely than career women to be critical about housework. Career women in Brazil are slightly more likely than stay-at-home housewives to find keeping house unrewarding.

Perhaps because they consider the housewife's lot confining and boring, consumers in the three Latin American countries are also more likely to believe that being a good housewife is more difficult than being a good professional. Men (66 percent) and women (69 percent) in Brazil are more likely to take this point of view than their counterparts in the other two Latin American countries. In Mexico, 46 percent of the women and 42 percent of the men take this position, and in Venezuela, 43 percent of the women and 45 percent of the men do so.[2]

All segments of women in Mexico are in fairly close agreement about this. Career women in Venezuela, however, are less likely (37 percent) than stay-at-home housewives (46 percent) to believe that being a good housewife is more difficult than being a good professional. The greatest contrast is found in Brazil. Brazilian career women are far less likely (50 percent) than Brazilian stay-at-home housewives (76 percent) to believe that being a good housewife is more difficult than being a good professional.[3]

Canada

Women in Canada take a more positive view of the housewife's role. Three out of four Canadian women say that being a good housewife is just as satisfying

144

as working outside the home. Their enthusiasm is in direct relation to their situation in the New Demographic spectrum. Almost nine out of ten stay-at-home housewives feel this way, compared to two out of three career women.[4]

West Germany

In West Germany, stay-at-home housewives and career women have diametrically opposed views about housework. Stay-at-home housewives are wildly enthusiastic about doing housework. Eighty-eight percent of them say housework is fun and 80 percent say that being a housewife is a pleasant and fulfilling occupation. Career women are far more likely to say that housework is a necessary evil (56 percent) or that housework is a daily drudgery with no visible results (26 percent). The two middle groups, plan-to-work housewives and just-a-job working women, are somewhere between the two extreme segments in their feelings about housework.[5]

Japan

Just over half of all women in Japan, both full-time homemakers and working women, believe that housewives have a narrow outlook. An equal proportion of stay-at-home housewives and just-a-job working women also feel this way. Plan-to-work housewives are particularly critical; they are more likely than any other segment to believe that housewives have a narrow outlook. Their viewpoint may, in part, be a reflection of their own aspirations to move beyond the horizons of their immediate households.[6]

Australia

Australian women have very strong priorities relating to the care and feeding of their families and households. More than nine out of ten say they are concerned about preparing enjoyable and healthy meals. Just under nine out of ten say they are concerned about having clean clothing for their families. They give a slightly lower priority to having a spotless house. Nonetheless, just under three out of four Australian women say they are concerned about this aspect of homemaking. Although all segments of women in Australia are concerned about these issues, they are of particular importance to the plan-to-work housewives and just-a-job working women. Each aspect of homemaking is of slightly less concern to the stay-at-home housewives and career-oriented working women.[7]

Husbands and Housework

Is housework only a woman's responsibility? What role should husbands play? We saw earlier that there is a certain amount of movement away from the traditional perception of marriage: the home is the woman's responsibility and the man's role is to go to work and support the family. Men and women in a number of these countries believe that husbands and wives should share in various aspects of homemaking responsibilities. The level of enthusiasm for shared responsibilities varies from country to country. It also varies somewhat among the four New Demographic segments.

In most cases stay-at-home housewives are least likely and career women are most likely to want to share household chores with their husbands. The differences between them, however, are relatively slight and stay-at-home housewives in some countries are far more advanced in their attitudes on these matters than even the most liberated career women in other countries.

West Germany

In West Germany, the answer appears to be that housework is a woman's responsibility. Half of all German women, both homemakers and working women, feel this way. Not surprisingly, more full-time housewives (55 percent) than working women (47 percent) believe that housework should be done by women.[8]

Canada

A very different attitude is discernible in Canada. An overwhelming four out of five Canadian women disagree with the idea that men shouldn't have to bother about housework. Only 12 percent of Canadian women take the traditional view that housework is a woman's responsibility, compared to 50 percent of German women who believe that women should do the housework. Although there is some variation among the New Demographic segments on this issue, the overwhelming proportion of all groups of women in Canada do *not* believe that men should not have to bother with housework. The level of opinion about this ranges from 69 percent among stay-at-home housewives to 92 percent among career women.[9]

Further evidence of the less conventional attitudes held by Canadian women is that more of them disagree than agree with the idea that a man loses his pride if he is able to have a job but stays home to look after the house and the children. Just 30 percent of Canadian women agree with this statement, but 50 percent disagree. Again, there is a range of response among the New Demographics. Stay-at-home housewives are least likely to agree with this position, and career women are most likely to do so. Even among stay-at-homes, however, a higher proportion disagree than agree that a man loses his pride if he stays home to look after the house and the children (40 percent agree and

44 percent disagree). More than twice as many career women take the non-traditional view (23 percent agree and 54 percent disagree).[10]

Latin America

The overwhelming majority of both men and women in the three Latin American countries believe that household tasks should be shared by men and women. In Brazil, 89 percent of the women and 79 percent of the men agree; in Mexico, 79 percent of the women and 77 percent of the men agree; and in Venezuela, 90 percent of the women and 83 percent of the men agree.[11]

There is some variation of response among the New Demographics. Career women in Brazil and Venezuela are most likely to feel this way. Ninety-four percent of career women in each country endorse sharing household tasks. But substantial proportions of stay-at-home housewives also believe that household tasks should be shared. Eighty-one percent in Brazil and 89 percent in Venezuela believe in sharing household responsibilities with their husbands.[12]

Enthusiasm for sharing household chores with husbands is slightly lower among women in Mexico. Just-a-job working women are more likely than career women to want cooperation from their husbands. Stay-at-home housewives are the least likely to believe that husbands and wives should share household tasks. Nonetheless, support ranges from a low of 77 percent among stay-at-homes to a high of 84 percent among just-a-job working women. In essence, this represents an extremely high level of endorsement of a nontraditional viewpoint.[13]

Canada

Ninety-six percent of Canadian women believe that if a woman works, her husband should share equally in the responsibilities of caring for their children. The responses of the four New Demographic segments are remarkably similar. Between 95 and 98 percent believe that husbands should share equally in the responsibilities of child care, if the mother works.[14]

Australia

Ninety-six percent of women in Australia believe that husbands and wives should share family responsibilities. There is very little variation among the New Demographic groups on this issue. Their responses range from a "low" of 93 percent among plan-to-work housewives to a "high" of 97 percent among career women. These differences are hardly statistically significant.[15]

Almost four out of five Australian women also believe that husbands and wives should share in the care of small children without regard to whether the mother works. There is some variation among the New Demographic segments, but it is not great. Predictably, stay-at-home housewives are least likely to expect husbands to share this work (74 percent), whereas the two working women groups are most likely to believe that husbands and wives should care for small children. Eighty-one percent of just-a-job working women and 80 percent of career women take this point of view. Plan-to-work housewives are closer to the two working women segments in their opinions on this issue (79 percent) than to their stay-at-home neighbors. Even though stay-at-home housewives are less likely than the others to believe that husbands should help care for children, it is still the dominant opinion among that group as well.[16]

Japan
Exactly three out of four Japanese women believe that husbands and wives should share in the care of small children. The responses of the four New Demographic segments in Japan are remarkably similar, with only a few minor variations in their levels of response. Stay-at-home housewives and just-a-job working women are slightly less likely (73 percent) than plan-to-work housewives (76 percent) or career women (77 percent) to say that husbands should share in child care.[17]

Who Should Do the Housework?

Women in various parts of the world agree about the cooperation of husbands and wives in the care of children and the home, but they diverge widely on how much cooperation they get in reality.

Japan
For example, Japanese women strongly endorse husbands and wives sharing in purchase decisions and in the care of small children, but they are less likely to believe that husbands should participate in such household chores as cleaning the house or shopping for groceries. Only 28 percent of Japanese women say that a married couple should share housecleaning tasks and only 27 percent believe they should share the chore of shopping for groceries.

Stay-at-home housewives in Japan are most likely to reject the notion of having their husbands cooperate in sharing household tasks, whereas working women are most responsive to sharing housework and shopping with their husbands. Nevertheless, enthusiasm for shared household responsibilities never rose above the 34 percent of career women who voted for help with cleaning the house and the 30 percent of just-a-job working women who said they would appreciate their husbands' help in shopping for groceries.[18]

Women and Homemaking

Australia

In sharp contrast, Australian women welcome their husbands' help in shopping for groceries and in cleaning the house. Seventy-two percent of women in Australia believe that husbands and wives should share in shopping for groceries. Plan-to-work housewives are least likely to feel this way (63 percent), and career women are most likely to do so (84 percent). This is one case in which the stay-at-home housewife is more enthusiastic about her husband's participation (71 percent) than either her plan-to-work neighbor or the just-a-job working woman (69 percent).[19]

Women in Australia diverge sharply from women in Japan on sharing responsibilities for cleaning the house. Two out of three Australian women approve of this. Support for it rises across the New Demographic spectrum. Stay-at-home housewives (54 percent) are least likely to support sharing, and career women (81 percent) most likely to.[20]

There are a number of specific household-related tasks that half, or more than half, of Australian women believe should be shared by spouses. In every case career women are most likely to endorse sharing. For the most part, stay-at-home housewives are least likely to do so. One exception is meal preparation: daily cooking and meal planning. Plan-to-work housewives are less enthusiastic than their stay-at-home neighbors about sharing these activities with their husbands, but the differences are slight. In each case career women are most likely to believe that spouses should share in planning and preparing meals.[21]

Stay-at-home housewives and career women in Australia differ most strongly over tasks that are usually considered "man's work," such as mowing the lawn and doing repairs around the house. Fewer than half of stay-at-home housewives believe that they should share these particular tasks with their husbands. Forty-six percent of stay-at-homes are willing to share lawn mowing with their spouses, compared to 62 percent of plan-to-work housewives and career women. Just-a-job women are slightly less enthusiastic: 55 percent of them are willing to take their turn at mowing the lawn.[22]

Doing the family laundry is the least popular of the eight household tasks studied. Just half of all Australian women are in favor of both spouses doing the laundry. Neither segment of housewives is particularly enthusiastic about this. Forty-one percent of the stay-at-home housewives and of plan-to-work housewives agree that husbands and wives should share in doing the laundry. By contrast, 68 percent of career women saw no reason why husbands should not share the laundry chores. As in most cases, just-a-job working women are in between. Fifty-five percent believe that husbands and wives should share responsibilities for the laundry.[23]

Even though stay-at-home housewives tend to be less responsive than career women to sharing specific chores with their husbands, with the exception of lawn mowing and home repairs, anywhere from 50 percent to 74 percent of stay-at-home housewives agree that it is a good idea for husbands to share specific household chores. For the entire list of household tasks, between 50 percent and 78 percent of all Australian women believe that husbands and wives should share responsibility equally. Even though career women tend to be most enthusiastic about sharing household responsibilities, this is a majority point of view among Australian women.[24]

How Much Do Husbands Really Help?

Women's enthusiasm for sharing household tasks with their husbands does not always translate into reality.

Canada

Only two out of five women in Canada say that their husbands help with the household chores. Stay-at-home housewives are the least likely of any segment of Canadian women to get help from their husbands (34 percent); career-oriented working women report the highest level of cooperation (45 percent). Canadian women also report getting help from their children. Twenty-two percent of total women, both full-time homemakers and working women, say their children help around the house. Just-a-job working women are slightly more likely than the others to get such help (25 percent); stay-at-home housewives are least likely to do so (19 percent).[25]

Australia

In "Home Truths," an intriguing study by the Clemenger group in Australia, researchers examined the attitudes and behavior of husbands and wives in the same household. Each partner was asked whether he or she did a fair share of work around the house. They were also asked whether they felt their partners did, as well. For the most part, the majority of both husbands and wives feel they are, in fact, doing their fair share. Seventy-eight percent of men and 71 percent of women feel they are doing their fair share of household tasks.[26] More women than men feel they are doing more than their fair share. Twenty-seven percent of women and 6 percent of men feel they are carrying an extra responsibility. Conversely, more men (16 percent) than women (2 percent) think they are not pulling their weight.[27]

We have seen that Australian women have strong expectations about the extent to which husbands should share in a number of household chores. The

Clemenger report gives us evidence on the extent to which husbands and wives allocate chores. The questions were asked in terms of whether the man under-took the chore on his own or shared it with his wife, and the report combines the two dimensions to indicate the husband's participation. We therefore have no way of knowing the extent to which the tasks are done by the man on his own or whether he shares responsibilities with his wife.

Among a list of specific tasks the husband does himself or shares with his wife, Australian husbands are most likely to work in the garden. A substantial number report they share in preparing breakfast (43 percent) and doing dishes (40 percent). One in three Australian men says that he shares in the grocery shopping or does it himself. Just over one in four (26 percent) says that he vacuums the house.[28]

Fewer are likely to report caring for children (21 percent). Men under thirty-five years of age, who are most likely to have small children in their households, are more likely to do so. Twenty-nine percent of men in this age group say they help care for their children. The remaining household chores get a negligible amount of cooperation from husbands. Sixteen percent help with the laundry and 15 percent of Australian men help prepare the main meal.

Men in their retirement years are most likely to participate in household chores. More than half of them say they prepare breakfast and do the dishes. Just under half share in shopping for groceries and one in four does the laundry. Middle-aged men, between thirty-five and forty-five years of age, are least likely to be involved in household tasks. Apparently, women in these households re-semble younger women in their attitudes toward the male and female roles, and husbands in this age group take a traditional viewpoint. At this age, "the men appear very much less flexible in their approach to who does what around the house."[29]

Working women get more help from their husbands than full-time home-makers: "In a household where the woman works, routine household chores were significantly more likely to be shared between partners. For example, part-ners were more likely to share the job of setting the table, doing the dishes, preparing meals or breakfast, vacuuming, and cleaning the bathroom." One young working wife observed, "But he does help with the inside chores as well. We normally take it in turns for cooking after work because we both work. That's one chore we both normally share."[30]

The researchers go on to say: "Although women in the work force generally get more assistance from their partners, career-oriented women were less in-clined to give their men credit than older women who work primarily for the income [just-a-job working women]. The partners of career-oriented working women were more inclined to describe tasks such as caring for the children, vacuuming, and doing laundry as ones that they share or that he does himself."[31]

Latin America

The overwhelming majority of both men and women in the three Latin American countries believe that household tasks should be shared between the husband and wife. In reality, husbands are far more likely to say they share in a variety of household responsibilities or do them on their own than their wives admit.

Brazil

In Brazil both husbands and wives agree that maintaining household or electrical appliances gets the greatest amount of attention from husbands. Eighty-five percent of men and 62 percent of women say that husbands participate in this activity.[32]

Brazilian husbands are also more likely to share child care than housework, but there is a wide discrepancy between the perceptions of women and those of men on the extent to which husbands help with children. Just 11 percent of the women say their husbands participate in five child-care activities, compared to 40 percent of the men who claim that they help with the children. Brazilian husbands are most likely to get up late at night to attend to children or to take their children to the doctor or dentist. They are somewhat less likely to accompany the maid when she brings the children to school. Approximately three times as many men claim to participate in each of these activities as their wives say they really do. Although the level of caring for small children is lower, three times as many husbands as wives say the men participate in this. The least frequently mentioned activity is taking children to school or fetching them home. Over twice as many husbands as wives say that husbands help in taking children back and forth to school.[33]

Finally, although the men in Brazil say they support sharing household responsibilities, they are least likely to participate in specific housecleaning and food preparation chores. In five tasks, 4 percent of women say they have help from their husbands and 12 percent of men say they participate in these tasks. Most frequently mentioned is cleaning the house; second, helping to prepare lunch or dinner over the weekend; third, washing dishes and cleaning the kitchen; fourth, preparing lunch or dinner on a weekday; and fifth, ironing clothes.[34]

Mexico

In Mexico, as in Brazil, husbands are more likely to help in the care of the children than in housekeeping chores. Again, as in Brazil, Mexican husbands are far more likely than their wives to claim that they help with either caring for children or cleaning. Both husbands and wives agree that husbands are more likely to help with children's homework than with child care. In each case twice as many husbands say they help with their children's homework as their wives report that their husbands do.[35]

On an average, wives say that only 3 percent of husbands participate in a variety of household chores. Even though husbands don't claim to do very much housework, they are more than twice as likely as their wives to say that they help with the mundane tasks. Both husbands and wives are most likely to say that husbands help with cleaning the bathroom and doing the dishes, although the level of such help is extremely low. Husbands are three times as likely as wives to say that they clean the house.[36]

Venezuela

In spite of their strong endorsement of sharing household responsibilities, husbands in Venezuela are also not likely to follow their words with action. As in the other two Latin American countries, they are more likely to help with children than housework. Again, they are far more likely to help with their children's homework than general child care. As in the other two countries, husbands are twice as likely to claim that they help care for their children as their wives say they do.[37]

Women in Venezuela say that they get only minimal help from their husbands with any of the household chores. On average, 1.5 percent of Venezuelan women say their husbands help with housework. Wives report that husbands are more likely to help with the dishes than any other particular chore in the house. Even though husbands don't claim a very high level of housework, they are far more likely than their wives to say they help around the house. An average of 8 percent of husbands claim to help with household chores. Husbands are most likely to say they wash the dishes and clean the house in general. They are also quite likely to say they cook and clean the bathrooms. As in the other two countries, there is a wide discrepancy between spouses' perceptions of how much husbands really help.[38]

Bringing Home the Groceries

No matter how women feel about housework or the role of the housewife, ultimately, someone has to shop for the food to be served at the table and to buy the various household cleaning products. It has been customary to assume that all of the family's shopping for food, groceries, and household supplies is done by the housewife, usually alone. Implicit in this is the assumption that shop-

ping gives the housewife a slight break in her routine, that it is a form of recreation. According to the evidence, this is a myth for many women.

Australia

In Australia, fewer than one in three women says she enjoys grocery shopping
and one in three actually dislikes it. The remaining are tolerant of the task. They
say they occasionally enjoy shopping for groceries. Stay-at-home housewives
are most likely to find shopping enjoyable. Forty-two percent like shopping,
but a substantial number (36 percent) do not enjoy it. The two working women
groups are less likely than either of the housewife groups to enjoy shopping,
but they are fairly tolerant of the chore.[39]

Shopping is not necessarily a lonely occupation. Just over half of all active
women in Australia do their grocery shopping alone, which means that almost
half have some company when they go to the market. Stay-at-home housewives
are most likely to shop with their husbands or with their children. As we move
across the New Demographic spectrum, each segment is increasingly likely to
shop alone. For example, 39 percent of stay-at-home housewives shop on their
own, but 62 percent of career women do so. Plan-to-work housewives are most
likely to do their shopping with either children or the whole family. Each segment of working women reports that their husbands or children accompany
them to the grocery store to a certain extent.[40]

About one in three Australian couples usually shops together or the husband does so on his own, but the big surprise is that husbands of full-time
homemakers are most likely to shop for the families' food and groceries. Fifty-
seven percent of men who are married to stay-at-home housewives share grocery shopping or do it on their own. Forty-five percent of husbands of plan-to-
work housewives participate in shopping for groceries. Conversely, only 24
percent of men married to career women participate in the chore. Husbands of
just-a-job working women are somewhere between. Thirty-two percent of them
share in the task or do it on their own.[41]

More than half of the older couples share the shopping chore, although 10
percent of men claim to do it alone. Among the younger couples where the wife
intends to work, almost one in three husbands always or generally does the
grocery shopping without her. An expectation of greater sharing of household
tasks is certainly evident among younger couples. The husband of a plan-to-
work housewife with young children at home said, "The food shopping is all
right because she gives me a list. She does the cooking so she's in charge of
making out the list and then I go along and abuse the list by buying other
things and leaving the odd bits off."[42]

Mexico

In Mexico both husbands and wives report that husbands are most likely to help in shopping for the family clothes either on their own or with their wives. Although more husbands than wives say they do such shopping, in each case they are twice as likely to acknowledge that the couple does this kind of shopping together as to say that the husband does it on his own. The main difference between the perceptions of each spouse is that husbands say they do more shopping than their wives give them credit for.[43]

Both husbands and wives are likely to say that husbands are likely to shop for personal care products. Again, these shopping trips are more likely to be joint than solo, and husbands are more than twice as likely to claim they do this than their wives admit.[44]

Finally, although husbands join their wives in shopping for food and do some on their own, they are less likely to do grocery shopping than to buy clothes or personal care products. Again, husbands are twice as likely as their wives to claim that they join in bringing home the family's groceries.[45]

Venezuela

The one generalization that holds across all three countries is that husbands claim to do more shopping than their wives admit they do. In Venezuela, as in Mexico, men are most likely to participate in buying family clothes. These shopping trips are more likely to be husband and wife outings than husbands shopping on their own. Nevertheless, there is a large discrepancy between husbands' and wives' views on how often husbands shop.[46]

Unlike husbands in Mexico, husbands in Venezuela are more likely to be active in the grocery store. Although the discrepancy between husbands' and wives' viewpoints holds, nonetheless, just under one in four Venezuelan women says her husband participates in shopping for groceries. Most of the shopping trips involve both spouses rather than the husband alone. Exactly twice as many husbands claim they shop for food as their wives give them credit for. Venezuelan wives are slightly less likely to agree that their husbands help buy personal care products. Again, the shopping trips for such products tend to be family outings rather than husbands on their own. Husbands are far more likely than their wives to say they do this shopping.[47]

Brazil

In Brazil there is clearly a partnership approach to grocery shopping. Fifty-three percent of the women and 68 percent of the men say that the husbands either share in the grocery shopping or do some of it on their own. Somewhat unexpectedly, both segments of Brazilian housewives are more likely than either segment of working women to have their husbands' cooperation in shopping for groceries. Stay-at-homes get more help from their husbands in this than any other segment of women.[48]

Husbands in Brazil are far less likely to participate in planning the family's shopping list. Just 8 percent of women and 22 percent of men share in making those decisions. Working wives, particularly those whose work is "just a job," apparently share this chore with their husbands to a slightly greater extent than do the full-time homemakers.[49]

The Careful Consumer: Checking the Labels

When Australian women do their grocery and household product shopping, they take a consumerist point of view. Just under eight in ten of all women in Australia now read labels more carefully than in the past. The two segments of housewives are more likely to report this than the two groups of working women. Nonetheless, the propensity to read labels carefully ranges from 75 percent among career women to 84 percent among stay-at-home housewives.[50]

Japanese women are also fairly sophisticated shoppers. Just under seven in ten consider industry standards and ingredients on labels carefully when they purchase food and household products. Career women are most likely to follow this practice. Seventy-six percent of career women check industry standards and ingredients, compared to 16 percent who say they don't bother to do so. Seventy-two percent of stay-at-home housewives check standards and ingredients.

Plan-to-work housewives in Japan are slightly less likely to shop in this fashion. Sixty-seven percent of them check industry standards and ingredients very carefully, compared to 16 percent who don't bother to do so. Just-a-job working women are least likely to do this kind of shopping. Still, they are far more likely to check industry standards than ignore them. Sixty-three percent of just-a-job working women check industry standards and labels, and 18 percent don't bother.[51]

Consumer Skepticism

Whereas Japanese women check industry standards when they shop, Australian women wish they had them. Australian women are skeptical about brand names. They continue to buy them, but believe there should be industry standard for quality beyond the promise of the manufacturer. Sixty-nine percent of both working women and housewives in Australia say that brand names are not enough and industry standards are needed. There is fairly consistent agreement on this issue across all four New Demographic segments. Plan-to-work house-wives and just-a-job working women are slightly more likely than women in the other two groups to stress the importance of industry standards, but the varia-tion is very slight. Sixty-nine percent of stay-at-homes and 68 percent of career women endorse the importance of industry standards.[52]

Another aspect of consumer skepticism in Australia is that more Australian women believe that product quality has not improved than believe it has. Only 31 percent say that product quality is better than it used to be; 47 percent disagree. Plan-to-work housewives are more tolerant of product quality than any other segment of women. Slightly more of them have a positive view of product quality (40 percent versus 36 percent). Just-a-job working women are most critical of product quality. More than twice as many of them say that quality has not improved as believe that it has. Career women are also more critical of product quality than either segment of housewives.[53]

The Strategic Shopper

Women in Australia have developed a number of specific strategies to enable them to get the most value for their money: comparing prices, stocking up on bargains, and buying in bulk. Almost nine out of ten say they are comparing prices more carefully. Plan-to-work housewives are particularly likely to com-pare prices (93 percent). Eighty-four to 85 percent of the other segments com-pare prices.[54] Just over three in five women in Australia stock up on bargains. Stay-at-home housewives are particularly likely and just-a-job working women are least likely to go bargain hunting. This could be a reflection of the time available to the stay-at-homes and the time pressures on just-a-job working women.[55] Just under three in five Australian women report buying in bulk. Plan-to-work housewives are most likely to do so (61 percent), and career women are least likely to (55 percent).[56]

Response to Generics

One reflection of consumer disenchantment with brand names is the extent to which shoppers respond to generic or no-name brands. In Australia 59 percent of all women believe that generic products benefit the consumer, and 24 percent disagree. Plan-to-work housewives and career women are more likely to en-dorse generic products (65 percent and 63 percent, respectively). Stay-at-home housewives are the least likely of any of the segments to believe that generics benefit the consumer. Nevertheless, just over half of stay-at-homes (51 percent) are favorably disposed toward the no-name brands.[57]

Although they endorse the concept of generics, they are less likely to believe that house brands are frequently better than nationally advertised brands. Just one in three Australian women thinks that house brands are better (33 percent), and just over one in three (36 percent) disagrees. Career women and stay-at-home housewives are more likely than the other two segments to endorse house brands. Plan-to-work housewives are least likely to do so.[58]

Even though only one in three Australian women believes that house brands are better, more than half of them (54 percent) are buying them more often, compared to 34 percent who say they are not. The plan-to-work housewives are the best customers for store brands. Sixty percent report buying them more often. They are followed by career women (56 percent), then stay-at-home housewives (54 percent). Just-a-job working women are the least interested in store brands (47 percent).[59]

Australian women are more responsive to generic brands in some product categories than in others. They are most likely to buy generic brands of paper towels (60 percent) and toilet tissue (58 percent). Just over half say they would buy generic brands of facial tissue and household cleansers. But fewer than one in four would buy generic brands of sanitary pads or tampons.

Plan-to-work housewives are most responsive to generic brands, particularly for toilet tissue, paper towels, and household cleaning products. Career women are most likely to endorse generic brands of paper towels and are second to plan-to-work housewives in endorsing generic brands of household cleaning products. Compared to the other three segments of women, stay-at-home housewives are less likely to consider generic brands of facial tissues or sanitary protection products.[60]

According to "Beyond the Stereotypes," two out of three Australian women buy generic or no-name products, at least in some product categories. Plan-to-work housewives are particularly likely to do so (85 percent), and stay-at-home housewives are least likely to (59 percent). Just-a-job working women (71 percent) are more likely than career women (62 percent) to buy generics.[61]

Women in Japan are less responsive to generic brands than their counterparts in Australia. One in three believes that no-name or generic brands are just as good as well-known brands. Almost as many (29 percent) disagree. The attitudes of Japanese women toward generic brands are fairly consistent through the four New Demographic segments. Plan-to-work housewives are slightly more responsive than the others to generic brands. They are followed in this by career women. Just-a-job working women are slightly less responsive than the other three segments to the notion of generic brands. Nonetheless, the variation among the four groups is fairly slight.[62]

Although not every country reported on women's concerns about product quality, product ingredients, distrust of manufacturers' claims, and responsiveness to generic or no-name brands, those who did so suggest a disquieting level of consumer skepticism. The better-educated and more affluent consumers, who are also the best customers for many products, are most likely to be concerned about these matters.

This healthy consumer skepticism should be taken as a warning to marketers. Clearly, labeling of product ingredients could serve as a reassuring sign that the manufacturer is proud of the quality of the product. It is also clear that any product improvement or tangible evidence of product quality should be communicated. But these improvements should be relevant to and discernible by the consumer and not merely a nuance meaningful only to the manufacturer.

And, of course, any communication about a product must acknowledge the general level of skepticism. In order to be credible, claims about the product in advertising must be based on reality and not merely generalized self-praise. Brand and company images are built on trust. Once that trust has been eroded it is very difficult to recapture it. A brand or company reputation is a precious commodity. It warrants careful cultivation and protection.

thirteen

Women and Food

THERE is probably no area of human behavior that is more sensitive to changes in attitudes and values than that of food. The pattern of meals, the way a family does or does not eat together, the way it sets the table, the extent to which meals are cooked from scratch, whether food is consumed in a traditional breakfast, lunch, dinner pattern or in casual snacking, and the way a family entertains, all reflect a constantly changing and complex kaleidoscope of tastes, values, and life styles.

Women in some parts of the world are concerned about nutrition, whereas women in other countries appear to ignore it. Consumers in some parts of the world are worried about the health implications of drinking too much coffee or smoking too much. Consumers in other parts of the world regard coffee and cigarettes as a matter of pleasure and personal taste rather than a health problem. The discipline of a diet may mean cutting down or cutting out pleasurable foods once a normal part of the menu. This affects the eating habits of consumers in some parts of the world. On the other hand, since people are not totally rational or unidimensional, they still find food a pleasure and an indulgence.

Eating at Home and Away

Italy

In Italy, of all the tasks necessary for running a household women most enjoy preparing and serving meals. They feel that cooking offers the greatest opportunity for creativity. There is very little difference among the four New Demographic groups in their approach to food, but women may approach this task differently: "The organization of this aspect seems to depend mostly on the structure and tenor of life of the family and by the hours of the different family members."[1]

Most Italian families tend to prepare at least one meal a day. The menus for these meals are quite traditional. Housewives tend to serve the main meal at midday, and they try to gather the family around the table at that time if at all possible. Of course, this depends on the schedules of family members. A major change in this century is that working people rarely come home for the midday meal. Therefore, the evening meal has become the most important meal of the day. In some families where children come home to eat the noonday meal even though the mother is at work, food is left out and ready for them to eat, but it is a meal that they eat alone and not around the family table.

Casual meals or snacks of sandwiches, toast, and so forth are rare among Italian families. They are sometimes prepared on Sundays or weekends in the summertime or when there is a program of great interest on television. Apparently, young people in Italy like casual eating and "consider it a moment of freedom and joy."[2] Mealtimes are nevertheless central to the fabric of family life. The daily meal is considered important and provides the one occasion during the course of the day in which the family shares its experiences and news.

There is a real difference between this kind of sociable, convivial family gathering around the dinner table and the eating patterns of women who live alone. In Italy unmarried women tend to eat their meals standing at the refrigerator rather than sitting down at the dining room table. Apparently, single women find mealtimes difficult because of the sense of isolation they feel when they eat alone. Some of them tend to avoid eating at home as much as possible. They solve the problem by going out for a meal with friends or even skipping a meal altogether.[3]

Eating away from home is common, particularly among women living alone and young couples without small children. Housewives with children occasionally go out on the weekends with their husbands and children, but they apparently prefer gathering the family and friends around the dinner table at home because they feel it is more intimate and easier to talk to each other. Women who work seem to go out to eat more often, both with their husbands and friends and colleagues from work.[4]

Japan

A similar divergence in the dining habits of single women and women living in a family group was observed in Japan. There is no major difference in attitudes to or the actual practice of eating out among the four New Demographic segments, but there are differences in attitude and practice between the single and married women.

Married women in Japan view dining out as a special occasion; they find eating in restaurants to be a festive treat. It is a special rather than a casual event. One housewife said, "I want to eat something I can't make at home or that tastes better in a restaurant than at home." Another woman said, "I want to eat delicacies that are in season."[5]

On the other hand, a relatively large number of single women tend to eat ordinary dinners away from home without feeling that such meals represent a particularly special occasion. None of these Japanese women feels that eating in a restaurant is a way of avoiding preparing a meal at home, but rather considers it either a festive outing for the married women or a more social experience for the single women.[6]

West Germany

About one in three German housewives and working women reports dining out in "good restaurants" at least once a month. Working women are just slightly more likely than housewives to do so. On the other hand, working women are more likely than full-time homemakers to go to ethnic restaurants. Although fewer of either group eat in fast-food restaurants or steakhouses, in each case the working women are more likely than full-time housewives to eat in these establishments.[7]

Australia

In Australia both segments of working women are more likely than either segment of housewives to have eaten in a restaurant in the past two weeks. Career women are most likely to have dined out, and plan-to-work housewives are least likely to have done so. An alternative to eating in a restaurant is to eat takeout food at home. Stay-at-home housewives (30 percent) are least likely to follow this practice. Both plan-to-work housewives and just-a-job working women are more likely (54 percent each) than career women (48 percent) to serve takeout food at home.[8]

Another alternative to cooking at home is to heat a preprepared meal. Stay-at-home housewives are least likely to do this (21 percent). There is very little difference among the other three groups in following this practice. Just-a-job working women are most likely to avail themselves of this convenience (27 percent). Plan-to-work housewives are just behind them (26 percent). One in four career women reports that they heat a preprepared meal at home. Although fewer stay-at-home housewives, who are often older women, use preprepared meals at home, those who do so are apparently very heavy users. They have served this kind of convenience food more than three times in the preceding two weeks. According to "Beyond the Stereotypes," it would seem that the one in five of the older women who eats convenience food relies on it fairly heavily.[9]

The most widespread custom among all segments of women in Australia is cooking a full meal and serving it at home. More than nine out of ten of all segments of women follow this practice. Plan-to-work housewives are most likely to cook a meal themselves. Between 90 and 91 percent of the other three groups prepared meals in the past two weeks. The stay-at-home housewives are most likely to have served a meal they cooked themselves.[10]

On the other hand, even though these women do a good deal of cooking, sometimes their meals are prepared by someone else in the household, particularly their husbands. Plan-to-work housewives are most likely to get help from their husbands, and stay-at-home housewives are least likely to do so. Fifty-seven percent of plan-to-work housewives say their husbands cooked a meal in the past two weeks, an average of 7.2 times. Only 28 percent of the stay-at-home housewives had help from their husbands, and the frequency was an average of 4.1 times in two weeks. More than half of each segment of working women had cooperation at a slightly less frequent rate than that enjoyed by the plan-to-work housewives.[11]

Diet and Nutrition

Consumers in many parts of the world express a growing concern about fitness and health. Some are motivated by vanity and strive to control their weight to maintain their best appearance. Others are aware that certain elements in their diets can help them maintain good health or prevent illness. The awareness of the importance of nutrition in keeping their families healthy is also reflected in increasing concern about the healthfulness of various foods. It is also reflected in changes in eating habits and menu selection, both in the food prepared at home and the foods ordered in restaurants.

Australia

A plurality of women in Australia believe that food today is not as healthy as it was in their parents' day. Just-a-job working women and plan-to-work housewives are most critical of the quality of today's foods. Although substantial proportions of stay-at-home housewives and career women are critical of today's foods, more of them believe that food today is as healthy as it was in their parents' day.[12]

The number-one health concern among Australian women is the need to maintain the right weight. Nine out of ten women in that country are concerned about weight control. Plan-to-work housewives and career women are particularly concerned about controlling their weight. Stay-at-home housewives are slightly less concerned about their weight. Nevertheless, 85 percent are concerned about maintaining the right weight.[13]

Almost as many women in Australia are concerned about eating a balanced diet. This is slightly more important to career women and plan-to-work housewives than to the others, although the variations are very slight. Just-a-job working women are a notch behind stay-at-home housewives in their concerns about a balanced diet.[14]

Of course, a sweet tooth is one obstacle to achieving a balanced diet. Overall, 85 percent of Australian women are concerned about eating too much sugar. This is especially important to stay-at-home housewives and slightly more important to career women than to the two middle groups. Between 84 and 89 percent of Australian women are worried about having too much sugar.[15]

Eighty-one percent of Australian women are concerned about too many chemical additives in foods; this is a particular concern for the two groups of housewives. Just-a-job working women are slightly less involved with this problem. Nonetheless, three out of four just-a-job working women care about chemical additives in foods.[16]

The problem of getting enough fiber in one's diet is a concern for stay-at-home housewives. They are followed by their plan-to-work neighbors. As with a number of other nutrition concerns, the two housewife groups are more conscious of this problem than are the two segments of working women. Just-a-job working women are least concerned about fiber. Nonetheless, three out of four express concern about this element in their diets.[17]

Eighty-one percent are concerned about eating or serving nonnutritious snacks. Plan-to-work housewives, in particular, care about nonnutritious snacks. They are followed by career women. Just-a-job working women are least concerned. Nonetheless, three out of four are concerned about the nutrition of the snacks they serve.[18]

Again, 81 percent of Australian women worry about eating too much salt. This is of slightly more concern to stay-at-home housewives and career women. Just-a-job working women are least troubled about eating too much salt.[19]

The problem of cholesterol worries three out of four Australian women. The age differences between the two housewife segments are apparent here. Stay-at-home housewives report the most concern about eating high cholesterol foods (84 percent); plan-to-work housewives report the least concern (69 percent).[20]

At a slightly lower level, Australian women are concerned about "too much alcohol." It is not clear whether this is for themselves or their families. Nonetheless, stay-at-home housewives are most concerned about too much alcohol (77 percent). They are followed by just-a-job working women (73 percent). Plan-to-work housewives are least troubled by this (62 percent).[21]

Great Britain

In Great Britain, the two working women groups are most likely to say they are cutting down their weight. Career women are most likely to say so (42 percent), followed closely by their just-a-job counterparts. Plan-to-work housewives are next, and stay-at-homes are least likely to say so (35 percent).[22]

United States

In the United States 35 percent of women say they are controlling their diets. Career women are more likely than any other segment of women to be doing this, and stay-at-home housewives are least likely. Married women are somewhat more likely than unmarrieds to be on a diet. In each case career women are most likely to diet.[23]

The motivations for dieting vary dramatically among the New Demographic segments in the United States. Although stay-at-home housewives are least likely to diet, those who do clearly do so for health reasons. They are most likely to be concerned about sugar, their cholesterol count, diabetes, heart disease, hypertension, and salt intake. Conversely, career women who diet do so mainly for weight control reasons, either to maintain their present weight or to lose weight.[24]

Aside from the time-honored practice of counting calories and attempting to eat a balanced diet, many women attempting to control their diets use a nonfood aid. The level of usage is minor: about 4 percent of women use a dietary pill, 3 percent try a meal supplement, and fewer than 1 percent use reducing candies to help them diet. One in five women does not use any nonprescription products. Career women are most likely to be careful in this regard and limit their supplementary use to products prescribed by their doctors. They are followed in this by just-a-job working women and to a lesser degree by plan-to-work housewives. Stay-at-home housewives are least likely to say they don't use nonprescription products.[25]

Health and the Grocery List

Australia

The intense concern about health and nutrition expressed by women in Australia is translated into changes in the foods they buy and serve and, most important, the foods they don't buy. Seventy-one percent of Australian women report that they are buying fewer snack foods. Stay-at-home housewives are slightly more likely than the other segments of women to have cut down on snack foods.[26]

Sixty-nine percent of all women say they are serving fewer convenience foods. Both groups of housewives, particularly the plan-to-work segment, are more likely than the two segments of working women to cut down on convenience foods.[27]

Although a substantial number of Australian women say they are serving fewer convenience foods, just over half say they are attracted by quick, easy products. Interestingly, the two segments of housewives are more likely than either type of working woman to find convenience products appealing.[29]

United States

In reviewing a range of low-calorie food and beverage products that are popular in the United States, all women are more likely than the total population to use such products. The incidence of use rises as we move across the New Demographic spectrum. For the most part, career-oriented working women are more likely than any other segment of women to use such products. They are followed in this by just-a-job working women and plan-to-work housewives. Stay-at-home housewives are least likely to use low-calorie products, although in some cases even they are above the norm of the total population.[29]

Diet cola is the most popular low-calorie product. Just under half of all women drink it. This is followed by diet soft drinks and yogurt. Each of these products is bought and used by just under two out of five women. One in four women reports specifically using low-fat yogurt. Eighteen percent of women buy and use low-fat cheese. This is the one low-calorie product that is purchased by more stay-at-home housewives than any other segment. They are followed in this by career women. Just-a-job working women buy less low-fat cheese than the national norm.[30]

Frozen low-calorie dinners or entrees, a relatively new product, have moved the relatively déclassé TV dinner to a level of acceptability among sophisticated consumers. This product gets its highest level of response from the two working women groups. Both segments of housewives are below the norm in buying frozen entrees. Frozen entrees are particularly appealing to career women, and have special appeal to unmarried career women.[31]

Coffee, Tea, and Soft Drinks

The general trend toward physical fitness and well-being has had a direct impact on the kinds of beverages people drink.

Australia

Fifty-nine percent of the women worry about drinking too much tea or coffee. This is particularly true of the stay-at-home housewife and less true of the plan-to-work housewife. In addition, 66 percent are serving fewer soft drinks, especially plan-to-work housewives.[32]

United States

In the United States there has been a growing concern about the harmful effects of caffeine, which is reflected in a decline in the extent to which people drink coffee and the increased interest in decaffeinated coffee. Currently, 58 percent of all women in the United States report drinking coffee. More of them are likely to drink traditional ground coffee than instant or freeze-dried coffee. Because of the increasing concern about caffeine, about half as many women drink decaffeinated ground coffee (24 percent) as regular coffee (49 percent).[33] There is little difference among the New Demographic segments in this area. Overall, unmarried women tend to be below the norm in drinking coffee. The one exception to this are the unmarried stay-at-home housewives, who are strong fans of decaffeinated instant and freeze-dried coffees. To a lesser extent they and unmarried, plan-to-work housewives drink the instant coffee that contains caffeine.[34]

All segments of married women are slightly above the norm in drinking regular ground coffee containing caffeine. Married stay-at-home housewives are particularly responsive to the decaffeinated form. They are also the only segment above the norm in drinking the decaffeinated form of freeze-dried coffee.[35]

Venezuela

Women in Latin America do not seem to be concerned about caffeine. Coffee seems to be a universal drink among women in Venezuela. Ninety-seven percent of Venezuelan women drink coffee regularly. Stay-at-home housewives are most likely to do so (98 percent); plan-to-work housewives and career women are slightly less likely to do so (95 percent).[36]

Brazil

Nine out of ten women in Brazil drink coffee regularly; this is generally the case across all segments. Just-a-job working women are slightly over that norm, and career women are slightly under it. Instant coffee is only a minor product in Brazil at the present time, but 12 percent of all women report drinking it. The two working women groups are more likely to use instant coffee than either type of housewife. Career women are most likely of all to drink instant coffee.[37]

Just under half of Brazilian women are tea drinkers (45 percent). The extent to which they drink tea rises as we move across the New Demographics spectrum. Just 42 percent of stay-at-home housewives drink tea, and 57 percent of career women do so.[38] Soft drinks are less popular: just over two in five Brazilian women drink soft drinks. Career women are more likely than any other segment of women to drink this beverage (48 percent).[39]

Mexico

There are some differences among Mexican women. In that country milk is more popular than coffee. Ninety-two percent of Mexican women drink milk regularly. Career women are more likely than any other segment to drink milk, followed by plan-to-work housewives. No fewer than 90 percent of any segment of women are milk drinkers.[40]

Coffee is less popular: 86 percent of Mexican women are regular coffee drinkers. Just-a-job working women are more likely than any other segment to drink coffee (90 percent). Career women are less likely than any other segment to be coffee fans (81 percent).[41] Just over half of Mexican women drink tea. Plan-to-work housewives are the greatest tea drinkers, followed by career women. Stay-at-home housewives are least likely to take tea. Just under half of Mexican women drink soft drinks. Career women and plan-to-work house-wives are least likely to drink them; stay-at-home housewives and just-a-job working women have the same level of consumption.[42]

Women and Alcoholic Beverages

Consumers' concern with health and fitness is also reflected in their changing tastes in alcoholic beverages.

United States

In the last decade or so in the United States there has been a move away from the darker spirits such as Scotch and bourbon to lighter drinks such as vodka. In turn, there has been a trend toward drinks with a lower level of alcohol such as wine and beer.[43] In the United States it has become completely acceptable to ask for a nonalcoholic drink at a cocktail party or a dinner party. A few years ago the introduction of mineral water reflected the change in consumers' attitudes toward drinking nonalcoholic drinks in a setting in which alcoholic drinks were normally served. This does not mean that people are not drinking all forms of spirits, but that there have been changes in taste and social acceptance of light and nonalcoholic drinks.[44] Recently, however, there has been a minor reversal of this trend. Some younger people, who probably began to drink during the white-wine-and-Perrier era, have begun to discover the stronger drinks of their elders. There is a move back to martinis and the darker, heavier liquors.[45]

168

Japan

Very few of the housewives in Japan drink away from home in the evening with someone other than a member of the family. Although they don't go out to drink themselves, they are not critical of the working women who do. Just-a-job working women and career women drink with their colleagues or co-workers, but the former tend to dislike the practice. The latter seem to go out drinking with their professional colleagues quite often without regard to whether it is personally enjoyable. Apparently, these women believe that to a certain extent it is necessary to drink with their colleagues as an extension of work.[46]

Just under half of active Japanese women drink some kind of alcoholic beverage (47 percent). Career women are consistently more likely than any other segment of women to drink alcoholic beverages, particularly wine. Plan-to-work housewives are second to career women in this.[47]

Nine percent of Japanese women drink whiskey. The two segments of working women are above the norm in doing so, and stay-at-home housewives are clearly below the norm. Five percent of Japanese women drink saki. Career women are far more likely than any other segment to do so, and both segments of housewives are relatively unlikely to do so. Just-a-job working women are over the norm in saki drinking, but career women are three times as likely as their just-a-job counterparts to drink it.[48]

Four percent of Japanese women drink wine. Career women are substantially more likely than any other segment of women to do so, and stay-at-home housewives are substantially least likely to drink wine. Five percent of Japanese women drink *shochu* (like vodka). Both segments of housewives are far below the norm in drinking this; career women are the only group above the norm in drinking *shochu*.[49]

Beer is a much more popular beverage. Forty percent of Japanese women drink beer; plan-to-work housewives are more likely than any other segment to be beer drinkers, followed by career women. Stay-at-home housewives are least likely to drink beer, and just-a-job working women are below the norm in this.[50] Awareness of imported beers is high among plan-to-work and career women. The relatively high rate of familiarity among stay-at-home women probably results from the custom of giving foreign beers as gifts. During the gift-giving season, festively packaged beer is a popular gift.[51]

Venezuela

In Venezuela beer is the most popular alcoholic beverage. One in three women drinks it. Although differences among the four New Demographic segments are slight, career women are most likely to drink beer, and stay-at-home housewives least likely; plan-to-work housewives and just-a-job working women are exactly between the two extremes.[52]

Just over one in five Venezuelan women drinks wine. Career women are most likely to, and plan-to-work housewives are least likely to, drink wine, rum, or whiskey. On the other hand, both groups of working women are more likely than housewives to drink alcoholic beverages. Career women are more likely than any other segment to do so.[53]

Mexico

Eighteen percent of Mexican women drink beer. The four segments of women differ by only one percentage from the norm.[54] Sixteen percent of Mexican women drink wine; the greatest support for this comes from the two working women groups, particularly career women. The picture is similar for brandy, although career women are more likely to drink wine than brandy. Finally, only 10 percent of all Mexican women drink rum, but more than twice that percentage of career women do so.[55]

Brazil

Twenty-eight percent of Brazilian women drink beer, and career women are more likely to drink it than any other alcoholic beverage. Just-a-job working women are slightly less likely than any other group to be beer drinkers.[56]

Seventeen percent of Brazilian women drink wine. Career women are significantly more likely than any other group to be wine drinkers, followed by their just-a-job working neighbors. Both segments of housewives are slightly below the norm in drinking wine.[57]

Sixteen percent of Brazilian women drink *Pinga e cachaca* (like Tequila). Plan-to-work housewives are least likely to do so; stay-at-home housewives are just under the norm. As in the other beverage categories, career women are more likely to drink this.[58]

Finally, 7 percent of women in Brazil drink whiskey. Plan-to-work housewives are less likely than any other segment to drink this spirit, and career women are most likely to do so. Just-a-job working women are more likely than either of the housewife groups to drink it.[59]

West Germany

In Germany women were asked which products they were least prepared to do without if it were necessary to economize. Eighty-two percent of German women are least prepared to do without food, alcohol, or cigarettes. The two groups of working women are least likely to want to give up these products;

plan-to-work housewives are more likely than any other segment to be willing to give up food, alcohol, or cigarettes.[60]

Women and Smoking

United States

In 1964, the surgeon general of the United States determined that smoking was injurious to people's health. As a result of that report, after some pressure, advertising for cigarettes was removed from television and radio. Cigarette manufacturers are required to post a warning on their packages. More than half of the American people believe there should be a ban on smoking in public elevators, movie theaters, buses, and that smoking should be restricted to special sections in restaurants. Exactly half believe that smoking should not be permitted in supermarkets and should be restricted to special lounges in travel terminals.[61]

The concern about public smoking is a reflection of the harmful effects of smoke even for a nonsmoker. Therefore, three out of four people believe "that when someone smokes near you, it's bad for your health," or that nonsmokers who are around smokers a lot are more likely to get lung cancer.[62] Given this negative climate, people who continue to smoke have obviously chosen to ignore the rational health appeals for not smoking. There has been a decline in levels of cigarette smoking in the United States. Currently, 32 percent of adults smoke cigarettes and 20 percent smoke a low-tar cigarette, which suggests they are concerned with minimizing the effects of smoking.[63]

Plan-to-work housewives are more likely than any other segment of women to smoke. They are followed by just-a-job working women. Career women are just under the norm in the extent to which they smoke, and stay-at-home housewives are least likely of any segment of women to smoke cigarettes. Among those women who do smoke, just-a-job working women are most likely to select the low-tar brands of cigarettes. They are followed in this by career women and finally by plan-to-work housewives.[64]

Unmarried women are more likely than their married counterparts to smoke cigarettes, but their behavior follows that of married women. Among the unmarrieds all three groups—plan-to-work housewives, career women, just-a-job working women—are strong supporters of low-tar cigarettes. Since unmarried stay-at-home housewives are far below the norm in smoking, they are equally far below in choosing low-tar cigarettes.[65]

Great Britain

In Great Britain, career women are least likely and plan-to-work housewives are most likely to smoke cigarettes. Although there are slightly more smokers among stay-at-home housewives (35 percent) than among career women (33 percent), fewer of them are heavy smokers (11 percent and 13 percent). More women smoke in the other two groups: just-a-job working women (40 percent) and plan-to-work housewives (41 percent). Fewer in the first group (14 percent) than in the second group (17 percent) are heavy smokers.[66]

Japan

In Japan women do not discuss the health aspects of cigarettes, and do not seem concerned about giving up smoking.[67] Stay-at-home housewives clearly dislike smoking and people who smoke. They especially don't care for women to smoke. In contrast, the other three segments of women perceive smoking as a matter of personal taste and not particularly related to gender. One young plan-to-work housewife said, "Smoking or not smoking has nothing to do with whether it's a man doing it or a woman. It's a personal decision on the part of the individual." A career woman who has given up smoking discussed it in terms of personal taste: "I just happen to be a person who couldn't see what was attractive about smoking when I tried it, so that's why I don't smoke today. It's a question of personal taste."[68]

Some working women are concerned that if a woman smokes at work, it might have a negative or unfavorable image. They feel that a woman smoking makes an unfavorable impression or weakens the image of seriousness or full commitment to her work. One just-a-job working woman said, "Many people have a poor impression of a woman who smokes." Another said, "I don't smoke when customers call. I feel that people don't consider that a woman who smokes is completely serious. It doesn't make a good impression."[69] A career woman described smoking as a form of relaxation rather than a part of her working day: "I don't smoke during meetings or when I am gathering information. Smoking is more of a relaxation, a bit of time off. If I smoke during work, I feel I'm using up time in that way."[70]

The evidence in this chapter suggests a number of fascinating speculations rather than definitive conclusions, partly because the participating countries reported on varying aspects of food, drink, and cigarettes. Nonetheless, that some countries chose to discuss certain issues and ignore others suggests that there may be differing priorities in those countries. Following are some of the hypotheses suggested by these data.

Women's presence in the work force appears to have an impact on the time of day the family meal is served. There also appears to be a greater propensity for working women and their families to eat in restaurants. The contrast between the convivial family meals of the married women and the lonely mealtimes of the unmarried appear to lead to more casual dining out for single women. This sort of issue would lend itself to quantification.

Similarly, some countries reported in detail about women's nutrition and health concerns and the ways that those concerns are expressed in the food they buy and serve. This may suggest that those concerns are important in particular countries. However, the fact that they were not reported by others does not mean that they do not exist. Again, this is the kind of issue that would lend itself to further study and verification.

However, just because consumers in some countries are deeply concerned about diet and nutrition does not mean that all the people in those countries follow such sensible precepts when it comes to the food they buy and serve. Certainly, the strong demand for diet books in the United States and reports about people continually going on and off diets are evidence that consumers are not totally rational or unidimensional. There seems to be a perpetual conflict between what we should do and what we want to do and nowhere is this more evident than in the areas of food and drink and smoking.

The very differences in the aspects of food chosen for discussion in each country suggest that there might be more cultural differences between countries in relation to food and drink than within countries. Similarly, the tantalizing contrast between women in the United States and Great Britain who are aware of the health aspects of smoking and women in Japan, who are apparently indifferent to the health problem of cigarettes, invites further study.

Another clue suggested in this chapter is the symbolic meaning of the family meal. This was discussed only in Italy. I speculate that the symbolism of the family dinner table is strongest in Latin countries. The emotional and psychological context in which food is served could have strong implications for marketers. On the other hand, no conclusions can be made without further study.

fourteen

Women and Fashion

THE way women approach fashion is a direct reflection of the way they spend their time. Housewives, for the most part, spend their days caring for their homes and families. Therefore, they dress simply or casually during the day. They tend to think of fashion as something reserved for special occasions. Stay-at-home housewives are less concerned with fashion than their plan-to-work neighbors. Although plan-to-work housewives also spend their days on child care and homemaking, they care more about how they look and take a keener interest in fashion.

By contrast, working women go out of the house every day, and they must be properly dressed and groomed for work. Both just-a-job working women and career women dress for work every day, but their emphasis is somewhat different. The working woman who thinks her work is "just a job" enjoys fashion for its own sake, according to her personal taste. The career women tend to be more aware of the impression they make on clients and colleagues. Working women spend more on clothes than either segment of housewives. Career women, the most likely to buy better-quality clothes, spend more money on fashion than any other group of women. Within these parameters there are some differences from country to country.

Great Britain

Housewives in Great Britain dress casually during the day and save their better clothes for social occasions. As one stay-at-home housewife said, "A housewife tries to look attractive in jeans." These housewives tend to dress quite differently on social occasions.[1]

There appears to be a class difference among women in Britain. Some of the more affluent women say they have dress allowances and, therefore, are able to buy what they need as they wish. But most of these women usually ask their husbands before spending money on themselves. Several of them say that their husbands tend to take a keen interest in the way they look and may actually accompany them on their shopping trips: "they regard the appearance of their wives as important to their own image." Several nonworking wives gave examples of the way husbands involve themselves in their wives' fashion expenditures. One said, "I don't dress myself, my husband does." Another reported, "I buy clothes for socializing as I need them. My dress allowance is for basic, everyday clothing, and the main items my husband buys."[2]

On the other hand, less affluent housewives apparently have to skimp and save to buy new clothes. Some of them make their own clothes, and some simply go without. One lower-middle-class housewife said, "I'd have to save from the housekeeping. I don't buy clothes often. I would rather wait and buy something nice and expensive than cheap and silly."[3]

One plan-to-work housewife complained that "the housewife has to be satisfied with what she's got." Another one described the initiative it took for her to buy something she wanted: "I bought a leather jacket before Christmas. I sold things and bought it. I had the satisfaction of buying it myself." In general, housewives spend less on clothing than either job- or career-oriented working women. Plan-to-work housewives are particularly likely to buy jeans and more likely than any other group of women to purchase jeans at all price levels.

The major difference, of course, between the life styles of working women and housewives is that working women go to their place of work everyday. This means that they need to dress for public appearances as a matter of course rather than occasionally dress for a social event.[4] Working women, especially the career-oriented and younger, just-a-job women, tend to take care of their appearance as part of their daily routine. Compared with housewives, they are likely "to buy clothes for themselves more often and generally to spend more money on themselves." As a matter of fact, although both groups of working women spend more on dresses and shoes than full-time homemakers, career women are more likely than any other group to shop in the upper-price brackets.[5]

One career woman explained, "You have more interest in clothes if you work. At home you tend to wear jeans or trousers and a sloppy jumper. You buy nice things to wear at work. It encourages you to diet and look after yourself better. You take more interest in yourself." Another said, "You take pride in your appearance. An extra half hour to put on your makeup, you have to decide what you're going to wear the next day and so on."[6]

Of course, the type of clothes they buy and the extent of their fashion consciousness relate to the work they do. "Women who work in factories, warehouses, or other jobs in which they do not meet the public do not need to look smart. They wear clothes that are practical for the job and which they do not mind getting dirty. Some are provided with overalls or uniforms or constantly driving from one place to another so that much of what they wear goes unseen."[7]

In contrast, career women and those just-a-job women who work in offices where they meet other people appear to feel obliged to dress well, because of their own pride and the sense that their appearance is part of their professional image. As one career woman explained, "It gives a good image to the public. If they see someone shabbily dressed when they come into your company, they will not think very highly of you. If you always look well groomed and smart, not necessarily fashionable, so long as you're smart, I think that's important."[8]

One young woman who thinks her work is "just a job" was also aware of the image aspects of her work: "I'm seeing clients in and out all day, so I have to be smart and presentable." Apparently, both career women and just-a-job working women who are aware of the image aspects of how they dress tend to favor classic styles that are smart rather than trendy. On the other hand, some young women say that although their work doesn't require it, they do enjoy dressing for work because of the self-esteem that being well dressed brings them: "I enjoy dressing up for work because I just feel better about myself. I don't really have to, I don't meet the public, but I want to."[9]

Some young career women report a psychological or emotional benefit when they shop for new clothes: "When I've gone out and bought something, it really cheers me up. It makes my day." Another said, "I buy clothes when I've got the money and when I feel like it. I will buy something if I feel a bit cheesed off." Because of the pleasure that they take in shopping and buying clothes, these young women say that the freedom to spend money on themselves is vital to them: "Most of my money goes on the house, but after that once all my bills are paid, nearly all my money goes on clothes."[10]

There is a real difference between the housewives with a clothing allowance or those who "fiddle" the housekeeping budget to buy clothes and young working wives and their husbands in how they deal with clothing expenditures. Working wives appear to enjoy the independence of selecting their own clothes and telling their husbands about it afterward, in contrast with the dependent behavior described by the more affluent housewives: "I don't want my husband thinking 'Oh, God, what a mess,' but I wouldn't like to have to ask him for twenty pounds for a dress. I like to say 'guess what I've bought . . . do you like it?'" Another said, "If I'm out and see a dress and have enough money, I'll buy it. He'll find out later."[11]

A young just-a-job wife explained both her sense of responsibility toward what the family can afford and her sense of independence in deciding how to spend their money: "I like to go out and buy it. If I think we can afford it, I'll get it even if it's a hundred pounds." On the other hand, another young working wife would consult her husband if her expenditure was over a certain amount: "If I was buying a dress for fifty pounds, I'd tell him first."[12]

In contrast with the extent to which these young working women are involved with fashion and enjoy buying and wearing new clothes, the older working women, particularly those whose work is "just a job," report that they don't go out socially very often and their work doesn't bring them in touch with the public. Therefore, they buy new clothes only when it is absolutely necessary: "I try to keep something reasonable for best, for going out, but I don't buy a lot of best clothes. You don't get the wear out of them." Another woman said, "I'm not one for going around shops and going through racks of clothes. I buy it when I need it, plus the fact that I couldn't afford to keep buying clothes."[13]

All women who work, both those whose work is "just a job" and career women, separate their fashion lives into work and personal time. Most like to change into something more comfortable when they come home from work. This seems to have a psychological benefit as well as a practical one. It separates their personal lives from their work lives and aids the relaxation process: "You come home and put your jeans and sweatshirt on and it's more relaxing. You're in a different frame of mind, whereas you couldn't be if you're stuck in a frilly blouse and skirt or whatever."[14] Of course, working women in England dress differently when they go out socially. They are less concerned about image in their personal wardrobes and dress to please themselves. They wear the kinds of clothes appropriate to the way they spend their personal leisure time.[15]

Japan

In Japan stay-at-home housewives are similar to their English counterparts in that they only dress up on social occasions. They don't go out very often and, therefore, their interest in clothes and fashion is rather low. One housewife explained her changing priorities in relation to fashion when she stopped working: "Once I stopped working I didn't have so many opportunities for going out anymore, so I don't get that feeling anymore of wanting a new piece of clothing." In addition, these women feel somewhat uncomfortable about spending money on clothing for themselves. They are aware that they are being supported by their husbands and some of them feel ill at ease about spending money they haven't earned themselves: "When I was working I could buy clothing because it was my own money I was spending. I'm not working now though and in the household budget many other things have priority over clothing for me."[16]

Stay-at-home housewives did not describe what they wear when they are at home alone. All groups of women were asked the criteria they use when they go shopping for clothing. Almost all of them talk about low price, comfort, clothes that are easy to move in, clothes that will last and are of good quality. Stay-at-home housewives particularly mentioned that the clothes they buy should meet their husbands' approval: "My husband is quite picky about my clothes, so whenever I go out to buy clothing, I always think about whether he will like the things I buy or not." They are also especially concerned about conforming to what is considered proper for their stage in life: "I don't like people to think 'oh, look at what she's wearing, it doesn't suit her at all at her age.' The clothes don't have to be expensive, but I choose things that will last and that are similar to what everyone else is wearing." Overall, the stay-at-home housewives mention "something my husband likes" and "something that is proper" as shopping criteria. The other groups of women choose clothes according to what they themselves like, but the stay-at-home housewives did not mention their own personal tastes as a guideline. They did not appear to use clothing as a way of expressing their taste or individuality."[17]

Although plan-to-work housewives have a life style similar to that of their stay-at-home neighbors, they differ in taking an active interest in fashion. Many are self-conscious about how full-time homemakers look. They feel that, by comparison, they are not nearly as fashionable as women who work. They themselves do not want to look like housewives. None of the stay-at-homes mentioned this concern. For example, a plan-to-work housewife said, "Women who work wear clothing that is more natural. However, full-time housewives wear showy clothing when going out because they may not have many opportunities for dressing up." This was echoed by another young woman who said, "Whenever I go to a PTA meeting, it always strikes me that the mothers are dressed to the nines."[18]

In common with the other groups of women, plan-to-work housewives say they choose clothing that is low priced, functional, of good quality, and long lasting. But they also want "something that suits my personal taste." One said, "I choose clothing seventy percent according to whether it is functional and thirty percent for how it looks. Lately, I only buy clothes that I like."[19]

"Something that suits my personal taste" was a standard that was also mentioned by Japanese working women. Plan-to-work housewives and just-a-job working women tend to place relatively more importance on their personal taste when selecting clothes. Some of the women said they bought specific brands or shopped in specific stores. Even though plan-to-work homemakers are full-time housewives, they use their own personal taste when choosing clothing, whereas stay-at-home housewives select their clothes to suit their husbands' preferences or what they think is considered proper.[20]

Just-a-job working women give primary importance to their personal preferences in buying clothing. Although both they and career women are in the work force, the attitudes of just-a-job working women to fashion do not appear to be influenced by the nature of their jobs. In common with the other women, they want to be able to wear the clothes they buy for a long time, but they are very aware of appearance: "There are certain colors and designs that I like. I always choose some particular designs." They make many comments about their own tastes. For example, "I always buy the same color," or "I never wear skirts," or "My clothes are all the same brand."[21]

Just-a-job working women were the only women who talked about the emotional release that comes from shopping for clothes. Some of them said that buying clothes was a diversion, a way of releasing stress: "Whenever something unpleasant happens at the office, I go straight to the department store and buy a whole lot of clothes." This group is the only segment of women who admit to being strongly influenced by brand names and fashion: "I like brand name articles. I always shop in one particular store and if I see something I like I will buy it regardless of price."[22]

On the other hand, career women are aware of the image aspects of the way they dress. They dress in a manner that will not offend people; they dress to appear professional, and to create a favorable impression. One woman said, "In my work I deal with customers so I have to dress in a way that will not offend." Some of them select their clothes to be compatible with the types of people whom they will meet: "Whenever I am meeting older people, I try to wear something conservative and neat looking." A display stylist explained that the way she dresses projects her professional competence: "I dress to make prospective clients imagine how good a display I can do. I have to play up to my clientele, so I dress accordingly."[23]

Career women also seem to be more organized in planning the clothes they buy or the way they will wear them: "I have to wear something everyday, so I plan a week's worth of outfits at a time. I think of the look that I want to project or what pieces go with each other." Another very organized career woman explained her fashion philosophy: "I buy good things I will be able to wear for a long time. Some of the clothes I own I have been wearing for ten years. I usually have ten outfits per season and wear them in rotation. That means I only have to wear one outfit about three times a month or ten times in a season, which means that my clothes last longer. If you own ten good outfits, you can wear them for ten years."[24]

Like the working women in England, Japanese career women differentiate between the clothes they wear to work and those they wear in their private lives: "I think I might dress differently if I wasn't working. I'd enjoy wearing an open shoulder shirt if I wasn't at work."[25]

Except for the just-a-job women, who are attracted to brand names, most

Japanese women tend to be indifferent to them. Nevertheless, quite a few of these women admit that they were attracted to brand names in the past.

> They were unable to give any clear reasons for their shift in interest, but some of them commented they had come to realize that good quality merchandise existed that was not a brand name product. However, the drop in the number of women interested in brand name goods seems to be closely connected with following very unusual brand names goods fever that took place in Japan. Five or six years ago brand name articles (Gucci, Louis Vuitton, etc.) enjoyed a huge boom in Japan. During this period it was considered a fashion status symbol to own one or more articles of brand name goods. Japanese women bought these goods in droves, not so much because of the excellent quality of the merchandise but because they did not want to be seen as unfashiona-ble. . . . However, so many women started owning imported brand name goods, that they stopped being considered status symbols. At the same time cheaply priced imitations of brand name goods started appearing on the market which reduced the buying fever considerably.
>
> At present a reaction to the boom in imported brand name goods seems to have set in. Women are less interested in brand names now. They feel they are being wise shoppers if they do not let themselves be influenced by brand names. In fact, it seems quite common to imply now that a woman who lets herself be influenced by the brand name on merchandise is not being a good shopper. Therefore, many of the participants who followed the trend of buying brand name goods a few years ago are now following the trend of not being interested in that kind of merchandise. However, interest in brand name goods has not completely died down. While it is now fashionable not to be so inter-ested in them, the popularity of brand name articles, both domestic and im-ported including those imported goods that were at the forefront of the boom of five or six years ago appears to have become firmly established.[26]

Although all groups of Japanese women say they are concerned about price, quality, and durability when they shop for clothing, the two segments of work-ing women spend more on clothing than do either segment of housewives. Career women are the most active consumers of clothes and fashion, followed by just-a-job working women. Even though plan-to-work housewives are more fashion conscious than their stay-at-home neighbors, their clothing expendi-tures are the lowest of any group of Japanese women.[27]

Interest in jewelry appears to cut across the New Demographic segments in Japan. Some women in each group wear jewelry, and some have simply never established the habit. Those who wear it enjoy it. Some say they find personal satisfaction in wearing jewelry. Several women, particularly the housewives, say their tastes in jewelry have changed over time. When they were younger they enjoyed having a wide choice and bought lots of "cheap things." They have begun to be more selective and concentrate on quality or on real jewels. A plan-to-work housewife said, "Whenever I buy expensive jewelry I choose carefully. I select pieces that I will not get tired of over the long run."[28]

Some women find that jewelry gets in their way or makes them feel self-conscious or overdressed. One stay-at-home housewife said, "I own jewelry but I hardly ever wear it because it seems such a bother." Another woman considered it "exaggerated to wear jewelry." A career woman explained that elaborate jewelry is not functional in a work setting: "There are only certain types of accessories you can wear when you're working. . . . The only kinds of jewelry I wear at work are petite necklaces, earrings, and rings."[29]

Australia

Two out of three women in Australia say they like to keep up with fashion trends. More career women and plan-to-work housewives are interested in fashion than stay-at-home housewives or just-a-job working women.[30]

There is a real difference among the New Demographic groups in their reasons for dressing well. Plan-to-work housewives and career women are more likely to reject "dressing because a man is present" than stay-at-home housewives and just-a-job working women who take the traditional viewpoint. Implicit in this is that career women and plan-to-work housewives are responsive to fashion and grooming for reasons beyond the traditional one of being attractive to men.[31]

Six in ten women in Australia say they have put off buying new clothing because of the economy, but career women are less likely than any other group of women to defer new clothing purchases. Both homemakers and working women in Australia are interested in keeping up with fashion.[32]

West Germany

Working women in West Germany appear to pay more attention to their appearance than homemakers. Both full-time housewives and women who work agree that they "like to look good." Slightly under four out of five homemakers feel this way, and slightly over four out of five working women agree. There is less agreement among them in the extent to which they "like to wear the latest fashions." Slightly more than half of the working women want to keep up with fashions, and fewer than half of the homemakers admit to being fashion conscious.[33]

The real differences in their approach to fashion and clothing are their criteria for buying clothes. Career women are more likely than any other group to stress quality, fashionable cut, and exclusivity. They are less concerned about reasonable price than the other segments of women. Along with plan-to-work housewives, they select clothing that is "pleasant to wear." Both career women and plan-to-work housewives are aware that when they go shopping for clothes, they ought to buy things that coordinate with the other parts of their wardrobes. On the other hand, plan-to-work housewives are less likely to stress quality, the type of fabric, or exclusivity.[34]

Stay-at-home housewives are least involved with wanting to look fashionable, if one judges by their lower level of concern with fashionable cut, fashionable color, or exclusivity. Just-a-job working women are interested in having the right fashion color, and even though they are somewhat more interested in exclusive fashion than either of the housewife groups, this is less important to them than it is to career women.[35]

Italy

The approach of Italian women toward fashion and grooming seems to take two different paths. On the one hand, some women are inner-directed, and use fashion as a means of personal expression or dress according to their moods so as to "feel in one's own skin." On the other hand, the outer-directed are concerned about their image and the situation in which they find themselves.[36]

Unlike the stay-at-home housewives in several other countries, stay-at-home housewives in Italy are somewhat involved in fashion. They fall into three groups:

1. *The Fashion-Oriented:* Those who say, "I like to dress well and make the most of myself." These women usually follow fashion trends fairly closely. They seem to spend enough money to achieve the looks they want, although they tend to spend more on quality than on designer labels. They dress well even at home and say they do it for themselves, for their own sense of self-worth. They also like jewelry and try to wear jewels when they are going out.

2. *The Comfort-Concerned:* Other stay-at-home housewives dress primarily for comfort. They say, "I like to feel comfortable and prefer casual clothing." They are less interested in fashion per se than with the price and quality of clothes.

3. *The Self-Expressive:* Still other stay-at-home housewives say, "I like to dress according to how I feel." These women are more impulsive in the way they buy clothes: "If I see something I like, I buy it." Of course, their impulses always function within the limits of their budgets and what is available to them. They might shop at all sorts of places from the marketplace to a downtown boutique.[37]

Plan-to-work housewives in Italy have a slightly different point of view. In Milan they change clothes before going out of the house. The more fashion conscious among them like to dress fashionably all the time to make the most of themselves. When shopping for clothing, they prefer quality and convenience. Within the limits of their budgets, they spend most for clothes to be worn on special occasions. They are less likely to shop impulsively, and are particularly likely to buy only a few things, but those will last. Only the more ambitious follow fashion trends. These women prefer to spend less on individual items so they can shop more often.[38]

Just-a-job working women are similar to plan-to-work housewives in their approach to fashion. Their clothing choices are strongly influenced by where they work. They try to be current and follow fashion trends. They say that because they go to work, they need to change their outfits more frequently. Therefore, when they buy clothes, they seek more variety and low prices rather than quality at a higher price. Their approach to fashion seems to change with age, as well. Younger working women follow fashion more closely. The not-so-young prefer to spend more money on fewer things of better quality.[39]

Age also seems to affect the approach of career women to clothes. Career women over forty are concerned about conformity. They are aware that the style of their clothes should be appropriate to the environment of the workplace. Above all, they are concerned about quality. Older career women are unlikely to do any impulse buying. On the other hand, younger career women think of fashion as a form of self-expression. They dress and make up according to personal styles. They feel the need to wear clothes that reflect "how they feel inside," and that express their identity. These young career women are impulse buyers, and they often make their choices on an emotional rather than a rational basis. Sometimes, they regret their choices.[40]

A small group of Italian career women are more casual and take no interest in fashion. These women try to spend as little as possible on clothing.[41]

United States

In the United States, working women buy more clothes, dresses, and shoes than housewives do. In every case, plan-to-work housewives are more likely than their stay-at-home neighbors to be involved in fashion as measured by the extent to which they have bought dresses or shoes in the last year or the average number of clothes they have bought and the dollar amount they have spent on them.[42]

By the same token, working women are more likely than either of the housewife groups to have been active consumers of fashion. Career-oriented working women dominate all measurable fashion activities. They have bought the great-

est number of dresses and shoes and have spent the most money for their fashion purchases.[43]

In the early 1980s retailers and fashion merchandisers became aware of the
potential value of the working women's market and that of career women in
particular. But many of them reacted to the changing nature of their customers
in a mechanical manner. They hypothesized that if career women are most
likely to spend money on clothes and need to be appropriately groomed for
their professional lives, they would automatically require man-tailored suits and
leather briefcases. This stereotype of the career woman was exacerbated by a
book written by John Molloy called *Dress for Success,* in which he advised
women to emulate men when they dress for careers.[44]

Many stores opened career departments that featured man-tailored suits that
were boringly alike and, of course, displayed the ubiquitous briefcase. Many
men's clothiers opened women's departments and some of them are extremely
successful in selling not just man-tailored suits but also classic and well-made
clothes less tied to the current whims of fashion. There is much evidence that
career women in the United States are particularly concerned about fashion as
a professional tool, but it is my judgment that this does not mean that they wish
to dress in a uniform manner or to imitate men.

As I move around in professional circles, I observe that the most successful
women are invariably well groomed but they do not dress alike. There is no
single uniform that exemplifies the way they look. Perhaps the best single ad-
jective to describe the special needs of career women is the word *appropriate.*
They must select their clothes and present themselves in a manner that is appropriate to their professional lives. As women move from working situations
in their own offices, to client meetings, to air travel, and to professional meetings, they meet all sorts of people in the course of the day. Therefore, their
clothes must be able to withstand many activities without looking crumpled or
requiring special attention. They need quality and durability in their clothes.
In addition, most women find that within the parameters of good taste and
appropriateness the clothes they wear should be attractive and becoming.

Several years ago there was a vogue for the phrase *investment dressing,*
which, perhaps, best expresses the approach of most career women to fashion.
They buy good quality clothes that can be worn for several years. This is perhaps the American version of wardrobe building, a very European notion that
serves most career women well.

As this is being written, the fashion press is touting short skirts. In many
ways, this particular fashion runs counter to most of the image needs of career
and professional women. A few months ago I was at a meeting with a group of

very senior businesswomen. We were taken behind the scenes at one of the major department stores where the director of fashion explained how they went about selecting fashion themes for the year. He told us they had decided to promote and feature short skirts as the dominant fashion for the coming season. Many of that group of highly successful women were of an age or figure type who would have looked ludicrous in short skirts. I walked out of the meeting with one of the younger, slimmer members of the group. I said to her that she was probably one of the few women in the room who could wear the new styles. She said, "I wouldn't dream of it. I've spent too much time trying to develop an image of credibility. That would absolutely undercut the way I want to appear in business."

At the present time, there is no way of knowing whether these new fashions will take hold or whether they are only a fad. Obviously, as fashions change, one's eye changes as well. What seems too long or too short at one moment seems perfectly appropriate at another. However, instinct tells me that this particular approach to fashion runs counter to the way women feel about themselves and the way fashion fits into their lives.

fifteen

Women and Grooming

THE way that women approach personal grooming, makeup, hair care, and fragrance is almost a direct reflection of the way they approach fashion. Stay-at-home housewives, who see fashion as something to reserve for special occasions, tend to feel the same way about makeup. Plan-to-work housewives, who aspire to be fashionable even though their daily activities are limited to home and family, take a livelier interest in makeup and hair care. Both just-a-job working women and career women see personal grooming as an extension of their need to be "put together" for work.

Great Britain

Stay-at-home housewives in Great Britain approach makeup in a haphazard way. Some wear it when they are at home, others do not. They tend to put makeup on before they go out, but they do not buy it frequently or spend much money on it. A stay-at-home housewife said, "I buy makeup on sale." Another said, "If I haven't got a lipstick, I go without." Clearly, cosmetics are not a major factor in the lives of these women.[1]

On the other hand, fragrance is important to them. They use it when they are at home as well as when they go out. They say it makes them feel feminine. A stay-at-home housewife said, "I never go without perfume. I never go around the house without it. It's feminine and it's nice." Another gave an amusing insight into her home life: "I put some on before I go to bed as well. I do it for myself. My husband's sinuses have gone anyway!" These housewives make a distinction between makeup, which is the face they present to the outside world, and fragrance, which they wear for their own personal pleasure. Yet plan-to-work housewives rarely buy perfume for themselves: they receive it as a gift. They make sure that their husbands know the type of perfume they like and wait for them to take the hint.[2]

A plan-to-work housewife described her daily grooming routine: "I have a shower every morning, wash my hair, and put my makeup on, for myself and other people's benefit." With today's simple hair styles, housewives normally wash their own hair. Most report doing so several times a week. Some of them treat themselves to a regular visit to the hairdresser for relaxation: "It's a woman's domain—the hairdresser. You sit and you're waited on."[3]

In Great Britain, working women do not "wear makeup at home, but most put some on when they go out. They do not seem to spend a large portion of their income on it. Apart from the odd lipstick or nail varnish in a new color, they tend to replace used items rather than buy on impulse. However, as they are out of the house more, the young working women use up their cosmetics more quickly so they need to buy makeup more frequently than the housewives do." One just-a-job working woman said, "I only wear it when I'm going out, just lipstick and a bit of eyeshadow." Another commented, "I find makeup is very expensive now to buy. Things I used to buy have tripled in price. It shows how often I buy it."[4]

Some young working women approach makeup as a daily ritual whether they are at home or away from home. One working wife said, "I wear makeup at home. I feel bare without it. I find it's just a ritual. I get up in the morning, have a bath, wash my hair and put on my makeup. Just occasionally, I think 'oh, I don't care today,' and I forget my hair and I leave off my makeup and somebody important always comes around." Another described her grooming regimen: "I wear it everyday. I just wear foundation, lipstick, and blusher during the day and at night I wear it heavier if I am going out."[5] A young career woman confirmed this: "It's part of going out . . . it's part of the whole process."[6]

Perfume is as important to some of these working women as it is to the housewives. Similarly, they do not usually buy perfume for themselves. They expect to receive it as a gift.

Most of the working women wash their own hair several times a week. They go to beauty salons for haircuts, and they enjoy being cared for: "I love going [to the hairdresser] . . . you just sit back and relax." Because of the time and cost involved, many of them do not go often, but there are a few who regard their hair as such an important feature that they have it done professionally on a regular basis. A young, married just-a-job working woman said, "I like changing it. My hair is never the same. I change it from month to month. My husband hates that." A career woman rationalized that she wouldn't indulge in her hairdresser regimen if she weren't working: "My hair is mousey color. Since I'm working I can really afford to have highlights and the perm done. I wouldn't bother with that and makeup if I wasn't working."[7]

According to the evidence, the two segments of working women spend more on lipsticks, moisturizing creams, and eye makeup than either type of housewife. They are also more likely to go to hairdressers and spend more money at the hairdressers when they do so. This is particularly true of career-oriented working women, who are more likely to be heavy users of cosmetic products and are most likely to have recently spent money on cosmetics and hairdressers.[8]

Japan

Women in Japan, across all New Demographic groups, agree that makeup is used in order to present a façade to the outside world. Their tendency to use it or not, in part, relates to whether they go away from home for social occasions or work. Since stay-at-home housewives tend to spend their lives closer to home, they are the least likely of the four segments of women to use makeup. Many of them say that lipstick is the only kind of makeup they use or consider necessary. Just as they don't take an active interest in fashion, they don't appear to see any purpose in makeup. One of them said, "I only use lipstick if I am at home. I hardly use any makeup when I go out." They tend to disapprove of women who use makeup in a manner that is conspicuous: "A woman . . . started working recently, but she seems to be using more and more makeup. She says she can't go out without makeup and that she doesn't want to see anyone if she doesn't have her makeup on. I wouldn't want to be like that."[9]

Some of the younger housewives in this group, however, are accustomed to wearing makeup every day, as a matter of course: "I put my makeup on right away when I get up in the morning. I don't take that much time on it but I do apply my makeup. Then I take care of cleaning and other chores . . . if I'm going out somewhere or to do shopping, I use lipstick again."[10]

Plan-to-work housewives in Japan tend to be more involved in activities outside the home than their stay-at-home neighbors. They are involved in hobbies or have gone back to school to train for the job market. Since they go out more often, they also tend to use makeup more frequently than their stay-at-home neighbors. Some of them, however, share the attitude that when they are at home they need not use makeup or need use only a minimum amount: "Usually I'm at home so I don't use makeup. I wear makeup if I am going shopping in a department store."[11]

They feel that makeup makes them more presentable, so they always use it when they meet with other people. A plan-to-work housewife said, "I'm old so I can't get away without makeup any longer. I always feel I should use makeup if I'm going to be meeting people, although I don't use it if I'm staying home." On the other hand, some of these housewives are concerned about the image they present to their husbands. Therefore, makeup becomes part of their daily grooming: "My husband wants me to have my makeup on and looking nice before he gets up. I feel that using makeup makes me pay more attention to my appearance." They appear to enjoy using makeup and sometimes change their "look" to be compatible with the clothing they wear.[12]

Both types of Japanese working women wear makeup as a matter of course when they go to work. A career woman said, "Wearing makeup helps me to switch gears as I leave the house. It feels good to wear makeup." Another explains, "Once you get used to wearing makeup, you don't feel at ease without it. Using makeup becomes a habit." Makeup, along with their style of clothes, helps them present a façade to the outside world: "If I don't wear makeup, my face just doesn't look the right color, and no matter what I wear I don't look attractive."[13]

On the other hand, Japanese working women, particularly career women, tend to compartmentalize their lives into time at work and personal time. Many of them don't wear makeup on their days off, unless they are seeing friends: "I don't want to wear makeup if I'm not going out. If I didn't have to meet people I wouldn't wear makeup."[14]

Just-a-job working women in Japan are less likely to differentiate between personal time and work time. Many of them do use makeup on their days off. Some wear lipstick only. They are less likely than career women to think of clothes and grooming from the standpoint of work. They simply follow their personal preferences or moods in deciding whether or not to use makeup. Some like to experiment and try different types of makeup. One just-a-job working woman uses makeup as a recreational activity: "Sometimes I put on a disco party at my house. The children wear makeup then, and I wear really loud clothes and makeup. It's really fun to try different colors on your face."[15]

Women in Japan take pleasure in the use of fragrance, toilet water, and perfume. In contrast to their use of makeup, some women use fragrance because of the way it makes them feel about themselves. A career woman expressed the pleasure that comes from using fragrance: "It gives me a lift to use a fragrance that I like." For others, fragrance is part of a daily ritual: one stay-at-home housewife said, "My perfume bottle is on my makeup table, and I just use it through force of habit." Another stay-at-home housewife said, "Using perfume is a part of my overall makeup routine." One just-a-job working woman articulated the self-delight she feels when she uses fragrance: "My reason for wearing perfume is self-satisfaction." On the other hand, another sees fragrance as part of her public persona: "I have to deal with people all the time and I don't want them to feel unpleasant, and that's why I started wearing perfume."[16]

Those who do not use fragrance or use it rarely say that, for a variety of reasons, they have never established the habit. Some have never found a fragrance they liked. Others don't like the odor of perfume when they're cooking or their husbands don't care for it. Some working women are self-conscious about using perfume at work because they think it might be too noticeable and detract from their image as professionals.[17]

Italy

Italian women tend to have two different attitudes toward fashion and personal care. Stay-at-home housewives who follow fashion trends use makeup and perfume as part of the daily routine. They "usually like to dress well even in the home and do it for themselves."[18] Women who are more concerned about feeling comfortable and prefer casual clothing are less interested in fashion and tend to use little makeup. These women, however, are concerned about caring for their skin. They often choose products that are hypoallergenic or available from the herbalist. Whether or not they use perfume seems to be a personal decision. Some use it scarcely at all; others consider it an essential element in personal grooming.[19]

The women who dress according to mood and shop on impulse are also impulsive in their use of makeup, perfume, or jewelry. Younger career women who use fashion as a form of personal expression use makeup in the same way. They feel that both fashion and makeup are a reflection of their inner selves and help them to express their identities.[20]

West Germany

One reflection of the importance of fashion and grooming to women is the extent to which they are prepared to give up certain products if they need to economize. In West Germany, career women are least likely of the four segments of women to be willing to do without their cosmetics and personal care products. Stay-at-home housewives are somewhat less willing than either plan-to-work housewives or just-a-job working women to do without cosmetic products. Not surprisingly, working women in Germany are more likely than full-time homemakers to use makeup every day or several times a week.[21]

United States

In the United States stay-at-home housewives are less interested in cosmetics than any other segment of women. The one minor exception to this is that they are slightly more likely than the other groups to use the traditional form of makeup, face powder. They are equal to their plan-to-work neighbors in the extent to which they use lipstick. Career women are more likely than either of the housewife groups to use lipstick and lip gloss.[22]

For every other category of makeup, working women in the United States are better customers than housewives; plan-to-work housewives are far more like working women than like their stay-at-home neighbors in the way they use makeup. Again, for every category, career women are by far the best customers of all. Thus, plan-to-work housewives are similar to just-a-job working women, but career women are slightly more active customers. Career women are particularly more likely than the other groups to use facial moisturizers and makeup foundation. Although all women, including stay-at-home housewives, are active users of fragrance, plan-to-work housewives are more like working women in their use of toilet water, cologne, and perfume.[23]

Australia

In Australia career women and plan-to-work housewives are particularly interested in keeping up with the latest hair styles, but homemakers are more involved than working women with the way they wear their hair. Career women seem to approach hair care products from a fashion perspective, and are therefore inclined to be strong supporters of the fashion use of hair-coloring products, permanent waves, and so forth. Stay-at-home housewives appear to use hair coloring for the more traditional reason of covering gray hair. All groups of women say they prefer to wear their hair shorter. This is particularly true of the stay-at-home housewife. All segments of women are also interested in products that improve the condition of their hair. This is especially important to stay-at-home housewives and career-oriented working women.[24]

Four out of ten women in Australia say they always buy the best skin care preparations. Such products are more likely to be bought by the two groups of housewives than either segment of working women. "Consistent with the importance of social interaction as a motivation for working, the career-oriented working woman is a substantial target for fashion-oriented products. Hair care products appear to achieve an almost universal penetration and use."[25]

In Australia, "the assumptions that career-oriented women tend to be staid and not particularly fashion conscious are unfounded. Of all women they feel the need most strongly to keep up with fashions and with the broader sense of changing style. To portray a business woman as a three-piece suit stereotype is unlikely to be relevant to the broad mass of women. From another angle portrayal of the 'typical housewife in the dressing gown and slippers/curlers in the hair' stereotype is unlikely to be based on the reality that is a stay-at-home housewife. In the majority of cases she maintains her interest in and knowledge of the fashions of the day."[26]

V

Changing Markets: The New Opportunities

IT has been customary for marketers to address the expensive or "big ticket" products and services such as financial products, cars, and travel to men. As a result, for the most part in many areas of the world products in these categories have not been marketed to women, leaving women an untapped opportunity.

It was not too many years ago in the United States that marketers of these products ignored the women's market. But as evidence of women's presence in the work force and of their market potential began to be recognized in the executive suites, many marketers began to address the women's market in the United States. In the following chapters I will consider several big-ticket product categories from the perspective of the New Demographics. I will examine the extent to which women are involved in purchase decisions or usage of these products and services and how each segment of the New Demographics behaves in relation to these categories.

Chapter Sixteen, "Women and Money," discusses women's participation in financial products and services. Among the areas considered are the extent to which husbands and wives share the financial decisions in the household. This is another specific application of the general concept of partnership marriage. This chapter also examines the traditional assumption that men are more financially competent than women and better at managing the household budget. The chapter reports on the extent to which each New Demographic segment participates in a number of specific financial activities such as savings accounts, checking accounts, credit cards, and investments. Finally, the chapter explores the "power" aspects of money, the implications for both husbands and wives when the husband is the only earner in the family, and how wives feel about being financially dependent on their husbands.

Chapter Seventeen, "Women and Cars," examines the car driving and buying behavior of women in a number of countries. It reports on the extent to which women hold driver's licenses, the number of miles they drive on the average, whether they live in a one-car or multicar household, and whether the most recently purchased car was a new or used model. Finally, it examines the crucial question of whether women participate in the car purchase decision. This chapter also explores women's attitudes toward cars and driving, and what they look for in a car.

Chapter Eighteen, "Women and Travel," examines the extent to which couples share in the decisions of where to go on their holidays, how much to spend, and how to get there. This chapter also reports on the travel behavior of women in a number of countries, the frequency with which they take holidays, whether they stay at hotels or motels, their means of travel to the vacation site and during the vacation, their international travel behavior, and their interest in cruise vacations and packaged holidays. Women's patterns of holiday travel are analyzed from the perspective of their place in the New Demographics and their place in the life cycle.

Action Implications

The major implication of this section is that marketers who have not considered women as customers for their products and services have overlooked a great opportunity.

1. The way to use these data in day-to-day marketing activities has been documented in the action recommendations in Part III. But since the products and services can be targeted to both men and women, factoring women into the target group obviously has the potential of expanding the scope of the market and, in turn, the returns to the marketer. A realistic way to approach the women's market in the product categories in question is an analysis of women's participation in the purchase decision. Thus, the New Demographic and life-cycle perspective can be applied to the share of the market that represents women customers.

   An example of this is reported in Chapter Seventeen, which discusses women and cars. A brief analysis revealed that, overall, women account for 44 percent of the total purchase decisions made for all cars bought new. Within the parameters of that 44 percent of women prospects, the New Demographic and life-style perspective identifies the value potential of each segment of women to the car market. This analysis can be applied to the women's share of any dual-gender product.

2. And, of course, if the New Demographic life-cycle perspective is built into the continuing series of steps that make up the marketing process, the positioning of the product and the communication of its benefits will be relevant to this newly discovered segment of consumers. It is particularly important for marketers unaccustomed to communicating with women to base their strategies and communications on the attitudes and perceptions of the consumers themselves to avoid the danger of stereotyping or alienating valuable prospects.

sixteen

Women and Money

T HE attitudes of men and women toward the role of women have obvious implications for whether or not a woman will enter the work force, and how she and her family will cope if she should do so. Less obvious is that attitudes toward the role of women also affect how a family makes purchase decisions, handles money, and buys and uses products.

In a traditional marriage, the husband earns and controls the money. He decides on all major purchases. The wife keeps house and cares for the children. Normally, she is given an allowance to buy food and household requirements. She might or might not have a personal allowance and, therefore, she might have to ask her husband's permission to buy things that are not included in the household budget, such as clothes and gifts, or she might eke such discretionary purchases out of her household allowance.

Traditionally, marketers have based their definitions of target groups on the perception of the differing roles of men and women. They marketed food, household products, fashions, and cosmetics to women. They addressed all big-ticket goods and services such as financial products, cars, and travel to men. The way a family handles its money and makes purchase decisions appears to be a direct reflection of perceptions of the male/female role.

Sharing the Purchase Decision

In many countries men and women endorse a partnership approach to marriage. Certainly, the decisions on how money is spent and how the household handles its financial affairs are direct evidence of the extent to which the partnership concept is accepted.

In five of the countries studied researchers explored the question of whether husbands and wives should share decisions on how the family spends its money, particularly for major purchases. The questions were phrased slightly differently from country to country but the import was similar. A dramatically high nine out of ten women in every one of the five countries endorse the concept of husbands and wives sharing in purchase decisions for major purchases.

In Venezuela 94 percent of all women and an equal proportion of men believe that husbands and wives should share the decision for major purchases. In every New Demographic segment, 92 to 95 percent of the women support the idea of sharing.[1]

Ninety-two percent of women in Australia believe that husbands and wives should share in the decisions. They go on to say that husbands and wives should also share responsibility for family finances. Eighty-eight percent of Australian women, both homemakers and working women, support this point of view. Eighty-five percent believe that husbands and wives should share the responsibility for the finances such as paying the monthly bills. Endorsement of shared purchase decisions is strongest among just-a-job working women (95 percent) and weakest among stay-at-home housewives (88 percent). Nonetheless, even among stay-at-homes close to nine out of ten want an equal voice in how the family spends its money.[2]

In Canada 92 percent of all women, both housewives and working women, believe that a woman should have a voice equal to that of her spouse in deciding how the family spends its money. Stay-at-home housewives are slightly less likely than the other groups to support this view. Nonetheless, 87 percent of stay-at-homes advocate husbands' and wives' sharing in purchase decisions. Career women are most enthusiastic about the partnership approach. Ninety-six percent of career women believe that husbands and wives should share in financial decision making.[3]

Eighty-nine percent of Japanese women, both homemakers and working women, endorse the partnership approach to deciding how a family spends its money. More plan-to-work housewives hold this opinion than any other segment of women (94 percent). Stay-at-home housewives and career women are equal in their desire to share purchase decisions with their husbands (89 percent), whereas just-a-job working women are slightly less likely to hold this attitude (87 percent).[4]

Eighty-nine percent of Mexican women and 87 percent of Mexican men vote for a partnership approach to purchase decisions. Although there is little variation among the New Demographic groups, it follows the pattern expected for the segments. Stay-at-home housewives are least likely to believe in shared purchase decisions (88 percent) and career women most likely to do so (92 percent).[5]

A somewhat different question was asked in West Germany. There men and women were asked to agree or disagree with one statement that "a man should have the last word in important decisions." These decisions might or might not be financial ones. Only one in three German women interviewed agrees with the statement; two out of three disagree.[6]

These figures represent what majorities of women believe husbands and wives should do. What is the reality?

United States

In the United States, 81 percent of married women share the decisions with their husbands about when to buy major household appliances, and 15 percent of women make those decisions themselves. Once the decision to buy the appliance has been made, wives are slightly more active in the selection of the model and brand. Seventy percent share the decision on the kind of appliance to buy, but 24 percent make that decision on their own.

If we combine the shared decisions with those that wives make on their own, we see that well over nine out of ten married women participate in the basic decision of when to buy a major household appliance as well as the specific purchase decision on the kind of household appliance to buy. This involvement of wives in the purchase of major household appliances cuts across all four New Demographic segments. Career wives are just a notch above the others in active participation in the decision process. Nevertheless, well over 90 percent of women in all segments are active players. Stay-at-home housewives are slightly more likely to participate in these decisions than their plan-to-work neighbors, but the difference is minimal (one percentage point).[7]

Financial Competence and Gender

The traditional notion that men are more able than women to handle money or make financial decisions is contradicted in every one of the countries that explored this issue.

Japan

In Japan, almost seven in ten women believe that the wife should be responsible for handling the family finances. As a matter of fact, stay-at-home housewives hold this opinion more strongly than any other segment of women (75 percent), and career women are less likely to insist that the wife take responsibility for family finances (61 percent).[8]

Stay-at-home housewives tend to be more traditional in their approach to issues and career women tend to be least traditional, but the responses of Japanese women to the question of the family finances is a direct reflection of the way husbands and wives manage their financial affairs in that country. It is traditional in Japan for the husband to turn his earnings over to his wife, who then organizes the family budget and gives him his spending money. Many businessmen receive perks on their jobs that enable them to dine in restaurants and enjoy other entertainment, thereby protecting the family budget. As a matter of fact, some companies pay substantial bonuses to their employees just so that the husband will have funds of his own.[9]

Australia

In Australia, fewer than one in four women believes that men are more capable of handling family finances than women. The overwhelming proportion of women in that country believe that they are every bit as capable as men of coping with family financial affairs. Even though this is the predominant opinion among all segments of women, stay-at-home housewives are more likely to believe that men are more capable of handling family finances, and career women are less likely to do so. The greatest contrast is between stay-at-home and plan-to-work housewives. The latter group disagrees more than any other segment of women that men are more capable than women in handling money.[10]

Similarly, two out of three women in Australia believe that women are more competent decision makers than men. In this instance plan-to-work housewives are slightly less likely than their stay-at-home neighbors to insist that women are more competent decision makers; not surprisingly, both groups of working women feel women are more competent decision makers. Career women hold this opinion more strongly than any other segment of women.[11]

Latin America

Even though we tend to think of Latin American consumers as very traditional, the reality is that neither men nor women in that region have condescending attitudes toward women's financial competence. High proportions of both men and women in the three Latin American countries disagree with the notion that men are more capable than women of managing the household budget.

There are clear divisions among the New Demographic segments on this issue. In each of the three countries career women are most likely to disagree with the idea that men are more capable than women in managing the house-

hold budget: in both Brazil and Venezuela, 83 percent of career women disagree; in Mexico, 72 percent.[12]

In each of the countries men are less likely than women to reject the traditional notion about relative competence in financial matters. Nonetheless, more
than half of the men in each of these supposedly "macho" societies take the
nontraditional viewpoint (from 51 percent in Mexico to 60 percent in Brazil).
Stay-at-home housewives in Mexico are less likely than any other segment of
women (only 55 percent) to believe that women are as capable as men in handling money. In Brazil and Venezuela, 70 percent or more of the stay-at-homes
take the nontraditional view. Just-a-job working women in Venezuela are
slightly less likely (68 percent) than other Venezuelan women to say that
women are financially competent.[13]

A more negative picture emerges when consumers in Mexico and Venezuela are asked to respond to the statement "normally women don't know how
to solve financial problems." Although more than half of the women in Venezuela (56 percent) and Mexico (52 percent) disagree with this idea, just under
half of the men disagree (47 and 49 percent, respectively). A high number of
both men and women chose not to answer.[14]

Australia

A large majority of Australian women believe that husbands and wives should
share the responsibility for family finances (88 percent) and the actual handling
of the finances (85 percent), details about keeping the budget, paying monthly
bills, and so on, and there are few variations among the New Demographic
segments. Career-oriented working women are most likely to believe in the
sharing of financial responsibilities by husbands and wives (91 percent), and
stay-at-home housewives are least likely to do so (84 percent). Just-a-job working women are more likely (90 percent) than either housewife group to opt for
shared responsibilities. Nevertheless, although working women demonstrate
the greatest enthusiasm for a partnership approach to money the lowest level of
support in either area comes from stay-at-homes for shared handling of monthly
finances (80 percent).[15]

United States

Women in the United States were not asked whether husbands and wives
should share in financial decisions; instead, they were asked how they do
handle financial matters in their households. Shared decision making is practiced to an overwhelming degree. Seventy-seven percent of all women say they
and their husbands share in the decisions on how much money to save or invest
and 76 percent say they share the decisions on what kinds of savings and in-

vestments to make. To a lesser degree the wives decide these things for them-selves. Ten percent of wives decide on the amount of money to invest and 8 percent decide on the nature of the investment. Therefore, 87 percent of women are involved in the family's financial planning and 85 percent of them are in-volved in the decisions on where to put savings and investments. The highest level of participation is found among career women: 91 percent decide how much to save or invest. The lowest level of participation is among stay-at-home housewives: 80 percent decide where to put savings and investments.[16]

Working women in the United States are particularly favorable to the part-nership approach to money matters. Seventy-nine percent of working women say that they and their husbands pool their salaries and use the combined amount for all household expenses, personal expenses, and savings. Career women are slightly more likely than just-a-job working women to do this, but the differences are not great (81 percent and 77 percent).[17]

By contrast, 10 percent of working women contribute something from their salaries for household living expenses and savings and keep the rest for them-selves. This approach is slightly more popular with just-a-job working women (11 percent) than with career women (9 percent) but, again, the differences are not great.[18]

A minority say that they live on one income and save the remainder of the second income of the other spouse after expenses from working. Six percent of all working women handle their money in this way. An equal proportion of just-a-job and career women follow this procedure. Just 4 percent say they live on the income of one spouse and the income of the other is used for that person's own purposes. Five percent of just-a-job working women and 3 percent of ca-reer women handle money in this fashion.[19]

The New Demographics and Money

United States

In the United States as in the other countries studied, career women are the most financially active group of women. Whether financial activity is measured by a savings account, a checking account, credit cards, or investments, career women are more involved in such financial activities than any other segment of women.[20]

For example, 47 percent of all people in the United States—men and women—have savings accounts. Working women, both job and career, are somewhat over the norm, whereas the two housewife groups are below the national average. Fifty-one percent of just-a-job working women and 59 percent of career women have savings accounts.[21]

Thirty-six percent of all people in the United States have checking accounts, but 47 percent of career women have such accounts. Just-a-job working women are above the norm, and both groups of housewives are below it. Twenty-nine percent of all adults have checking accounts that pay interest. Both types of housewives as well as just-a-job working women have such accounts but at a lower level than the national average. On the other hand, career women are above the norm: 32 percent have such accounts.[22]

Travel and entertainment credit cards are owned by 29 percent of the people in the United States. Career women are substantially above the norm in owning a credit card, such as American Express or Diners Club. Forty percent of career women have this kind of credit card; housewives and just-a-job working women are far less likely to have such cards. Twenty-two percent of stay-at-home housewives, 23 percent of plan-to-work housewives, and 24 percent of women who say their work is "just a job" have cards.[23]

More people report having a bank credit card: 41 percent of adults have one. Again, career women are far above the norm: 58 percent of career women carry a bank credit card (Visa or MasterCard). All other groups of women are below the norm in having such cards, although their usage increases as they move across the New Demographic spectrum.[24]

Forty-three percent of people in the country have charge accounts at a department store. Both groups of housewives are slightly under the norm in having department store charge cards: 39 percent of stay-at-homes and 38 percent of plan-to-work housewives. Just-a-job working women are somewhat above the national average: 46 percent have department store charge cards. Again, career women dominate the market. Sixty percent of career women have department store charge cards.[25]

Investments present a similar picture. Just 16 percent of all adults in the United States own some form of securities, stocks, or bonds. This does not include savings bonds, which are often given to children as a form of savings. In this case stay-at-home housewives are somewhat over the norm in being investors, but career women have the highest level of investment of any segment of women. Plan-to-work housewives are least likely to be involved in investing, and just-a-job working women are far below the norm in having investments.[26]

Great Britain

Career women in Great Britain tend to be the most financially active of all segments of women. They are significantly more likely than other women to have their own current bank accounts, to have check guarantee cards, cash dispenser cards, or credit cards. They are also far more likely than the other groups of women to have insurance on their homes as well as the contents and to have car insurance they have taken out themselves. They are also more active in investment matters, more likely to have stocks and shares, and national savings certificates.[27]

For the most part, stay-at-home housewives are least likely of all women to have their own bank accounts, credit cards, check guarantee cards, and so on. On the other hand, stay-at-homes are more likely than their plan-to-work neighbors to be involved in investments, although not to the same extent as career women.[28]

Plan-to-work housewives are most likely to participate in a joint bank account, rather than have their own. Career women are slightly less likely than other segments of women to have their names on joint bank accounts. Stay-at-home housewives are least likely to have their own life insurance, home insurance, or car insurance.[29]

In Great Britain women and men deal with money according to which spouse is more comfortable with handling financial matters. Both working women and housewives talk about shared decision making, which cuts across occupational lines. The major difference between full-time homemakers and working women is, of course, that housewives are dependent on their husbands for their personal spending money and working women are not.[30]

Some of the upper-income homemakers cross the boundaries when their husbands give them formal allowances. According to one woman, "I have my money quarterly in advance. I have a current account and a deposit account. My quarterly dress allowance goes into my deposit account which is entirely up to me what I do with. My quarterly housekeeping goes into my current account, and if I can make anything out of that, it's mine. I find I can quite comfortably dress myself out of my housekeeping account."[31]

Several commented that by having accounts funded by their husbands, they feel a sense of independence because their use of those accounts is entirely discretionary: "I have one or two accounts which he funds from his salary, but I feel I'm buying independently when I use those accounts." Another said, "I have my own account because he gives me an allowance. I like that. You'd miss the independence if you'd been used to it from working."[32]

Not all homemakers enjoy the independence of receiving an allowance. Although some of the less affluent housewives participate in joint checking accounts and some of them might have credit cards, they tend to feel less free to use those accounts or credit cards without discussing their expenditures with their husbands. They feel they need their husbands' agreement to spend more than twenty-five or fifty pounds.

On the other hand, some of them report buying small items for themselves through "fiddling the housekeeping." Since these women do not have personal

spending money or allowances from their husbands, they accept this as a normal and legitimate practice to avoid having to ask for every penny they want to
spend. Some of them actually fund savings accounts through the small amounts
of money left over from their housekeeping budgets or from contributions their
children make toward their board. When these women spend the money they
have saved from their housekeeping funds, they don't discuss it with their husbands. As one stay-at-home housewife said, "He doesn't even know about it."
Another said, "It's nice to be able to buy yourself a pair of shoes without having
to ask for them."[33]

The main difference between full-time homemakers and working women in
relation to money is that the working women contribute to the family's income.
Therefore, they have a much greater sense of financial independence and don't
need to resort to subterfuge. Some actually insist on keeping their own funds
separate from those of their husbands. As one just-a-job working woman said,
"Joint account? You're joking. I don't want him to get his little maulers on it."
Another explained, "It's my own, so my husband can't get his hands on my
money. It's *our* money really, but if we had a joint account, it would be *his*
alone."[34]

Not all working women insist on keeping their funds separate from those
of their husbands. Some of them regard their joint earnings as earnings for the
household. On the other hand, the feeling that they have contributed to the
household income gives them a sense of freedom in how they spend their
money: "You work to earn money for the family, but when you have your own
money, you don't worry too much about overspending the housekeeping." The
sense of financial independence contributes to a feeling of equality in the marriage. As one of them said, "We want the same status as a man, to go to a pub
or buy a meal without asking for extra or having to break into the housekeeping." Another explained, "My husband is very generous, but I enjoy and find
it necessary to have my own money. If I want something I don't have to ask for
some extra."[35]

Aside from a sense of financial independence, there is little difference between how full-time housewives and their husbands and two-paycheck couples
manage money. In some cases the wife pays the bills and keeps the budget, and
in some cases, the husband does. This is true for both working wives and those
who are supported by their husbands. Apparently, the choice of which partner
keeps the accounts seems to be a matter of interest and financial ability rather
than occupational status of the wife. A stay-at-home housewife said, "I handle
all the money in our place . . . I'm better at it. I pay the bills and give him what
he wants. So I can make quite a bit and save it. He wanted it that way." Another
explained their partnership approach in managing money: "I look after all the

money even though it's ours. He tells me what goes in, I say what he can have.
I have my own credit card. *I feel it's our money*. I don't think of it as my money."
A career woman said, "We've just one bank account. Everything goes into it.
If anything needs paying, we just take money out and pay it. What's left is left,
and we spend it as we go along. If he earns more, he doesn't *have* more. *We
share it totally.*"[36]

Other women contribute to the household finances, but leave it to their
husbands to deal with the details. A just-a-job woman said, "I'm terrible with
money. I agree with him and give him all my pay. But if I want anything, I
usually get it. I never want for anything." Another working wife, who apparently feels more competent in these matters, said, "We have one bank account
in joint names. I've always worked in finance, so he leaves it to me. But we
make joint decisions. He knows what's going on. I sort it out."

In the households of both working women and full-time homemakers, major financial expenditures appear to be a shared decision. Again, there is little
difference in this between full-time housewives and working wives. A plan-to-
work housewife said, "If it's something big, we discuss it and go to buy it
together." A just-a-job working woman said, "Big items like a TV are joint decisions, you choose them together." This position is echoed by women throughout the New Demographics spectrum.[37]

West Germany

Full-time homemakers and working women in West Germany "have become
respected bank customers whether investing or taking out credit. Nearly two-
thirds of all women save a fixed amount every month, and almost half of them
are interested in investing money." There is remarkably little difference between
housewives and working women in these matters. Working women are just
slightly more likely to say they are interested in investing and to have a regular
savings program.[38]

In specific financial activities, German career women are more financially
active than any other segment of women. Having a savings account seems to
be almost universal in Germany. More than nine out of ten of all women report
having a savings account. One hundred percent of the career women interviewed have savings accounts. Just-a-job working women are least likely to have
them, although their savings activity is very high: 87 percent of just-a-job working women have a savings account. More than nine out of ten homemakers
have such accounts. Plan-to-work housewives (94 percent) are slightly more
likely than their stay-at-home counterparts (91 percent) to have savings accounts.[39]

Almost half of German women report having a life insurance policy. Stay-at-home housewives are least likely to participate in this financial activity (42 percent), and career women are most likely to do so (58 percent). Plan-to-work housewives and just-a-job working women are between these extremes (47 percent and 48 percent, respectively).

Four in ten German women have a savings program. Again, career women are most likely to do so. Two out of three career women have a savings program, but only one in four plan-to-work housewives has one. Stay-at-home housewives are slightly more likely to be involved in this than their plan-to-work neighbors (32 percent). Just-a-job working women are substantially more likely than either segment of housewives to have savings programs, but not to the same degree as their career counterparts.[40]

One in three German women have savings in a mortgage bank. Again, the career woman is most likely to do so, and the plan-to-work housewife is least likely to do this: 58 percent of career women and only 16 percent of plan-to-work housewives have savings in a mortgage bank. Stay-at-home housewives are more active in this (28 percent) than plan-to-work women, and just-a-job working women are more likely than either of the housewives to have this program (38 percent) but not nearly to the same degree as the career women.[41]

Only a small number of German women invest in stocks and bonds (6.6 percent). The degree to which they are involved in investments is a direct reflection of their situation in the New Demographics spectrum. Stay-at-home housewives are least likely to invest. They are followed by plan-to-work housewives. Just-a-job working women are more likely to have investments, but career women are the heaviest investors of any segment of women.[42]

In view of this pattern of financial activity, it's not surprising that career women are most likely to have paid for purchases with EuroChecks in the past month. Fifty-eight percent of them report having done so. This is more than twice the number of plan-to-work housewives who have made out such checks (26 percent). As with the other financial activities described, stay-at-home housewives are more likely than plan-to-work housewives to participate in this activity (34 percent). Just-a-job working women are more likely than either segment of housewives to have used EuroChecks (37 percent), but not nearly to the same extent as career women.[43]

One clue to why plan-to-work housewives want to go to work is that they are less likely than any other group of women to prefer to wait before buying something new. Almost one in four plan-to-work housewives says she doesn't like to wait but would prefer to buy on credit. The other three segments of women are more conservative in buying products if they don't have the money to pay for them. "Women who plan to return to work save with the intention of improving their financial situation, but this group is also the most prepared to take out credit to enjoy things they want today." Furthermore, women have become less dependent on their male partners in dealing with money. Nearly a third of nonworking women have checking accounts as a means of noncash payment, and almost two-thirds of career women have them.[44]

Australia

Men and women in Australia were asked whether they or their spouses feel any need to justify expenditures to each other. Stay-at-home housewives are significantly less likely to share expenditure of household income; they are more likely to claim that neither they nor their husbands feel the need to justify the way they spend money. On the other hand, plan-to-work housewives are more likely to say that they need to justify expenditures (27 percent) to a greater extent than they believe their husbands do (21 percent). Men are more likely to believe that they and their wives are equal in the extent to which they justify expenditures to each other. On the other hand, women generally believe that there is a lot less sharing by husbands.[45]

Working wives were asked whose income is used to pay for a number of items. The purpose was to see how women's incomes are spent within the household. Most items are bought by "our income," the joint household income. Working women tend to spend their own income on clothing, hairdressers, cosmetics, small food purchases, pharmaceuticals, and to a lesser extent the main grocery bill. Although the differences are small, just-a-job working women more than others tend to use their own salaries for food, and career-oriented women are more likely to spend their own money on clothes and grooming, hairdressers, and cosmetics. "Overall, working women and more so career-oriented women appear to organize themselves into a more independent financial arrangement, but also rely more on each partner reporting back to the other about the expenses each is incurring."[46]

Passbook savings accounts are the most prevalent kind of bank account among all groups of women in Australia. As a matter of fact, more women (67 percent) than men (60 percent) report having them. Plan-to-work housewives are most likely to have an account. On the other hand they are less likely to be financially active in other areas, less likely to operate checking accounts, investment accounts, or building society passbook accounts, and least likely to hold accounts in their own names. According to "Beyond the Stereotypes," "This seems to reflect the limited household finances resulting from a single breadwinner and the financial constraints imposed on young families."[47]

In general, Australian working women are more financially active than the housewives, and career-oriented women are the most active group of all. They are more likely than any other segment of women to have checking accounts, bank investment accounts, building society passbooks, investment accounts, and credit union accounts. Interestingly, they are also more likely to answer a question about finances with specifics, whereas stay-at-home housewives are most likely to avoid answering. The stay-at-homes are less likely than working women to have a credit union or building society account, but they are more financially active than their plan-to-work neighbors. Just-a-job working women are more likely than stay-at-home housewives to have bank savings accounts, and they are identical to the stay-at-homes in the degree to which they have checking accounts or bank investment accounts, as well as building society investment accounts. Although not at the same level as career women, just-a-job women are more likely than either group of housewives to have building society passbook savings accounts or credit union savings accounts.[48]

There are real differences between the two segments of working women and the two segments of housewives in relation to credit cards. Bankcard is the most widely held credit card in Australia, carried by 35 percent of the women and 42 percent of the men. Just under half of career women (49 percent) and more than two in five just-a-job women (43 percent) have Bankcards. By contrast, only one in four plan-to-work housewives and three in ten stay-at-home housewives have a Bankcard. A similar pattern was found for retail store cards. Although one in four women has them, they are more likely to be held by working women than housewives. Career women are more likely to carry charge accounts at retail stores than any other group of women, but stay-at-home housewives are more likely than their plan-to-work neighbors to have department store charge cards.[49]

The use of travel and entertainment cards is not high among Australians. Men are more likely than women to have either American Express or Diners Club cards. Working women are more likely than housewives to have such cards.[50]

One indicator of women's financial independence is the extent to which they have ever discussed financial matters with their bank managers without the presence of their husbands. For the most part, most women have not had this kind of discussion. Career women, however, are significantly more likely than any other segment of women to have dealt with a bank manager without benefit of their spouses, and stay-at-home housewives are least likely to have done so. Interestingly, the percentage of men who have discussed financial matters with a bank manager without their spouses is the same as the percentage of career women who have done so (21 percent).[51]

Men in Australia are far more likely to organize their own comprehensive insurance programs rather than plan them jointly with their wives. Seventy-five percent of men report organizing comprehensive insurance themselves, compared to 47 percent of women who have done so. The two groups of working women are slightly more likely to handle this matter themselves. This is one case where just-a-job working women take the lead over career women: 54 percent of the former organize their own insurance, compared to 49 percent of career women. Stay-at-home housewives are slightly more likely than their plan-to-work counterparts to handle this matter on their own: 44 percent of stay-at-home housewives and 42 percent of plan-to-work housewives organize their own comprehensive insurance.[52]

Canada

The desire for financial equality and autonomy is very strong among all women in Canada. They believe almost universally (97 percent) that a woman should make it her business to know the amount and location of the family savings and financial assets. This attitude is found among both housewives and working women. In addition, nine in ten Canadian women believe that women should have their own money for personal use and savings over and above household requirements. Working women are just a shade more likely to feel this way, but the differences between the two segments of working women and the two segments of housewives are minor. Almost seven in ten believe that a married woman should be financially independent by having her own income or savings. Again, just-a-job working women (73 percent) and career women (74 percent) are slightly more likely to feel this way than stay-at-home housewives (65 percent) and plan-to-work housewives (64 percent).[53]

By the same token, eight out of ten Canadian women reject the traditional approach to money, "that a married woman should leave major financial decisions to her male partner/spouse." Career women in particular (86 percent) reject this notion, but 72 percent of stay-at-home housewives do so as well. It is not surprising, therefore, that a major reason why women work is "because some financial independence is important to me." Again, this is more important to career women (84 percent) than to women who say their work is "just a job" (74 percent).[54]

Consistent with the Canadian woman's strong desire for financial equality, women have a strong voice in a number of financial activities and decisions. They either take the responsibility for many activities on their own or share them jointly with their husbands. For the most part, only a small minority leave financial matters to their husbands alone. For example, 44 percent of Canadian women are responsible for preparing the household budget and 40 percent prepare the budget jointly with their husbands. This pattern is consistent among all segments of women. Career women and stay-at-home housewives, however, are slightly more likely than the others to have a strong voice in the family's budget process. Just-a-job working women are slightly less likely than the others to be involved in planning the budget. Just under eight in ten women in this category participate in the process.[55]

Canadian women play a very active role in a long list of financial matters. Eighty-five percent of Canadian women are involved in deciding the amount of money to be saved in the household; 83 percent either choose or share in choosing the savings institution; and 82 percent are either responsible or share the responsibility for making deposits to financial institutions. Seventy-eight percent are either responsible themselves or share responsibility for paying household bills. An equal number are responsible for choosing credit cards for the household. Just over three out of four are either responsible or share responsibility for choosing investments, and exactly three out of four are responsible for selecting an institution for a loan. All segments of Canadian women are involved in these activities, but career women are more likely than any other group to be active in them and stay-at-home housewives are least likely to be involved.[56]

In more specific terms, two out of three have regular savings accounts. The two working women groups are more likely than housewives to have an account, and stay-at-home housewives are more likely than their plan-to-work neighbors to have one. Personal checking accounts are held by just over half of all Canadian women. Career women are more likely than any other segment to have an account.[57]

Daily interest savings accounts are held by 45 percent of Canadian women. Again, working women are more active in this regard than the housewives; of all segments, career women are the most active. A smaller number (28 percent) have a joint savings and checking account. Among New Demographic segments, plan-to-work housewives (24 percent) are less likely than any other segment to have such accounts. The same proportion of stay-at-home housewives and career women have this kind of account. Daily interest checking accounts are held by 21 percent of Canadian women. Although working women are more likely than housewives to have one, career women are most likely of all groups to have one.[58]

In mortgages, personal loans, or auto loans, career women are more active than any other segment of women in Canada. This is also true of investments. Whether it is a registered retirement savings plan, a registered home ownership savings plan, Canada savings bonds, or other government or corporate bonds, career women are more likely than any other segment of Canadian women to participate. This is also true of common or preferred stocks, mutual funds, term certificates, or guaranteed investment certificates, even though investments are far from universal among Canadian women.[59]

This is equally true of pension plans at work, personal life insurance policies, or group life insurance policies. Working women, both job and career, are more likely to participate in these activities than housewives, but in every case career women are more likely than just-a-job working women to do so.[60]

Three out of five Canadian women have or regularly use credit cards, but, again, career women (74 percent) are most likely to have them. Plan-to-work housewives (55 percent) are slightly less likely than any other group of women to have or use credit cards. Bank cards, Visa, and MasterCard, are the most popular general credit cards among all women. Career women are slightly more likely to have Visa cards, followed by plan-to-work housewives. Just-a-job working women (30 percent) are slightly more likely than any other segment of women to have a MasterCard, followed by career women. Plan-to-work housewives are more likely than their stay-at-home neighbors to have such cards. Three out of four Canadian women have a department store charge card. These are most frequently held by stay-at-home housewives and just-a-job working women (79 percent), followed by career women (74 percent) and plan-to-work housewives (72 percent).[61]

If financial activity is measured by the number of times in the past month in which particular financial behavior occurred, career women are more financially active than any other group of women. Whether making a deposit to, or a withdrawal from, a savings account, writing a check for personal or household expenses, visiting a bank branch, seeking outside financial advice, using an automatic teller machine, or using a credit card, career women are more likely than any other segment of Canadian women to carry out financial transactions.

The Power of Money

One aspect of the traditional arrangement—that a husband goes to work and supports the family while the wife stays home and takes care of the house and children—means that the husband is the only member of the family to earn money. This has a "power" implication for some men and women.

Brazil

An intriguing question was asked in Brazil. Working women and men were asked how they felt about the statement: "Husbands (men) have a great deal more power when only they bring money home." This question was asked only of working women, so we don't know how housewives feel about the issue. Nonetheless, there is a real contrast between the way Brazilian men and working women feel about this subject.

Although more women disagreed with this point of view than agreed with it, about two in five working women, both those who think their work is "just a job" and those who are career oriented, say they believe that when men are the only breadwinners it does give them more power in the household. There was an amusing difference of opinion between men and women on this issue. Only a minority of men agreed with this assessment. The vast majority (82 percent) disagreed that earning money gave them power in the household.[62]

Australia

We have observed that the major difference between full-time homemakers and working women in relation to money is that homemakers are dependent on their husbands for allowances or for spending money. "Beyond the Stereotypes" reports that the majority of women at home "would prefer to have income in their own names." Sixty-two percent of plan-to-work housewives and 50 percent of stay-at-home housewives claim that they would like to have money of their own.[63]

An even stronger statement was presented to the women and men who participated in this study: "half of their spouse's income should legally belong to me." A remarkable two out of five women, both working and not working, feel this way. Not surprisingly, men were far less likely to accept this point of view, but a sizable minority did endorse it. One in four men agree that legally half of the spouse's income should belong to the wife. Endorsement of this somewhat radical notion is a reflection of the concern about financial independence which troubles housewives. One young mother who is a full-time homemaker said, "I'd like his salary to be split in half and then each contribute the same amount into housekeeping. I think that's fair. He's working at home. So, he can pay me by giving me half."[64]

One reason many of these presently nonworking women were uncomfortable about being dependent on their husbands' incomes is because many of them had worked in the past and had the sense of financial independence that comes with earning their own money. When they moved from financial independence to dependence on their husbands, many of them found it extremely difficult to adjust to the change. As the author of "Beyond the Stereotypes" says, "This may be something men find hard to sympathize with." Two comments from young housewives illuminate this attitude: "I don't hold the money at all. I wish I did. I get child endowment which I sneak off and spend and it's terrific." and "I find it so hard suddenly being dependent on him."[65]

Women on three continents have a strong desire to participate in the decision-making process for financial activities; indeed the partnership approach to financial matters seems to be a reality in a number of countries.

The assumption that men are more financially competent than women is

rejected by majorities of women in a number of countries. Women's participation in financial activities is not only endorsed, it appears to be practiced.

Career women are the most financially active of all segments of women in
every country that reported on these matters. The major difference between
working women and housewives is that working women enjoy some financial
independence in dealing with money matters, whereas housewives are dependent on their husbands. Nevertheless, the desire for financial independence is
important to housewives as well as to working women.

Finally, how powerful is the power of the purse? This issue was discussed
specifically in only two countries. Men and women in Brazil disagree on how
much power the husband wields when he is the only breadwinner in the family.
Housewives in Australia chafe at being financially dependent on their husbands. This is another clue as to the reasons that plan-to-work housewives aspire to enter the work force and earn their own money.

seventeen

Women and Cars

I T isn't too many years ago that the conventional wisdom decreed that the car market was a man's market. A woman may have picked the color of the upholstery, but men decided which cars to buy. In those days women were the marketing targets for food, household products, fashion, and cosmetics. Men were the customers for all big-ticket purchases: travel, financial services, and cars. What are the current realities?

Great Britain

In Great Britain two out of three people hold a current driver's license. Both segments of housewives and just-a-job working women are below this norm. Stay-at-homes are least likely to be drivers (45 percent), and plan-to-work housewives and just-a-job working women have a similar rate of participation (56 percent and 58 percent, respectively). On the other hand, career women are far more likely than the average Briton to have a driver's license (78 percent).[1]

Career women's involvement with cars and driving is also reflected in their rate of membership in driving organizations such as the Automobile Association. The national rate of membership is 23 percent. Career women are the only group of women who are substantially over that level: 33 percent are members. Career women are also better customers for gasoline than the average Briton or any other segment of women.[2]

On an average, adults in Great Britain drive their cars about seventy-four miles a week. Career women are just under the national average: they drive an average of seventy-three miles a week. The other segments of women, however, are far less likely to be frequent drivers. Stay-at-home housewives drive an average of thirty-three miles a week. Plan-to-work housewives and just-a-job working women drive their cars an average of forty-four and forty-five miles a week, respectively.[3]

Three out of four adults in Great Britain have cars in their households. The two groups of housewives are slightly less likely than the average Briton to live in a car-owning household. Sixty-nine percent of stay-at-home housewives and 71 percent of those who plan to go to work have cars in their households. Just-a-job working women are above the average (76 percent) and career women are substantially above average (85 percent) in living in a car-owning household.[4]

Twenty-one percent of adults in Great Britain live in a two-car household. Again, two-car ownership tracks with the hierarchy of the New Demographics. Both housewife groups are less likely than the average Briton or working women to live in a two-car household. Just-a-job working women are also under the norm: 20 percent live in a two-car household. On the other hand, career women are substantially above the national average: 33 percent of career women have two cars.[5]

Twenty-two percent of people in Great Britain report that the last car purchased was bought new. Stay-at-home housewives (24 percent) are slightly above that norm. Career women (31 percent) are more likely than any other group of women to say the last car bought in their households was new. Just-a-job working women (18 percent) are less likely than any other segment of women to have bought their last car new. Plan-to-work housewives (20 percent) are also below the average for new car purchases.[6]

Only a handful of women made that car purchase decision themselves. Even so, career women (16 percent) are more likely than any other segment of women to have selected their cars on their own. Plan-to-work housewives (4 percent) are likely to have selected their own cars, and stay-at-home housewives and just-a-job working women are far less likely than career women to select their own cars (6 percent and 7 percent, respectively).[7]

On the other hand, approximately half of the women in all segments participated in the purchase decision either on their own or with their husbands. Their tendency to participate increases according to their place in the New Demographic spectrum. Stay-at-home housewives are least likely to have participated in the car purchase decision (47 percent), whereas career women are most likely to have done so (61 percent).[8]

The importance of career women to the car market is indicated by other evidence. Just 24 percent of all adults paid for their own cars. Career women are just above that norm: 25 percent of them paid for their own cars. Just-a-job working women (11 percent) are more likely than stay-at-home housewives (8 percent) and plan-to-work housewives (7 percent) to have paid for their own cars.[9]

Many housewives defer to their husbands when buying a new family car. Their husbands may ask their opinions, but "most women seem happy to go along with their husband's choice so long as they like the look of it and feel comfortable driving it." A plan-to-work housewife said, "We discussed what was the right size and what we could afford to spend." A stay-at-home housewife said, "I don't think it matters so long as it has four wheels and gets you from A to B."[10]

The housewives are far more likely to be involved in the purchase decision if the car is to be the wife's car, the second car in the family. They care about the size of the car, how it handles, and if it would be easy to park. "Those who have no money worries are more concerned with looks than practical matters."[11]

Some working women share cars with their husbands; and single women buy and drive their own cars. According to one report, "[women] tend to see a car as important in their lives. For some it is the only practical way of getting to work. But even where suitable public transport is available, the car is often regarded as essential. To some, particularly the young unattached, it is a mark of independence, a passport to freedom. And although practical aspects matter, image can also be important."[12]

Working women are far more specific than housewives in their evaluation of the qualities they look for when buying a car. Aside from appearance, they are concerned about the economy of the car, the reliability of repairs, comfort, and luggage space. These concerns illustrate the fact that they are aware of the functional aspects of the cars they buy.[13]

Married working women are not likely to buy cars without consulting their husbands, but they appear to have considerable freedom of choice: "Within the price range that we could afford, I chose my car." If the husband is the principal driver, he may choose it: "I went with him on the test drives, but he bought what he wanted because he drives it."[14]

Australia

In Australia, only 9 percent of all women do not have a car in their households. Predictably, housewives rather than working women are less likely to have cars at home. Forty-five percent of women and 48 percent of men live in a one-car household; 37 percent of women and 41 percent of men have more than one car. Career women are dramatically more likely than any other segment of women or than men to live in a multicar household. Fifty-three percent of career women have more than one car; they are followed by just-a-job working women (47 percent). At the other end of the scale, 28 percent of stay-at-home housewives and 34 percent of plan-to-work housewives live in a household with more than one car.[15]

217

Just under three out of four Australian women participate in the car pur-chase decision. Forty-three percent chose their cars themselves and 30 percent shared the decision with their husbands. Overall, career women are slightly more likely to have participated in the purchase decision. The real difference between working women and housewives is the extent to which working women made the decision on their own. Fifty-one percent of career women and 47 percent of just-a-job working women chose their cars themselves.[16]

Italy

In Italy, full-time homemakers and working women respond to cars on two levels. First, on a rational, functional level they consider the car basic transpor-tation, granting them mobility and independence. From this perspective, the important characteristics of a car are the economy of gas and maintenance. They are also concerned with maneuverability in driving and parking. These attributes add up to "the image of the classical utilitarian car." In many families this is the second car and usually the one used by the woman of the house.[17]

Second, these women respond to the emotional side of car ownership and driving. The car becomes an extension of their own personalities, or presents an image with which they can identify or they would like to project. They are particularly sensitive to the appearance and speed of the car. The emotional aspects of car ownership are particularly important to stay-at-home housewives and career women. Some feel that having a car is necessary in today's society. One woman said, "I don't care much about it as long as it's fast." Others feel that a car has to be practical, economical, and comfortable. The car must have an attractive design. For others a car has to be fast, sporty, and aggressive. Finally, it should be a multipurpose vehicle that can go anywhere.[18]

Venezuela

Car ownership is not as common in Latin America as it is in Italy and Australia and therefore may not have the same meaning in those countries. Sixty-nine percent of all women in Venezuela live in a car-owning household. Career women are more likely than any other segment to have cars in their homes (77 percent), followed by stay-at-home housewives (71 percent). Plan-to-work housewives are the least likely of any segment of women to live in a car-owning household. One in four Venezuelan women lives in households with more than one car. Again, career women are more likely (33 percent) to live in a multicar household, and plan-to-work housewives are least likely to do so (18 percent).[19]

Just under one in four Venezuelan women has a car that she regards as her own personal car, not simply the family car. Career women (41 percent) are far more likely than any other segment of women to have their own personal cars.

Just-a-job working women (28 percent) are more likely than either of the house-wife groups to have their own personal cars, and plan-to-work housewives (15 percent) are least likely of any group of women to drive their very own cars. Fifty-two percent of Venezuelan women selected their cars themselves and an-other 18 percent shared the decision with their husbands. This means 70 per-cent of women who own personal cars participated in the car purchase deci-sion. Conversely, 23 percent of husbands selected their wives' personal cars without consulting them.[20]

As in other car-related activities, career women are far more likely to have selected their cars themselves. Seventy-one percent of career women who own personal cars chose the make and model. When this is combined with those who shared in the purchase decisions, the result is 85 percent of career women who own a personal car participated in the purchase decision for that car. Al-though plan-to-work housewives are less likely to live in a car-owning house-hold and far less likely to have their own personal cars, those who do so are second to career women in having participated in the decision. These home-makers are more likely than career women to report a shared decision (22 per-cent); 52 percent made the decision on their own. Thus, 74 percent of plan-to-work housewives participated in the purchase decision for their own personal cars. Just-a-job working women (61 percent) and stay-at-home housewives (59 percent) are less likely than the other two groups to have participated in pur-chase decisions.[21]

Only 12 percent of women in Venezuela plan to buy a car sometime in the next year; 6 percent of the purchases would be new cars and 4 percent would be used cars. Just-a-job working women are slightly more likely than the other women to anticipate buying a car (18 percent) in the near future. More than half of them (10 percent) plan to buy new cars. Conversely, stay-at-home house-wives are least likely to plan on buying a car (8 percent); their intentions are fairly evenly split between new and used cars.[22]

Brazil

In Brazil, women have a similar level of car ownership, but the consumer pat-terns are somewhat different from those in Venezuela. Sixty-eight percent of women live in car-owning households. Stay-at-home housewives are more likely than any other segment (79 percent) to live in a household that owns at least one car. Only 53 percent of just-a-job working women live in car-owning house-holds. Fewer women in Brazil (11 percent) have more than one car in their households. Again, stay-at-home housewives (15 percent) are slightly more likely than women in any other group to live in multicar households, followed by career women (12 percent). The two middle groups are below the norm.[23]

There is another pattern in the ownership of personal cars. Thirteen percent of Brazilian women have their own cars. Personal car ownership is dominated by career women (24 percent), followed by just-a-job working women (15 percent). Although stay-at-home housewives live in the most car-oriented households, they are less likely than any other group of women to have their own cars (9 percent).[24]

Among those women who claim to have their own personal cars, 51 percent selected the car themselves and 21 percent shared that decision with their husbands. Twenty-three percent said their husbands made the decision without consulting them. Career women are more likely than any other segment of women to have selected their cars themselves (60 percent). When sole and shared car decisions are combined, 79 percent of career women who own personal cars had a voice in that purchase decision. By contrast, 60 percent of stay-at-home housewives had a voice in the decision.[25] Between these extremes, 65 percent of just-a-job working women had a voice in the purchase decision for their personal cars; 46 percent made the decisions on their own. Plan-to-work housewives are second to career women in having influenced the decision. Seventy-five percent said they had a voice in the car decision.[26]

Still another picture emerges when we consider who paid for the woman's car. Twenty-eight percent of women car owners said they paid for the cars themselves; 14 percent shared the payment with their husbands; and 58 percent said the car was bought by their husbands or someone else. Only 7 percent of stay-at-home housewives paid for their own cars, and 93 percent said the purchase was made by their husbands or another family member. On the other hand, 49 percent of career women paid for their own cars; another 24 percent shared the payment with their husbands; and 27 percent said the payment was made by their husbands or another family member. Just-a-job working women are far more likely than either segment of housewife to have paid for their personal cars. Thirty-five percent bought them themselves; another 24 percent shared the cost with their husbands for a total of 59 percent contribution to the car purchase. Fifteen percent of plan-to-work housewives paid for the cars themselves; another 4 percent shared the purchase with their husbands; and almost 82 percent said that the cars were paid for by their husbands or another family member.[27]

Mexico

There are fewer car-owning households in Mexico than in the other two Latin American countries, and the car-related behavior of Mexican women is somewhat different from that of women in Brazil. Fifty-eight percent of women in Mexico live in a household that owns at least one car. Twenty-one percent of the women have more than one car. Twenty-four percent drive their own personal cars.[28]

There is sharp differentiation among the New Demographic segments in Mexico in relation to all aspects of car ownership. Career women dominate the picture. Eighty-five percent of career women live in a car-owning household, and 43 percent, more than twice as many as the average, live in a multicar household. Although only 24 percent of all women drive their own cars, 63 percent of career women have their own cars. Stay-at-home housewives are slightly more likely than the other groups to live in a car-owning household or multicar household; but they are less likely than either of the working women groups to have their own cars. Twenty-six percent of just-a-job working women drive their own cars, compared to 20 percent of each type of housewife.[29]

Women in Mexico are slightly less likely than women in the other Latin American countries to participate in the car selection process. Forty-two percent selected their own cars, and 17 percent shared the decisions with their husbands, for a total of 59 percent participation in the selection process. Only 32 percent of stay-at-home housewives, 41 percent of just-a-job working women, and 64 percent of career women selected their own cars. Seventy-nine percent of stay-at-home housewives and 74 percent of plan-to-work housewives did not pay for their cars. Working women took a more active role in paying for their cars: 55 percent of career women paid for their cars themselves, and another 8 percent shared the cost with their husbands. Similarly, 40 percent of just-a-job working women paid for their own cars, and another 19 percent shared the costs with their husbands.[30]

Only 13 percent of women in Mexico plan to buy a car in the near future. More of them plan to buy used (8 percent) rather than new (3 percent) cars. Stay-at-home housewives are least likely (10 percent) to anticipate buying a car soon. On the other hand, 20 percent of career women plan on buying a car in the near future, and they are evenly divided on new and used cars. Fifteen percent of each of the two middle groups, just-a-job working women and plan-to-work housewives, plan to buy a car in the near future, and this is more likely to be a used rather than a new car.[31]

United States

In the United States, 82 percent of people over the age of eighteen have a driver's license. Although the majority of active women drive, career women are most likely to have a driver's license (90 percent). Eighty-five percent of just-a-job working women, 74 percent of plan-to-work housewives, and 66 percent of stay-at-home housewives are drivers.[32]

The amount of driving women do is in direct correlation with their place in the New Demographics. Stay-at-home housewives are least likely to drive their cars frequently; their annual median mileage is 3,500 miles. The annual mileage for plan-to-work housewives is 4,400 miles. Both groups of working women use their cars more than the housewives. Just-a-job working women drive 6,000 miles per year, and career women drive 8,700 miles per year.[33]

The automobile marketer might say that it's true that these women drive cars, but are they potential customers? Do they really buy the cars they drive? Let's consider car decision makers.

Some women buy their own cars without consulting anyone else: 68 percent of new car purchases are sole decisions. Two out of five of the decisions are made by women. Some car decisions are shared decisions: 32 percent of all decisions are shared and women participated in over half of the decisions. If we combine all sole and shared purchase decisions for all new cars bought in a household, the ratio of men to women decision makers is 56 to 44 percent.[34] Clearly, the car market is no longer a man's market: almost half of current car prospects are women and their business is worth pursuing.

But which women are the best prospects? Are all women equally good prospects for cars? How do you find out which women represent the best potential? The New Demographic and life-cycle perspective can help us. We isolate only those women who are car decision makers. We give double weight to those women who bought their cars by themselves and single weight to those who shared in the decision. This kind of analysis enables us to define the relative value of the New Demographic and life-cycle segments to the car market. From this perspective, career women are particularly valuable car prospects. Twenty-seven percent of all women are career women and career women represent 44 percent of women car decision makers. However, life cycle plays a role as well. Unmarried working women, both job and career, are also especially important for the car marketer. Only 22 percent of active women are unmarried working women, but they represent 38 percent of all women who choose cars. Forty percent of women prospects live in two-paycheck households. Married career women are particularly valuable customers. There are 16 percent of them in the population, but they represent 24 percent of the women's car market.[35]

We can no longer accept the conventional wisdom that the car market is a man's market or that women only choose the color of the upholstery. Forty-four percent of current car prospects are women, and their business is worth cultivating.

Identifying which women are the most promising prospects is only the first step for marketers. We are long past the kind of advertising that shows a beau-

tiful woman in an evening dress being driven to a country club, or the housewife driving children to scout meetings in a station wagon.

The key to communicating with these very discriminating consumers is
credibility. Marketers must take women seriously as customers. Listen to their
needs. Treat them with respect. And above all, don't condescend. If automotive
marketers take women seriously as customers, they must project that in the tone
of their advertising and in how they deal with women in the showroom. And,
if they do, they will get their share of this relatively untapped dynamic segment
of the car market.

eighteen

Women and Travel

TRADITIONAL thinking has defined the travel market as primarily a man's market. The assumptions behind this view were that men were the only people who traveled for business and men made the decision and financial arrangements for family holidays. Regardless of whether these assumptions were ever valid, they are not valid today.

Business travelers are situational travelers; their trips are essential to the conduct of their business. And although they have no choice about whether or not to travel, they usually have a choice in how they get there: the selection of an airline, train, or car rental service as well as where they will stay when they arrive. Most analyses have shown that even though the people traveling on business are a minority of the population, they represent an extremely heavy user group. Therefore, the travel industry has courted their business. This is reflected in the multitude of facilities and conveniences tailored to the needs of the business traveler: special departure lounges, carry-on luggage racks, computerized car rentals, car rental credit cards, and simplified hotel reservation services.

By contrast, pleasure travel is discretionary. Pleasure travel occurs only because the holiday traveler thinks it would be more fun to spend a vacation away than at home. Consumers have many choices in how they spend their discretionary dollars. Their decisions appear to be a combination of available funds, attitude, and life situation. Studies done over the years suggest that there are factors other than demographics that predispose people to travel for pleasure. I speculate that the "outward bound" attitudes of working women and their tendency to seek broader horizons are likely to predispose them to pleasure travel.

I also speculate that the stay-at-home housewife is more likely to focus her interests on her home, her family, and her community ties and, therefore, would be less likely to have the money or the inclination for travel vacations. Nevertheless, it would be highly simplistic to characterize the women's market as monolithic. Not all working women are alike, and they do not represent equal potential as customers for travel. I speculate that women's prospective response to travel holidays is necessarily affected by whether they are tied down by family responsibilities, self-supporting, or are part of a two-paycheck household.

In a speech in 1973 entitled "Working Women, the Invisible Consumer Travel Market," I reviewed a cross-section of travel advertising and concluded that working women were, in fact, totally ignored by travel marketers as potential customers for business travel: "We see an endless parade of businessmen carrying attache cases, getting on and off planes, in and out of cars and hotels. But nowhere is there any indication that a woman ever travels on business."

This was not a surprising conclusion at that time because there was almost no recognition of women's presence in the business world. But women were equally invisible in advertising for holiday travel. "The only time the little woman emerges in a travel commercial is as an airline stewardess or a Hertz or Avis reservations clerk. If she is a passenger, she is a backdrop to a small baby or an adoring bride clinging to her husband. Nowhere is there any indication that a single girl or a pair of women may take a vacation trip alone. Somehow the news about this important market segment does not seem to have penetrated the executive suites where serious marketing decisions are made. We suspect that travel marketing decision makers still view women through the stereotypes of the 1950s."

In recent years many travel marketers have become aware of the potential of the women's travel market in the United States and have begun to address this previously untapped segment. But not all of them have done so, and not all of them have done so effectively.

Unfortunately, the traditional perspective is still pervasive in many parts of the world. Indeed, most of the travel information reported by the participating countries focuses on pleasure or holiday travel rather than business travel. Therefore, this chapter will concentrate on women's patterns of holiday travel.

Holiday Travel Decisions

The tendency for husbands and wives to share decisions on how the family spends its money at home carries over to decisions on where to go and how much to spend on holidays.

Italy

In Italy in 1972 a group of married women reported on how they made decisions on their holidays. Just over half said they and their husbands shared in
the decision on the types of vacations they would take. In a 1981 study, married
couples, both husbands and wives, as well as some who were living together
without benefit of marriage, reported a greater degree of shared decision making when it comes to holidays. Seventy-three percent of these couples reported
that they shared the decision in planning their vacations or holiday travel.[1]

Latin America

Almost half of the couples in Mexico and Venezuela also report sharing in the
decisions in planning their vacations. In both countries, the husbands are more
likely than the wives to claim shared decision making. Forty-four percent of
women in Mexico say they share the vacation-planning decisions with their
husbands; 55 percent of the men claim to share those decisions. Similarly, 45
percent of women in Venezuela say they and their husbands plan vacations
together; 51 percent of the men claim the vacation planning is joint.

United States

In the United States nine out of ten married women say that they and their
husbands share the decisions on where to go on their vacations. Six percent of
wives make the decisions on their own and 4 percent of husbands make the
decision alone. There are minor directional differences in the way that the New
Demographic wives and their husbands handle the decision-making process,
but the overwhelming majority of husbands and wives take a partnership approach to the vacation travel decision.

Stay-at-home housewives are slightly more likely than the other segments of
women to participate in the process. Plan-to-work housewives and career
women are slightly less likely to share in the decision but slightly more likely
to make that decision alone. Exactly nine out of ten just-a-job working women
share the decisions with their husbands, but their husbands are slightly more
likely than husbands of women in the other segments to make the decision
alone.[2]

Overall, 85 percent of all women share the decisions with their husbands
on how much money to spend when they take a vacation. In this instance,
husbands are slightly more likely to decide on the amount of money to be spent
(9 percent), compared to wives who make the decision alone (5 percent). Although the majority of the New Demographic segments participate in the process with their husbands, there are slight differences among them. Plan-to-work
housewives are slightly less likely to participate in decisions on how much

money to spend (82 percent), whereas slightly more of the stay-at-home house-wives share the decisions (84 percent). In homes of housewives, 10 percent of the husbands make the decision on how much money is to be spent on a vacation.[3]

On the other hand, more career wives share the spending decisions with their husbands (91 percent) and their husbands are least likely to make that decision on their own (5 percent). Just-a-job working wives are somewhere between. Eighty-five percent of them share in the decisions on how much money to spend on vacations. Their husbands have a stronger voice than the husbands of career women in how much money to spend (9 percent), but 6 percent of just-a-job wives make that decision on their own.[4]

Both marital status and place in the New Demographic spectrum affect women's travel patterns. For example, 37 percent of all adults who took a vacation in the United States in the last twelve months stayed in a hotel or a motel. Marital status seems to be the discriminator among women. Thirty-seven percent of married stay-at-home housewives stayed at a hotel or motel, compared to 20 percent of unmarried stay-at-homes. Similarly, 38 percent of married plan-to-work housewives stayed at a hotel or motel on a vacation in the past year, compared to 18 percent of the unmarried plan-to-work housewives.[5]

Just-a-job working wives are far more likely to have patronized hotels or motels on their last vacation (44 percent), compared to their unmarried counterparts (33 percent). Both married and unmarried career women are above the national average in patronizing hotels and motels on holidays. Career wives are slightly more likely to have done so (51 percent) than career women who are not currently married (47 percent).[6]

Seventeen percent of all adults in the United States report having flown on a domestic airline in the last twelve months. Working women are far more likely than housewives to be checking in at airline counters, and career women are more likely than any other group of women to travel by air. Again, marital status is a key discriminator. Twenty-five percent of career wives have taken a domestic airline trip in the past year, but 29 percent of unmarried career women have done so. Unmarried women who say their work is "just a job" are just over the norm in airline travel, at 18 percent.[7]

Ten percent of people in the United States report having flown overseas sometime in the past three years. As in the case of domestic travel, career-oriented working women, both married and unmarried, are most likely to be international travelers. Fourteen percent of career wives took an international plane trip in the past three years; 16 percent of unmarried career women did so. No other segment of women, either married or unmarried, is above the national average in international travel.[8]

Cruise vacations are patronized by only a small segment of American consumers. Since the numbers are small, I will comment on directional patterns but these should be considered with caution. Fewer than 2 percent of Americans took a foreign cruise sometime in the past three years. Plan-to-work housewives, both married and unmarried, are not responsive to this kind of travel. Among married women, career wives are most likely to have taken such a trip. Both working wives who say their work is "just a job" and married stay-at-home housewives also participated in foreign cruises slightly more than the national average. Unmarried stay-at-home housewives are as likely to take foreign cruise vacations as their career counterparts. Unmarried working women who say their work is "just a job" are just at the national average in taking foreign cruises. The figures for stay-at-home housewives, both married and unmarried, may reflect a segment of affluent, older women.[9]

Domestic vacation cruises have a very low level of national participation. Fewer than 1 percent of all adults took such a trip in the past year. Married working women and unmarried stay-at-home housewives are most responsive to this form of travel. Just-a-job working wives are particularly likely to take domestic cruises. They are followed by unmarried stay-at-home housewives and by career wives. Married stay-at-home housewives are far less likely to take this kind of vacation. On the other hand, plan-to-work housewives, both married and unmarried, are completely out of this market.[10]

It is clear that working women are more valuable customers for travel than their nonworking counterparts. It is even clearer that career women are more valuable travel customers than women who say their work is just-a-job. We also see that their situation in the life cycle impacts on their response to travel and in the specific types of holiday trips that they take.

Great Britain

In Great Britain, "most full-time housewives have at least one holiday a year and some of the more wealthy couples take numerous short breaks. As with all purchases, the decision is usually made jointly, although either husband or wife may be the instigator and handle the arrangements. The type of holiday chosen varies widely according to circumstances, previous experience, and personal preferences. Whether at home or abroad, package deal or privately arranged, self-catering or full board, the accent is on relaxation and a complete change from normal routine." Many women work primarily to finance vacations for themselves and their families. "Part of their income may be set aside specifically for this purpose. Nevertheless, as a rule they seem no more likely than housewives are to influence their husbands in the choice of holiday and again the initial suggestion and arrangements may be made by husband or wife. Rarely is the whole issue left to her."[11]

Once again, data on the travel behavior of the New Demographic segments underscores the value of career women to the travel market. Thirty-eight percent of all adults in Great Britain have taken at least one holiday in the past year. Both working women who say their work is "just a job" (41 percent) and career women (42 percent) are more likely to have taken a holiday in the past year. Seventeen percent of people in that country took two holidays in the past year. Stay-at-home housewives conform to the national average, but plan-to-work housewives are below it (12 percent). On the other hand, both just-a-job working women (20 percent) and career women (21 percent) are more likely to have taken two holiday breaks in the past twelve months.[12]

Only 8 percent of all people in Great Britain took three or more holiday interludes in the past year. Career women are more likely than any other segment of women to have done so (11 percent). Just-a-job working women conform to the national average, and stay-at-home housewives (7 percent) and plan-to-work housewives (5 percent) are below the national average.[13]

The most popular means of holiday transportation is by car. Thirty-one percent of all adults in Great Britain drove their cars when they took their last vacations. Just-a-job working women are slightly more likely than the average to have taken a driving holiday (35 percent). Career women conform to the national average, and stay-at-home housewives (29 percent) and plan-to-work housewives (28 percent) fall below the national average.[14]

The next most popular form of holiday travel is by scheduled and chartered airlines. Ten percent of adults in England traveled by scheduled airlines when they took their holidays in the past twelve months. Almost twice as many career women as the national average traveled air (19 percent). Just-a-job working women are above (11 percent) and plan-to-work (9 percent) and stay-at-home housewives (8 percent) are below the norm.[15]

Ten percent of people in Great Britain took a holiday trip by means of a chartered airline. Again, career women (14 percent) and just-a-job working women (11 percent) are above the norm in having done so. Stay-at-home housewives (9 percent) and plan-to-work housewives (7 percent) are slightly less likely to have taken a chartered airline.[16]

Eight percent of people in Great Britain took a packaged holiday abroad in the past year. As in the other forms of holiday travel, the two groups of working women are more likely than their housewife counterparts to have used this form of travel. Eleven percent of career women and 10 percent of just-a-job working women took a packaged holiday abroad in the past year. Five percent of people in Great Britain took two packaged holidays in the past year. Again, working women are more likely than either type of housewife to have done so: 8 percent of career women and 6 percent of just-a-job working women did so. A very small number of British people, around 3 percent, took three or more such trips in the past year. Career women are just over that figure, stay-at-home house-wives conform to the national average, just-a-job working women are below the average, and plan-to-work housewives are lowest ranked.[17]

Thirty-seven percent of people in Great Britain traveled by air in the last three years. Just-a-job working women conform to the national average in air travel. The two housewife groups are below and career women are above the national average: 54 percent of career women traveled by air in the past three years.[18]

The major destination of air travel for 23 percent of all adults in Great Britain is Europe. Again, the two groups of housewives are below the norm. Just-a-job working women are just above the norm (24 percent) and career women are significantly above it (39 percent).[19]

One in four people in Great Britain stayed at a hotel in the past year. As with the other forms of travel, the two segments of housewives were slightly less likely than the national average to have stayed at hotels. Twenty-two percent of stay-at-home housewives and 20 percent of plan-to-work housewives say they stayed at hotels in the past year. Just-a-job working women are just under the norm at 24 percent. On the other hand, career women were far more likely than any other segment of women to have stayed at a hotel in Great Britain in the past twelve months. Thirty-seven percent report having done so.

Australia

In Australia as in the other countries reporting on women's travel behavior, career women are the most active segment of women in the travel market. Forty-eight percent of all women have taken a holiday within their own state in the past two years. Stay-at-home housewives (41 percent) are least likely to have done so, and plan-to-work housewives (46 percent) and just-a-job working women (47 percent) are more likely to have done so. Career women, on the other hand, are more likely than any other women to have taken a holiday in the past two years within the state (56 percent).[20]

Forty-six percent of all women report having taken an interstate holiday within the past two years. Plan-to-work housewives conform to the average, whereas stay-at-home housewives and just-a-job working women are below the norm (44 percent). Career women are slightly more likely than any other women (48 percent) to have taken an interstate holiday in the past two years.[21]

Fifteen percent of all women taking an interstate holiday traveled to their destinations by air. All segments but career women are below the norm in having done so; at 20 percent, career women are well above the norm.[22]

Six percent subscribed to a packaged holiday for their interstate vacation trips. Stay-at-home housewives conform to the norm, and plan-to-work and just-a-job working women are below the average. Career women (10 percent) are more likely than any other women to have taken an interstate packaged holiday in the past two years.[23]

Exactly 32 percent of Australian women traveled overseas on a holiday in the past two years. Stay-at-home housewives (27 percent) and plan-to-work housewives (25 percent) are less likely to have done so, and just-a-job working women (34 percent) are more likely to have done so. Again, career women are more likely than any other women to have traveled overseas: 42 percent of career women took an overseas holiday in the past two years.[24]

Not surprisingly, most of their overseas travel was by air. Twenty-eight percent of all women in Australia traveled to their holiday destinations by airplane. Stay-at-home housewives (24 percent) and plan-to-work housewives (23 percent) are below the norm, just-a-job working women conform to the norm, and career women are substantially above the national average (36 percent).[25]

Sixteen percent of Australian women traveled to their overseas holiday destinations through a packaged tour arrangement. This holiday was particularly appealing to stay-at-home housewives (19 percent). It was far less appealing to plan-to-work housewives (7 percent). Again, just-a-job working women conform to the norm (16 percent) and career women are above the norm (21 percent).[26]

The Changing Travel Market

Married women have an active role in making the decision on how and where the family is to spend its vacations and how the travel dollars will be spent. Whether they are married or single, working women are more likely to be active participants in the travel market than are full-time homemakers. With very few exceptions, career women are the most active travelers of all.

Whereas women were invisible in travel advertising in the early 1970s, they are far from invisible in the United States today. Since those early days, travel marketers have, in fact, recognized the value of the women's market in general and the working women's market in particular. In more recent years travel marketers have gone to great lengths to study the desires and needs of women travelers and to address them in their services as well as in their communications. For example, several years ago a major hotel chain instituted consciousness-raising sessions for its staff, which included a film of hypothetical travel situations such as a woman checking in at the registration desk and a woman entertaining a male client in the dining room. In each situation the film recorded the different ways that men and women were treated by the hotel staff. The moderator then suggested procedures that would put women guests at their ease.

The changing market has also affected hotel design. For example, in past years the bar section in a hotel was usually a dark, leathery enclave reminiscent of a men's club. Now, in addition to such bars, many hotels have open lounge areas that are well lit where a woman would feel perfectly comfortable entertaining a man, meeting with another woman, or having a drink alone. Although women traveling alone tended to be made uncomfortable in hotel dining rooms and restaurants, more hotels have learned how to greet them and make them feel welcomed.

All of these changes took understanding, time, and effort on the part of managements. Since travel is a service or an experience, instead of a product in a package, clerks, stewardesses, waiters, and others can make the experience pleasant or unpleasant. Cultivating the women's travel market goes beyond advertising to training and sensitizing the retail staff.

I have reported some of the changes that have taken place in the travel market in the United States because it is possible that travel marketers in other parts of the world have not capitalized on the enormous potential of women as prospects for travel.

VI
Changing Audiences

In Part VI I explore the differences among the New Demographic groups in regard to media and advertising applications. I explore whether they have distinctive patterns of media use as well as how they respond to advertising.

Chapter Nineteen, "Women and Media," reports on the media women in the countries studied watch, read, or listen to, and compares the media tastes of each of the New Demographic groups with those of the population as a whole. Some countries reported on the tastes of women consumers in terms of particular programs and particular magazines. The Latin American countries also reported on consumers' evaluations of the media.

Chapter Twenty, "Women and Advertising," reflects the varied aspects of advertising reported by the participating countries. These include their feelings about advertising overall, the degree to which it influences their purchase behavior, and the role of advertising in their lives. Some countries discussed elements of advertising that improve or lower their opinions of advertising overall. Finally, this chapter discusses the extent to which consumerist and governmental groups are concerned about the stereotyping of women in advertising and specific actions taken to improve the situation.

Action Implications

1. For the marketer who has applied the New Demographic and life-cycle perspective to the women's market, the differing desires, needs, and behavior of the various segments of women have been built into the marketing process. By the time the marketer is ready to communicate with prospective consumers through advertising and to place that advertising in the media, a number of strategic decisions have been made. The target

group has been defined, the relevant benefits and attributes of the product have been identified, the context within which the product is bought or used has been studied, and the relative value of the various segments within the New Demographic and life-cycle grid have been identified.

Therefore, the best way to apply this approach to media selection would be to apply the grid to the media possibilities in each country. In those countries that have the New Demographic questions built into standard media studies, the marketer is able to select the media that best fit the purposes of the campaign. For example, instead of generalizing about the media tastes of stay-at-home housewives compared to career women, it is possible to define precisely which women in each of the New Demographic segments are in the market for a particular product. Therefore, the media plan can be targeted very precisely to the users or prospects most relevant to the strategy.

2. The application to advertising is equally straightforward. If the consumer needs and attitudes of the New Demographic and life-cycle segments have been built into the marketing process, they are also built into the creative strategy. The most direct way to ensure that the communication to the desired prospects is relevant to them is to obtain their responses at an early stage in the creative process. In this way, advertising imagery, usage context, and tonality will reflect the responses of the target consumers. This is the best way to develop advertising that is personally involving and relevant to those consumers. Following this procedure would ensure against alienating these desirable customers by inadvertent or inappropriate stereotyping or imagery.

nineteen

Women and Media

THE New Demographic segments of women are distinctive in their self-perceptions, their attitudes toward work, and their attitudes toward life itself. In order to link an understanding of the differences among this spectrum of women to marketing and advertising applications, we need to learn whether they have distinctive patterns of media use. Do they respond differently to the media choices in their countries? What do they watch, read, or listen to? How do the media tastes of each of the New Demographic groups vary from those of the population as a whole?

The media available vary from country to country, and the sources of media information in each country are equally varied. The United States, Canada, and Great Britain have regular syndicated media-reporting services that include the four major media: television, radio, magazines, and newspapers. The United States and Great Britain have incorporated the New Demographic questions into the standardized services. Therefore, we are able to analyze the media behavior of the New Demographic segments in those countries.

The standard media services in Canada and West Germany do not, as yet, include the New Demographic questions. Therefore, we are able to report on the media behavior of housewives and working women, but not of the four New Demographic segments. In the remaining countries the media information was gathered by means of customized surveys not part of standard media reports. Regrettably, we have only limited media information from Italy and Japan.

The Electronic Media

TELEVISION

Television is the dominant medium in every country studied.

United States

In the United States, usage of daytime television is reported in terciles, that is, the extent to which the total population watches daytime television is divided into equal thirds of heavy, medium, and light viewing.

Housewives are far more likely than working women to be heavy viewers of daytime television, since they are at home and available to watch it. Stay-at-home housewives are slightly more likely than their plan-to-work neighbors to be heavy viewers of television during the day. Conversely, working women, who are not normally available to watch television during the day, are relatively light viewers of the medium. Career women are even less likely than their just-a-job counterparts to watch daytime television.[1]

Theoretically, all four segments of the New Demographics would be available to watch TV during the evening. In the United States this is labeled prime time television. Of all segments of women, the stay-at-home housewives are the heaviest viewers, followed by plan-to-work housewives. Just-a-job working women are somewhat less likely than either of the housewife groups to watch television during the evening. Again, career women are the lightest viewers of all.[2]

Canada

In Canada, 65 percent of housewives watch television during the day before five o' clock. This is more than double the proportion of working women who watch television during daytime hours. Only 31 percent of working women are viewers of daytime television.[3]

Both housewives and working women are available to watch television during the evening, between seven and eleven o'clock, and the great majority of them do so. Housewives are slightly more likely (92 percent) than working women (88 percent) to view prime time television.[4]

When we examine the intensity of their viewing, it is clear that Canadian housewives are much heavier viewers than their working counterparts: 32 percent of housewives are among the heaviest viewers; only 13 percent of working women are in that segment. Conversely, only 13 percent of housewives are among the lightest viewers, and 25 percent of working women are among the lightest viewers.[5]

Great Britain

In Great Britain the Target Group Index defines heavy viewers as people who watch television four or more hours a day; medium viewers are those who watch two to three hours a day, and light viewers watch one hour a day or less.[6]

Housewives in Great Britain are far more likely than working women to be heavy viewers of ITV, the commercial television channel. British women's involvement with television follows their place in the New Demographic spectrum. Stay-at-home housewives are the heaviest viewers; they are followed by housewives who plan to return to work. Just-a-job working women are less likely to be heavy viewers than either group of housewives, but they are far more likely to watch television than their career-oriented counterparts.[7]

West Germany

In West Germany the heaviest viewers are those who watch television daily; heavier viewers are those who watch television several times a week; medium viewers watch once a week; lighter viewers look at television one to three times a month; and the lightest viewers never watch or rarely look at television.[8]

The majority of housewives and working women are among the heaviest or heavier viewing segments. Therefore, the majority of them watch television at least several times a week. German housewives, however, are far more likely than German working women to be heavy television viewers. Sixty-eight percent of housewives watch television every day, compared to 50 percent of working women. Conversely, 38 percent of working women look at television several times a week; only 24 percent of housewives watch that infrequently.

Brazil

In Brazil, television-viewing behavior is reported in terciles of light, medium, and heavy viewing. The majority of all women in Brazil are heavy viewers of television. The two segments of housewives, however, are substantially more likely to be heavy viewers than are the two groups of working women. Eighty-one percent of stay-at-home and of plan-to-work housewives are heavy viewers, compared to 65 percent of just-a-job working women and 64 percent of career women.[9]

Mexico

In Mexico, television-viewing behavior is also reported in terms of heavy, medium, and light viewing. The level of heavy viewing is somewhat lower than in Brazil. Plan-to-work housewives are most likely to be heavy viewers: 76 percent of plan-to-work housewives are heavy television viewers. Sixty-seven percent of stay-at-home housewives and just-a-job working women are heavy viewers. A substantial number of career women (60 percent) are heavy viewers, but career women are less likely than the other segments of women in Mexico to be heavy viewers.[10]

Venezuela

Women in Venezuela are also involved with television. As in most other countries, housewives are more likely than their working counterparts to be heavy viewers. In Venezuela plan-to-work housewives are the heaviest viewers of all (83 percent), followed by their stay-at-home neighbors (81 percent). An identical proportion of the two segments of working women are heavy viewers: 73 percent of just-a-job working women and of career women are in the heavy viewing group.[11]

Japan

In Japan, in the two largest metropolitan areas, Tokyo/Yokohama and Osaka/Kobe, 34 percent of all active women watch television for twenty-three hours or more a week; 41 percent watch for less than twelve hours a week.

The two housewife groups are more likely than the two segments of working women to watch television frequently. Plan-to-work housewives, however, are the heaviest viewers of all. Just-a-job working women watch less than either segment of housewives, but they are slightly more likely than their career counterparts to be fans of television.[12]

Australia

Housewives in Australia are also more likely than working women to be strong supporters of television. In that country, however, the plan-to-work housewives are the heaviest viewers. They are more likely than their stay-at-home neighbors to be among the heaviest viewers, who watch television thirty-one or more hours a week, and among the heavy viewers, who watch between twenty-one and thirty hours a week. Australian stay-at-home housewives are second to their plan-to-work neighbors in heavy viewing of television. Just-a-job working women are less likely to be among the heaviest viewers, and career women are least likely to be heavy viewers of television.[13]

Women in Australia were asked whether or not they were watching more television today than a year ago. According to their responses, 19 percent of all women, both working women and housewives, are watching more television than a year ago; 72 percent are not watching more television.

Although significantly more Australian women in every New Demographic segment are watching more television today than a year ago, more stay-at-home housewives (30 percent) have increased their viewing, followed by plan-to-work housewives (24 percent). Very few just-a-job working women (13 percent) and career women (10 percent) watch more television today than in the past.[14]

Stay-at-home housewives are most likely to be constant viewers of nearly every program type studied. They are more likely than any other segment of women to look at early evening news, on both public and commercial stations. The just-a-job working women are second to stay-at-homes in watching commercial early evening news. They are followed by career women. Plan-to-work housewives are least likely to watch the news programs.[15]

Again, stay-at-home housewives are the most consistent viewers of current affairs programs. Plan-to-work housewives are most likely to be occasional viewers of such programs. Just-a-job working women are slightly more likely than career women to watch them, but their viewership is far below that of stay-at-home housewives.[16]

Stay-at-home housewives are also the strongest fans of long-running, evening series programs, followed by just-a-job working women. Plan-to-work housewives rank third and career women rank last in viewing this type of program.[17]

The two segments of housewives are strong fans of the police and detective shows; the two segments of working women are far less likely to watch such programs regularly.[18]

Although both types of housewives are more likely than either segment of working women to watch comedy shows, plan-to-work housewives are the greatest fans of comedy programs, followed by the stay-at-homes. Just-a-job working women rank third and career women fourth.

Stay-at-home housewives are also enthusiastic fans of sports programs. They are far more likely than any other segment of women to watch them regularly. Plan-to-work housewives tend to be occasional viewers.[19]

The stay-at-home housewives are more likely than any other segment of women to watch game shows. They are followed, in order, at a far lower level by plan-to-work housewives, just-a-job working women, and career women.[20]

RADIO

United States

In the United States the radio-listening patterns of the New Demographic segments are almost diametrically opposed to their television-viewing behavior. Stay-at-home housewives are the heaviest viewers of television, but the least likely to be heavy listeners to radio. Radio appears to be a working woman's medium: just-a-job working women, more than any other segment, listen to it frequently. Plan-to-work housewives are more likely than career women to be categorized as heavier listeners.[21]

Canada

We do not know the radio-listening patterns of the four New Demographic groups in Canada, but we do know that working women are slightly more likely than housewives to be the heaviest listeners to the medium. Conversely, housewives are more likely to be the lightest listeners.[22]

Great Britain

The pattern of radio listening is somewhat different in Great Britain. Plan-to-work housewives are more likely than any other segment of women to be fans of radio. They are followed closely by just-a-job working women. Stay-at-home housewives and career women are least likely to be heavy listeners to independent local radio.[23]

West Germany

Working women in West Germany are also slightly more likely than housewives to be strong supporters of the radio medium. Working women are more likely to be found in the heaviest listening category, which is defined as people who listen to radio daily, and less likely to be in the lightest category, people who never listen to radio or listen to it rarely. For the most part, however, the listening profiles of housewives and working women are not too dissimilar.[24]

Brazil

Although the majority of all segments of women in Brazil are heavy radio listeners, their interest in radio is far less intense than their interest in television. Unlike the New Demographic segments in the United States and Australia, stay-at-home housewives in Brazil are most likely to be the strongest fans of radio. Plan-to-work housewives rank second, just-a-job working women rank third, and career women are least likely to be heavy listeners of radio.[25]

Mexico

The pattern among women in Mexico is somewhat different. Again, their level of radio listening is far lower than their level of television viewing. Within those parameters, plan-to-work housewives are most likely to be found in the heavy listening category; they are far more likely than any other segment of women to turn their radios on frequently. They are followed by career women, who are followed fairly closely in heavy listening by stay-at-home housewives. Just-a-job working women are the least likely of any segment of Mexican women to be active radio listeners.[26]

Venezuela

Women in Venezuela resemble women in the other two Latin American countries in being less supportive of radio than they are of television. Nonetheless, the responses of the four New Demographic segments are somewhat different. Just-a-job working women in Venezuela are most likely to listen to radio. They are followed closely by plan-to-work housewives. Career women are the least likely to be fans of radio. Stay-at-home housewives rank above the career women but below the plan-to-work housewives.[27]

Australia

Stay-at-home housewives in Australia are less likely than plan-to-work housewives to be strong fans of radio. The former are behind just-a-job working women in being heavy listeners, but they are less likely than any other segment of women to listen to a moderate degree, and they are most likely to be nonlisteners.

Plan-to-work housewives are the strongest supporters of radio in Australia. They are far more likely than any other segment of women to be heavy listeners. They are also more likely to be moderate listeners. Just-a-job working women are slightly more likely than career women to be heavy listeners, but a high proportion of both segments of working women listen to radio at a moderate level of eleven to thirty hours a week.

The structure of working women's days becomes apparent when we examine the times of day at which they listen to radio. Three out of four just-a-job and career women listen to radio between 5:30 a.m. and 9:30 a.m., while they are getting ready for work or driving to work. Housewives are less likely to listen at that time. Plan-to-work housewives are more likely than their stay-at-home neighbors to turn on their radios during the early morning hours. Conversely, working women are far less likely than housewives to listen during the morning hours between nine o'clock and noon. Plan-to-work housewives are more likely than stay-at-home housewives to turn their sets on at that time as well.

The two groups of housewives are almost identical in the extent to which they listen between noon and four o'clock. Although working women listen less than housewives in the early afternoon, the differences between the two groups are less dramatic at that time. Just-a-job working women are more likely than career women to listen during the afternoon hours, but are not as likely to do so as the housewives.

Working women, particularly career-oriented women, are likely to turn on their radios again while driving home from work, between four o'clock and seven o'clock. At that time, plan-to-work housewives are far more likely than their stay-at-home neighbors to listen to radio.

241

Plan-to-work housewives are similar to the two segments of working women in listening during the evening hours between 7:00 P.M. and midnight; stay-at-home housewives are far less likely to turn on their sets then. Plan-to-work housewives and career women listen to radio to the same degree during the evening. Just-a-job working women listen to the radio during the evening hours slightly more than the other two groups.[28]

There is an unusual agreement between the two extreme segments in their interest in listening to Australian Broadcasting Corporation radio on an average weekday. This is the noncommercial, government-sponsored station, comparable to public broadcasting in the United States. Career women are more likely than any other segment of women to listen to ABC Radio and they are closely followed by stay-at-home housewives. On the other hand, plan-to-work housewives are least likely to listen to this network; just-a-job working women are somewhere in the middle.[29]

The pattern of radio listening offers another contrast to television viewing. Although far more of each segment say they are not watching television more often than a year ago, the opposite is true of radio. Twice as many women in Australia say they are listening to radio more often than last year (62 percent). With minor variations this pattern is fairly consistent across all New Demographic groups. Just-a-job working women are least likely to say they are listening to radio more often than in the past (58 percent). Career women and plan-to-work housewives are also listening to more radio these days (63 percent for both groups). Stay-at-home housewives are also listening more often (61 percent).[30]

Australia also reported on how the four New Demographic segments respond to different types of program formats. It is here that their personal tastes and preferences emerge. There are sharper differences between stay-at-home housewives and their plan-to-work counterparts than between other groups of women. For example, the most popular program format is "middle-of-the-road" radio (light FM). Stay-at-home housewives are least likely to listen to it, whereas just-a-job working women are the heaviest supporters. Plan-to-work housewives tie with career women in their interest in "middle-of-the-road" radio.

Conversely, "beautiful music" and "talk back" shows, which are next in popularity among all women, have special appeal to the stay-at-home housewives and are least attractive to plan-to-work housewives. The two segments of working women are more supportive of "beautiful music" than are the plan-to-work housewives, but are less enamored of it than are the stay-at-homes. Just-a-job working women are more likely than career women to listen to "talk back" radio. Career women and plan-to-work housewives are the least likely to listen to this kind of program.

A dramatic contrast emerged in relation to FM "soft music." Stay-at-home housewives are least likely to listen to this kind of program, whereas plan-to-work housewives are its strongest fans. They are followed by just-a-job working women. Career women are slightly less interested in it, but they are far more so than stay-at-home housewives.

The pattern is repeated for pop music. This is least appealing to stay-at-home housewives and most appealing to those who plan to go to work. The two segments of working women have the same level of interest, which is slightly lower than that of plan-to-work housewives.

Sports programs are the only type of program that has fairly universal response from all four segments of women, with plan-to-work housewives being just one percentage point behind the other three. This is a rare instance of agreement between stay-at-home housewives and the two segments of working women.

Stay-at-home housewives are least likely and career women are most likely to listen to FM "rock music." In this instance, just-a-job working women and plan-to-work housewives are far closer to career women than to stay-at-home housewives, who barely listen to this type of music at all.[31]

The Print Media

MAGAZINES

United States

The response of the New Demographics to magazines in the United States is almost directly opposite to their interest in watching television. Stay-at-homes are by far the lightest readers of magazines. Career women are clearly the heaviest readers among any segment of women. They are least likely to be light readers and most likely to be heavy readers of magazines. Both plan-to-work housewives and just-a-job working women are among the heaviest readers. Nevertheless, more plan-to-work housewives are among the heavier readers, and fewer of them are among the lightest readers, compared to just-a-job working women.[32]

Canada

In Canada in general, working women are more likely than housewives to be strong supporters of magazines. They are most likely to be found in the top two quintiles (heaviest and heavier), whereas housewives are most likely to be found in the lowest quintiles (lighter and lightest readers of magazines).[33]

Great Britain

In Great Britain, heavy magazine readers are defined as women who read at least three out of four issues, medium readers read one or two out of four issues, and light readers read less than one in four issues. Assessments are based on women who read two categories of magazines: general magazines and women's magazines. Career women are most likely to be very heavy readers of general magazines, compared to the other three segments of women. Stay-at-home housewives and just-a-job working women are heavy magazine readers, whereas plan-to-work housewives rank just below these two segments as heavy readers. Among those in each segment who are medium-level readers, the order is just-a-job women, plan-to-work housewives, and stay-at-home housewives.[34]

Although the conventional wisdom is that women's magazines are particularly attractive to housewives, the reality is that career women are not only the heaviest readers of general magazines but also the heaviest readers of women's magazines. Just-a-job working women follow career women in readership of women's magazines. The two types of housewives tie in the extent to which they are heavy readers of women's magazines, but the plan-to-work housewives are more likely than their stay-at-home neighbors to read one or two out of four issues.[35]

West Germany

In Germany there is slightly less difference between working women and housewives in their magazine readership. According to Media-Analyse, housewives are slightly more likely to be the lightest readers and working women are more likely to be heavier and medium readers. The differences between them, however, are slight.[36]

Differences appear when we examine the types of magazines they read. Working women are more likely than housewives to be above the norm in reading women's magazines, fashion magazines, and illustrated magazines. In every case working women are above the norm and housewives are below the norm in reading those publications.[37]

Australia

In some countries career women are clearly the heaviest magazine readers among all segments of women. This pattern is not repeated in Australia. The magazines most frequently read are the general interest ones, and plan-to-work housewives in Australia are most likely to read them. Just-a-job working women rank second, career women rank third, and stay-at-home housewives rank fourth. Nevertheless, between 70 and 80 percent of all four segments of women read general interest magazines.

The real surprise is homemaking magazines. One might have assumed that stay-at-home housewives would be the main audience for homemaking magazines, but they are least likely to read them. Career women are the strongest supporters of homemaking magazines. In descending order, career women are followed by just-a-job working women and plan-to-work housewives. These three segments are far more likely than stay-at-home housewives to read homemaking magazines.

Although business magazines are less likely to be read by women, it is somewhat surprising that career women are no more likely than their plan-to-work neighbors to read business publications. Just-a-job working women are just one percentage point behind these two segments. Stay-at-home housewives are least likely to be interested in reading about business.[38]

Overall, stay-at-home housewives (44 percent) and plan-to-work housewives (45 percent) are more likely to say they have increased their magazine reading than just-a-job working women (36 percent) and career women (38 percent).[39]

Japan

In Japan, 48 percent of active women have bought a magazine during the past month, and the purchases of individual segments conform to their position in the New Demographics spectrum. Stay-at-home housewives are least likely to have bought a magazine and they are substantially below the norm in purchasing magazines. Plan-to-work housewives are also below the norm but are more likely than their stay-at-home neighbors to have bought a magazine in the past month. Just-a-job working women are just above the norm and career women are more likely than any other segment of women to be readers.[40]

Within these parameters, each of the New Demographic segments responds to individual magazines somewhat differently. For example, 30 percent of women in Japan have read the magazine *Friday* (like *People*) in the past month. All but career women are slightly below the norm in reading this. Thirty-seven percent of career women have read *Friday* in the past month, compared to 27 percent of stay-at-home housewives. Twenty-eight percent of plan-to-work housewives and just-a-job working women read it in the past month.[41]

The magazine *More* (like *Vogue*) was read by 21 percent of women in the past six months. As in the case of *Friday*, the magazine draws its greatest readership from career women: 28 percent of career women have read *More* in the past six months. During the same period, stay-at-home housewives are least likely to have read it (16 percent). Plan-to-work housewives are slightly above the norm in reading it (22 percent), and just-a-job working women are slightly below the norm (20 percent).[42]

Nineteen percent of Japanese women have read the publication *Croissant* (like *The Ladies' Home Journal*) in the past two months. The audience for this magazine is somewhat different from the others. Stay-at-home housewives are slightly more likely than any other segment of women to read it (21 percent). Career women are above the norm (20 percent), and just-a-job working women and plan-to-work housewives are below the norm (17 percent and 18 percent, respectively) in reading *Croissant*.[43]

Focus (like *People*) has a much smaller audience. Only 6 percent of Japanese women have read *Focus* in the past month. There is also a greater contrast between the readership of career women and the other three New Demographic segments. Although the overall level of readership is low, 50 percent more career women than the average read this magazine in the past month. Nine percent of career women read *Focus*. On the other hand, 4 percent of plan-to-work housewives, 5 percent of stay-at-home housewives, and 5 percent of just-a-job working women read *Focus*.[44]

We also have information from Japan on the purchase of novels, which offers another pattern of readership. Twenty-two percent of active Japanese women bought a novel in the past month. Both segments of housewives are below the norm in this. Plan-to-work housewives are least likely to have purchased a book in the past month. Just-a-job working women conform to the norm, but career women are 50 percent above the norm.[45]

NEWSPAPERS

United States

In the United States women respond to newspapers according to their position in the New Demographic spectrum. Housewives are the least likely to be the heaviest readers of newspapers, but stay-at-home housewives are more likely than their plan-to-work neighbors to be heavier readers of newspapers. Just-a-job working women are below the norm of the heaviest readers, but they are more likely to be in that group than either of the housewife segments. They are also less likely than the housewives to be very light readers of newspapers. Career women are the heaviest newspaper readers.[46]

Canada

Three out of four Canadian women read a daily newspaper sometime in the past seven days. Career women are most likely to have done so, followed by just-a-job working women. The two housewife groups are somewhat behind the two working women segments in reading daily newspapers. Plan-to-work housewives are just one percentage point above stay-at-homes in this activity.[47]

Whether we consider the number of papers read, the number of hours in the day spent reading them, and the number of days in the week in which they read papers, Canadian career women are most likely to read newspapers. Just-a-job women are second to career women in newspaper readership. Stay-at-home housewives are more likely than plan-to-work housewives to read newspapers. The only exception to this pattern is the average number of hours spent reading newspapers on the weekend. Career women still dominate this picture, but stay-at-home housewives are slightly more likely than just-a-job working women to spend time reading newspapers over the weekend.[48]

Great Britain

Women in Great Britain have a different pattern of newspaper reading. The Target Group Index defines heavy readers of newspapers as people who have read at least three out of four issues, medium readers as those who have read one or two out of the last four issues, and light readers as those who have read less than one in four issues. Working women are more likely than housewives to be heavy readers of newspapers, and just-a-job working women are the heaviest newspaper readers. More of them are heavy readers and fewer of them are light readers. Career women rank second as heavy readers. Stay-at-home housewives are more likely than their plan-to-work neighbors to read newspapers.[49]

West Germany

Housewives in West Germany are more likely than working women to be the heaviest readers of newspapers, that is, people who read a newspaper every day. Conversely, there are more working women than housewives among those who read newspapers several times a week. Regardless of their occupations, however, German women are very responsive to newspapers: 74 percent of housewives and 67 percent of working women read newspapers daily. Not surprisingly, working women are more likely than housewives to read financial papers. In fact, working women are 25 percent above the norm of readership of financial papers, and housewives are substantially below the norm.[50]

Latin America

In the three Latin American countries career women are consistently the heaviest readers of newspapers, even though the absolute levels of readership vary markedly from country to country.

Newspaper reading is a very strong habit in Venezuela. Three out of five of the housewives and the just-a-job working women are heavy readers of newspapers, and 77 percent of career women are heavy readers. Only a minority of any of the segments of women are light newspaper readers.[51]

In Mexico approximately one in four housewives and just-a-job working women are heavy readers of newspapers; they are more likely to be medium readers. On the other hand, almost half of career women are heavy readers and they are far less likely than the other segments to be light readers.[52]

Housewives and just-a-job working women in Brazil are most likely to be light newspaper readers. Plan-to-work housewives and just-a-job working women are slightly more likely than the stay-at-home housewives to be heavy readers. Although the level of career women's readership is not nearly as high as it was in the other two Latin American countries, it is substantially higher than that of any other segment of Brazilian women. Career women are almost equally divided among heavy readers, medium readers, and light readers.[53]

Australia

Four out of five Australian women (82 percent) read a morning newspaper, but, again, their levels of reading follow the pattern of the New Demographic segments. Stay-at-home housewives are less likely than any other group of women to read morning newspapers (70 percent); plan-to-work housewives are far more likely to read newspapers in the morning (85 percent). The two segments of working women are almost universally likely to read the morning papers: 93 percent of just-a-job working women and 96 percent of career women are morning newspaper readers.

Afternoon papers tend to be less accessible to women at home. It is simply easier for working women to buy a newspaper on their return from work. Although readership of afternoon papers is lower than that for morning papers, there is less difference in the reading levels of housewives and working women. Two out of three Australian women read an afternoon newspaper (66 percent). Stay-at-home housewives are least likely to read one (63 percent), whereas just-a-job working women are most likely to do so (72 percent). Readership of Sunday and weekly papers is similar to that of afternoon papers. Overall, stay-at-home housewives are least likely to read newspapers and plan-to-work housewives resemble women who are already in the work force in their reading habits.[54]

Comparison of the Four Media

In Latin America, respondents were asked directly to evaluate various media: television, radio, newspapers, and magazines. The respondents were asked which of the media are most informative, most credible, and most entertaining, and which presents the best advertising.

Regardless of the specific dimension that was being measured, television was the dominant medium in the three countries. It was voted the most informative, the most credible, and the most entertaining, and the medium that presents the best advertising by large majorities of consumers.[55]

Innovative

Nevertheless, there are variations from country to country. For example, 86 percent of Venezuelan women and 83 percent of Brazilian women consider television the most innovative of the four media; only 66 percent of Mexican women term it the most innovative. Women in Mexico are slightly more likely than women in the other two countries to say that radio and newspapers are somewhat innovative. Their support for these two media is far below their support for television as an innovative medium, however. Nonetheless, 14 percent consider radio and 9 percent consider newspapers as the most innovative. By contrast, only 3 percent of women in Brazil and 5 percent in Venezuela consider radio the most innovative. Just 1 percent of Brazilian women and 4 percent of Venezuelan women consider newspapers as the most innovative.[56]

Entertaining

There is stronger agreement on the entertainment value of television. Eighty-five percent of women in Venezuela find television the most entertaining medium; 75 percent of Brazilian women and 74 percent of Mexican women say it is the most entertaining. Women in those two countries are somewhat more likely than Venezuelan women to find radio entertaining, and Mexican women are more likely than the others to say that newspapers are entertaining.[57]

Similarly, when asked which of the four media is the best way to pass the time, television is most strongly endorsed by women in Venezuela (84 percent). Seventy-six percent of Mexican women and 71 percent of Brazilian women say that television is the best way to pass the time. Although all other media receive minority votes, women in Mexico and Brazil are slightly more likely than Venezuelan women to say that radio is a good way to pass the time.[58]

Informative

Women in the three countries also strongly endorse television as the medium that is most informative in telling them about what is happening in their countries and in the world. Seventy percent of women in Mexico, 69 percent in Venezuela, and 66 percent in Brazil consider television the best source of information.[59]

There are slight differences in the support given to other media. Women in Venezuela are more likely to choose newspapers (21 percent) over radio (9 percent) as a good source of information. Women in Brazil rate them equally (17 percent). Mexican women are slightly more likely to endorse newspapers (15 percent) than radio (12 percent).

Convincing

Television is also perceived as the most convincing medium and the one that consumers find most credible. In each case, women in Venezuela are slightly more positive about the credibility of television than their counterparts in Mexico and Brazil: 71 percent of Venezuelan women say that television is most convincing. They are less likely than women in the other two countries to find radio a convincing medium (8 percent), and slightly more likely to find newspapers convincing (16 percent).[61]

Credible

Sixty-three percent of Mexican women and 62 percent of women in Brazil find television the most credible medium. Radio is a distant second choice: 15 percent in Mexico and 16 percent in Brazil. Similarly, 67 percent of women in Venezuela find television the most credible medium; newspapers are a distant second choice (18 percent).[62]

Interesting Personalities

Women were also asked which of the media presents the most interesting presenters or personalities; television was the overwhelming favorite. Eighty-six percent of women in Venezuela choose television and only 4 percent choose radio. In Mexico, 79 percent choose television, 10 percent choose radio, and 6 percent choose newspapers and magazines. Television also dominated in Brazil: 72 percent choose it, 8 percent choose radio, and 8 percent choose newspapers.[63]

Best Advertising

Finally, women in all three countries think the best advertising is found on television. Women in Venezuela and Brazil are almost in agreement on this (88 percent and 87 percent, respectively). Seventy-five percent of Mexican women think the best advertising is on television. Twelve percent of Mexican women, more than in the other two countries, think the best advertising is on radio. Women in Mexico (7 percent) are also more likely than women in Venezuela or Brazil to say that newspapers have the best advertising.[64]

Response of the New Demographics

Although television is the dominant medium among the four New Demo-graphic groups in all three countries, there are some minor variations in their responses. For example, stay-at-home housewives in Brazil are consistently the most enthusiastic about television in answer to any question about the four media. Career women are consistently less likely to vote for television even though it is still their main choice.[65]

Another instance of their diversity is that 78 percent of stay-at-home house-wives in Brazil say television is the best way to spend leisure time, but only 53 percent of career women agree with this. Even though television is their main choice, more career women than women in the other groups find radio, maga-zines, and newspapers rewarding for their leisure time.[66]

Similarly, 69 percent of stay-at-home housewives in Brazil find television the most credible medium and only 56 percent of career women agree. They are slightly more likely than the other groups to say that newspapers inspire their trust; plan-to-work housewives and career women are slightly more likely to mention radio as a credible medium.[67]

There are similar differences among women in Venezuela. Again, even though television dominates their responses, career women are slightly less likely than the others to find it the most convincing medium. They are more likely than the other three segments to say that newspapers are convincing and inspire their confidence.[68]

The picture is similar in Mexico. Working women are less likely than housewives to find television the most credible medium. Career women are far less likely than the others to say that television inspires their confidence even though it is their overriding first choice. In each case they are more likely than the other segments to consider newspapers convincing or credible.[69]

There are real differences in how the four New Demographic segments of women use and respond to media. Although television is the dominant medium in every country studied, it is particularly appealing to housewives and slightly less appealing to working women. There is almost a direct relationship between a woman's place in the New Demographic spectrum and her involvement with television, the greatest involvement being found among stay-at-home house-wives and the least involvement being found among career women.

Radio tends to be more of a working woman's medium. Patterns of radio listening vary from country to country. The divergence between plan-to-work housewives and stay-at-home housewives becomes very clear in the way they respond to radio. Plan-to-work housewives in every country are very responsive to radio, whereas stay-at-home housewives tend to be far less involved with it. In most countries, just-a-job working women are more interested in radio than their career counterparts.

The educational level and range of interests of career women are reflected in their commitment to magazines. In every country studied, career women are the heaviest readers of magazines and tend to be responsive to many types of magazines. Again, for the most part, their interest is a direct reflection of their place in the New Demographic spectrum, with career women being most likely to read magazines and stay-at-home housewives least likely to do so.

Similarly, career women tend to be most responsive to newspapers. With very few exceptions, the newspaper reading patterns of the New Demographic segments reflect their place in the spectrum, with stay-at-home housewives least likely to read newspapers and career women most likely to do so. There is a minor variation in this pattern in Great Britain, where just-a-job working women are more likely than career women to read newspapers and stay-at-home housewives are slightly more likely than plan-to-work housewives to be newspaper readers.

There are country-by-country variations in the relative dominance of the four media. Although television dominates in all countries, it is particularly important in Latin America. The levels of newspaper reading are somewhat lower in Latin American countries, but are very high in Australia and West Germany, where the literacy rate is also very high.

twenty

Women and Advertising

THE diversity of the women's marketplace around the world and the changes in women's aspirations, life styles, and consumer behavior have clear implications for the way we talk to them in advertising. In one sense, this entire book deals with the subject of women and advertising. Many of the changes that have taken place in women's lives challenge some of the traditional assumptions about the target groups for advertising campaigns. Advertising is the final manifestation of the marketing process, in which decisions are made about the consumers to whom the campaign is addressed, the strategy for reaching them, and the tone of the advertising communication.

If advertisers understand the dynamics of the women's market in each of the countries studied and if they seek to understand the self-perceptions and attitudes of the various segments of women within those markets, at the very least they will reexamine the ways in which they define their target groups and thereby challenge the traditional assumptions about how women feel and what women want.

The specific subject of advertising was not pursued in every one of the countries studied. In some countries researchers examined the economic role of advertising, in others they explored women's feelings about advertising, and in still others they investigated aspects of advertising that please women or alienate them. In Italy, for example, women discussed their feelings about advertising overall, and the degree to which they believe it does or does not influence their purchase behavior. In Japan women discussed the role advertising plays in their lives and their feelings about it, but they didn't comment on specific advertising executions or imagery. In the three Latin American countries, researchers obtained quantified responses to a number of aspects of television advertising, both positive and negative. They did not deal with details or tonalities of execution.

In Great Britain women discussed the specific advertisements and commercials they liked and disliked. They explained which elements were positive or negative. They were also shown a reel of commercials and invited to comment on the ways in which women were portrayed in them. This focused the discussion on specific advertising tonality and casting.

In Australia and Canada researchers did not explore women's attitudes toward advertising per se, but some of the general findings suggest that women in both countries have a healthy skepticism about business in general, which could be challenging to the advertiser who wants to defend the reputations of advertised brands.

In Canada, for example, 71 percent of women believe that "most big companies are out for themselves." Only 10 percent disagree. This attitude is fairly consistent among all four New Demographic segments, but both groups of housewives are slightly more negative toward big companies than working women.[1]

Women's Responses to Advertising

Italy

Women in Italy are quite negative toward advertising, overall. They have two main complaints about it: first, advertising is too invasive, too repetitive, and too "pounding." Italian women find the intrusiveness of advertising very disturbing, particularly in television advertising. Second, advertising "takes up too much room," particularly in print. They acknowledge, however, that advertising gives them information about products. They find this is particularly relevant for advertising campaigns which tell them about new products which are on the market and the benefits that those products might bring.[2]

In Italy, the four groups of women differed from each other in their perceptions of the extent to which advertising does or does not influence their own personal behavior in the marketplace. Stay-at-home housewives are generally critical of advertising, and particularly irritated by the "invasiveness" of advertising. They tend to defend themselves by setting up "an attitude of counter dependence." Apparently, they feel they can resist the sales messages aimed at them.[3]

Plan-to-work housewives "feel much more conditioned by advertising in their purchase behavior and at times they manifest an attitude of fear because they experience advertising as a hidden persuader from which it is difficult to defend one's self." Plan-to-work housewives also complain about the intrusiveness and repetitiveness of advertising, but they are particularly concerned about advertising as an attempt to manipulate them and their children. They believe "it has a negative influence on their children, both because it looks for consumer behavior in them as well as influencing their attitudes and their language." In addition, "it presents situations that are unrealistic and hardly credible."[4]

Just-a-job working women in Italy agree with the others about the irritation and intrusiveness of advertising, but they are more positive about the content of the advertising they see and the information it imparts about the products advertised. They are also responsive to the entertainment value of advertising. They think that "original or fun television advertising is pleasing," and they enjoy watching it. Unlike plan-to-work housewives, just-a-job working women feel that advertising has only a limited impact on their purchase behavior. They feel they can "defend themselves" from the influence or conditioning advertising tries to impose on them.[5]

The Italian career women expressed a "wide range of attitudes toward advertising ranging from total refusal to a critical interest." Their feelings vary according to the medium. They criticize television advertising as most irritating because it interrupts the programs they are watching, and they find the intrusiveness of television commercials unpleasant, and "pounding." Their comments on press advertising suggest that they are not particularly aware of it or respond to some of it with aesthetic interest. They are aware of outdoor or billboard advertising, which attracts their curiosity and "a critical or aesthetic interest." Career women appreciate the informative function of advertising, but complain that much of the advertising they see has little information content.[6]

They also note "the spectacular character of advertising," and are aware of the emotional character of the images projected by advertising. Advertising imagery arouses their curiosity and interest, but to a certain degree they find such imagery perplexing. Career women take a sophisticated view of the advertising medium. They recognize that it is an efficient means of communication, and some even try to analyze the elements that make the messages work. They try to reason backward, from the ad to the concepts the advertisers are trying to communicate to the public.[7]

In general, Italian career women say they have noticed changes in advertising communications in the past few years. The messages have become more refined and tend to create an effect or an image that surrounds the product rather than specifically detailing the qualities of the brand advertised. They respect advertisers as able people, and believe that advertisers are aware of cultural fashions and use this knowledge to offer products as various solutions to current problems.[8]

Japan

Women in Japan focus their attention on the function of advertising as a source of consumer information about how products work or the specific benefits of advertising. Much of their concern centers on whether or not they are influenced to buy products because of advertising.

For the most part, Japanese women are quite tolerant and accepting of advertising. Their only major criticism is that there is simply too much of it. A career woman said, "I like advertising but when there's *too much* of it, it gets tiring."

On the one hand, some Japanese women insist they are not influenced by advertising. One stay-at-home housewife said, "I don't go out looking for products just because I've seen them advertised. Ads are just ads as far as I'm concerned." Career women echo this view. On the other hand, a just-a-job working woman who said that advertising was of only limited influence in her case went on to explain how specific advertisements had described a particular product improvement or benefit that she had clearly internalized as a result of seeing the ad: "The only kind of product where ads influence purchase in my case is candy and snack foods (because the children want them). For other products it's not the advertising that makes me want them so much. When I see ads, the things I think of are 'oh, that product has gotten a lot more convenient' or 'it costs less than when I bought it.'"[10]

Many Japanese women appreciate advertising as a source of information about products. A plan-to-work housewife said, "When I am looking at a particular article that I want to buy, I look at ads." A stay-at-home housewife also said, "When I haven't decided what brand I want to buy, I refer to ads for information." The same statement is voiced by women in all four New Demographic segments. A stay-at-home housewife confirmed the wisdom of the time-honored advertising strategy of creating consumer involvement with the product by offering a recipe or a service suggestion: "When I see a print ad on making sushi, for example, I read every word of it although I never remember who it was that was sponsoring the ad."[11]

Japanese stay-at-home housewives are particularly responsive to advertising that gives them detailed explanations about products rather than simply mood or image. For that reason they prefer print advertisements to those that appeal simply to the eye or the ear: "I don't pay so much attention to commercials on radio or TV. A well-written print ad though means to me that the company

sponsoring it is reliable." This was a common view among stay-at-home housewives.[12]

The perception of advertising as fostering consumer trust in the advertised
brand cuts across the New Demographic spectrum. A stay-at-home housewife
said she would select an advertised product over an unknown brand: "You
remember seeing the ad. If you go to the supermarket and see two identical
products side-by-side on the shelf at the same price . . . one a well-advertised
brand and the other a brand you never heard of . . . you feel like buying the
one you saw advertised." A career woman said, "You tend to develop a feeling
of trust toward products that are well known because they are often advertised."[13]

Working women in particular find advertising enjoyable and entertaining.
These women are less likely to discuss the information aspects of advertising.
A just-a-job working woman even said, "I videotape television commercials that
I like." A career woman described the pleasure she takes in advertising: "Ads
are very interesting now. TV commercials are more interesting than the pro-
grams."[14]

Latin America

Consumers in Mexico and Venezuela are intensely critical of the sheer amount
of advertising and clutter on television. Eighty-four percent of women in Venezuela think there is too much advertising on television, and only 5 percent
disagree. Similarly, 79 percent of women in Mexico complain about the amount
of television advertising, and only 7 percent feel it is not a problem. This
strongly critical feeling about advertising is found in all four New Demographic
groups in both countries. In both countries, however, career women are more
critical than any other segment of women.[15]

It is common to say that many people complain about advertising on television, but few do something about it. In Venezuela, however, 50 percent of
the women say there is so much advertising on television "that it makes me
change the channel." On the other hand, 18 percent of women are not motivated to change the programs they are watching. Although women in Mexico
also complain about the amount of advertising, they are less likely to take action. Thirty-nine percent of them are motivated to change channels, but 35
percent are not. Career women are more likely than any other segment of
women to take this kind of action, both in Mexico and in Venezuela.[16]

By contrast women in Latin America see the entertainment value of advertising as one of its more positive aspects, although even here their comments
are far blander than the intense criticism about the quantity of advertising on
television. For example, 48 percent of women in Venezuela say that television

commercials are original, but 18 percent disagree. Similarly, 41 percent of women in Mexico believe that television advertising is original, but 28 percent disagree.[17]

Again, more women in Mexico and Venezuela say that advertising is amusing, but fairly substantial groups in each country do not find television commercials amusing. In Venezuela 35 percent find commercials amusing, and 28 percent do not; in Mexico, the figures are 38 percent and 31 percent, respectively.[18]

There was some difference between women in the two countries on whether television advertising is pleasant to watch. In Venezuela 34 percent of women think television commercials are pleasant to watch, and 21 percent disagree. On the other hand, in Mexico actually only 30 percent think that advertising is pleasant to watch, and 31 percent disagree. Similarly, in Venezuela 30 percent think television advertising shows a sense of humor, and 26 percent think it does not. In Mexico, 29 percent think advertising has a sense of humor, but 35 percent think it does not.[19]

In Venezuela 43 percent of women believe that television advertising attracts people's attention and 42 percent believe it does not. Women in Mexico are more likely to say that television advertising attracts attention (45 percent) than disagree (25 percent). In Venezuela 36 percent of women always pay attention to advertising, but 26 percent don't. In Mexico only 21 percent always pay attention to advertising, and 47 percent do not.[20]

Substantial numbers in both countries say that advertising makes people buy things they don't really need. In Venezuela 43 percent of women agree that advertising manipulates consumers to buy unnecessary products, and 42 percent disagree. Women in Mexico are particularly concerned about this aspect of advertising. Fifty-two percent say that advertising makes people buy things they don't need, 28 percent don't think this is the case.[21]

Stay-at-home housewives and just-a-job working women in Venezuela are slightly more positive than negative about the potential of advertising to persuade people to buy products they don't need. Plan-to-work housewives are absolutely neutral on the subject; the same number agree as disagree with this point of view. Career women, however, are particularly critical of the manipulative potential of advertising. All groups of women in Mexico are critical of this aspect of advertising. Stay-at-home housewives are slightly less critical than the others. Nonetheless, the predominant opinion among all segments is that advertising does, in fact, manipulate consumers.[22]

A more positive aspect of the role of advertising is its consumer benefits: the function of advertising to inform consumers about the products available to buy and the ways those products will work. This elicited quite a favorable response among women in Venezuela. Forty-nine percent appreciate the consumer benefit aspect of advertising, compared to 22 percent who disagree that product information is useful to them. In Mexico 39 percent of women agree that there are consumer benefits from advertising, but 33 percent do not.[23]

Although all segments of women in Venezuela are positive about the consumer benefits of advertising, their enthusiasm varies according to the New Demographic spectrum. Stay-at-home housewives are most likely to appreciate this aspect of advertising, whereas career women are least likely to do so.[24]

By contrast, the two housewife groups in Mexico are more positive than negative about the consumer benefits of advertising, and the two groups of working women are more negative than positive. The strongest opinions are held by stay-at-home housewives and career women. Forty-two percent of stay-at-home housewives feel that advertising provides benefits to the consumer; 28 percent disagree. On the other hand, 44 percent of career women believe that advertising does not provide benefits to the consumer; 27 percent appreciate the consumer benefit aspect of advertising.[25]

Great Britain

The responses of women in Great Britain to various advertisements cut across the New Demographic typology. Researchers commented, "We were surprised at the extent to which responses were similar across all four groups of women. Even without exposure, the same commercials were mentioned as popular and realistic, while those that cause irritation or resentment tended to be the same in all groups." A campaign that receives the most spontaneous positive mention is one for a food product that features a mother in a series of situations with members of her family. A stay-at-home housewife said, "The family's typical, they come in all over the place, she's got smart answers and puts them down in a natural way." The comments from women in other groups are similar.[26]

Their spontaneous criticism of advertising focuses on advertisements for cleaning products and toilet soap. According to British researchers, "women object to advertising which appears to exaggerate the importance of household chores or suggests that housewives are only (or especially) concerned with getting things cleaner, whiter, softer, or fresher, for example. Such aspects may be relevant to a housewife, but not significant enough to feature as a topic of conversation between friends." This sort of advertising is particularly irritating to stay-at-home housewives, who are probably the target consumers for these campaigns. A stay-at-home housewife speculated, "It makes me wonder if these ads are made by men. It's what they think women say to each other."

Clearly, women "dislike advertising which makes them feel that the advertiser considers women to be unintelligent, inefficient, and unable to make decisions for themselves." They particularly resent commercials in which the advertiser preaches to them or one housewife tries to explain the product to another.[27]

Women in Great Britain also dislike ads that make exaggerated claims, either by direct comparison between the advertiser's brand and another brand or by the implication that using the advertised brand may change the user's life. This criticism is voiced equally by stay-at-home housewives and career women.[28]

They particularly resent ads which condescend to women. A plan-to-work housewife criticized one commercial as "irritating, repetitive . . . we're not damned imbeciles that we need the woman to keep on about it."

They are also annoyed by ads that show an idealized and unrealistic picture of women. Soap commercials elicit criticisms from housewives and working women alike for their glamorized version of the wife and mother. A plan-to-work housewife said, "She doesn't look like a housewife, she's too pretty. She wouldn't get her hands dirty. She'd never lose her temper. She's so dressed up." A career woman was equally critical: "The woman's not like a mum. She's a model, overglamorous. People aren't like that." Some were upset by ads that "exploit women" by using them as sex symbols to attract attention. One of the young working women who is a daily commuter from the suburbs to central London voiced a strong objection to large posters showing scantily clad women: "The TV ads don't annoy me. The tube or rail ads do where they're selling tights or stockings or underwear and you just see guys there ogling this huge poster. They always show someone sexy and beautiful. There are still some in Victoria Station and they guys just stand and watch. There are women getting raped everywhere, and it's not surprising. I feel it puts things into guys' minds." Other young women agree with her.[29]

Like women in other countries, British women respond in a positive manner to advertisements based on realism and intelligence. A 1960s commercial called "Men Make Better Cooks" showed a husband cooking a meal for his wife. Apparently, he left the kitchen in a mess with the implication that his wife would clean it up. This commercial "stands the test of time well. Some women say that their husbands leave the kitchen just like that when they cook. On the other hand, a few women consider that the commercial does not reflect today's role sharing practices adequately. A [husband] of the 1980s would cook more often and perhaps do the washing up as well."[30]

Another 1960s commercial for a detergent showed a mother interacting with her children. "It strikes the right note with some mothers . . . the 'mum' is real and her caring attitude to her children is noted and appreciated. However, even here there is some suggestion that she is too traditional . . . to typify the housewife today." Again, women's responses to this ad cut across their position in the New Demographic spectrum. A more recent commercial for the same product is applauded for the "apposite way it portrays the mother, son, and life today."[31]

A cosmetic commercial that depicts a romantic misunderstanding between a young girl and her beau evokes personal identification from women, even though the situation is not relevant to their current lives. A stay-at-home housewife said, "It's the sort of thing I'd have done twenty years ago. It's nice." In contrast, a deodorant commercial showing an airline hostess getting ready for her day and in a work setting elicits mixed responses. Even though British housewives express a certain resentment of career women, they are able to relate to the commercial quite positively. A plan-to-work housewife said, "She's got a job, a career, no constraints. It doesn't irritate me, she's not too perfect." But because the commercial uses a shower scene to demonstrate the use of the product, it also elicits criticism for using the woman as a sex object. This attitude also cuts across the New Demographic segments. A just-a-job working woman said, "It uses a body to sell it. It's the sex part to sell the soap, and it makes you feel inferior." Another commercial in the same campaign begins with a similar shower scene and elicits the same reaction. A stay-at-home housewife said, "Pure sex again. They're selling that soap to a man, not a woman. It's titillating men. It's a gimmick to sell the soap." A career woman agreed, "It belittles women, using their bodies."[32]

Consumer Attitudes to Advertising

In the 1970s the American Association of Advertising Agencies conducted a study on consumer attitudes toward advertising. The results of this study revealed that three aspects of advertising are crucial to consumers' opinions of the industry. "If consumers think that the advertising they see provides consumer benefits that help them to choose the products they buy, that it is pleasant or entertaining to look at, and not boring or offensive, and that it is credible, their overall perception of advertising will be positive."[33] The same issues—consumer benefits, credibility, and enjoyment—also dominate the responses of the women in the countries discussed here. Women who felt that advertising tells them things they need to know about products in order to make a brand choice are positive in their responses. Women who find advertising pleasant, amusing, and enjoyable to watch, also express positive attitudes toward advertising.

On the other hand, when women in these countries feel that advertising manipulates consumers and persuades them to buy things they don't need or fails to tell them what they want to know about products, they have a negative view about advertising and tend to distrust the advertiser. The most intense criticism of advertising is the sheer amount of it and its resulting intrusiveness, particularly on television.

Advertising Imagery

Women in Great Britain are the only ones who considered the imagery of specific advertisements. The themes in their discussions are similar to those in a study of how American women respond to advertising that was conducted in the late 1970s, even though the specific stimuli used in the U.S. study were different and a number of years have elapsed since the study was conducted.

The advertisements that elicited the most positive responses from American women evoked emotional involvement or personal identification with the contemporary roles of women. Women also responded positively to advertising that showed husbands participating in the care of children and in household chores. They identified with advertising that showed the multiple roles of today's women, and they responded positively to contemporary imagery of women, particularly those that showed women playing many different roles in our society. They appreciated ads that reflected diversity, of both life style and motivations.[34] They liked advertising that showed respect for women's intelligence and judgment as consumers. They appreciated commercials that treated women with respect, whether they were in a purchase situation or not.[35]

American women were ambivalent about any commercial that dealt with sex. The same execution could elicit two totally conflicting responses: "It's more teasing than sexy and I find that appealing," or "It is suggestive and I find that commercial offensive." They were also embarrassed by sexy treatments because they normally watch television in their living rooms with their husbands, families, and visitors.[36]

They were particularly critical of advertising that went beyond being mildly sexy or romantic and actually showed women as sex objects. They disliked an execution when it not only showed the sensuality or sexiness of the woman, but also implied that she was preening herself in order to get a man. One particular commercial went beyond the generalized sex object approach to the ultimate implication of showing a man reacting overtly to the attractions of a fashion model who is wearing the advertised bra. The women felt this portrayal was indeed degrading to women.[37]

They were also critical of advertising that implied that women can't cope or make a purchase decision without a man. They rejected strongly the traditional image of the helpless little woman turning to a man for advice. Particularly

262

interesting was the fact that all women, especially housewives, took as a personal insult any advertising that implied that family laundry or housework was the woman's responsibility.[38] By extension, they perceived any implication that her performance of chores is less than perfect as condescension. Any execution that treats both men and women as incompetent, childish, or dimwitted was rejected.[39]

The notion of advertising personal products on television was a particularly sensitive one to many women. Since television is a public medium, they resent a personal product being shown on the screen. Another aspect of the resentment against the invasion of privacy is the sense that advertisers focus on the intimate aspects of women's lives but not those of men.[40]

Sexist tonality was the most negative issue of all. Some advertising was perceived as sexist because of semantics. Other commercials were considered sexist because of the attitude toward women implied in the strategy. For example, the unfortunate use of the word *girl* instead of *woman* triggered strong reactions. Again, women objected to the assumptions behind the story in a ten-year-old tire commercial. Women felt that the problem presented in the ad applied to both sexes, not just women. One viewer explained, "Instead of saying 'no man around,' I'd sooner have it say 'when there's no help around.' Some men couldn't help even if they were there."[41]

Implications for Public Policy

The way women are shown in advertising is of concern not only to consumers and the advertisers who wish to reach them but also to public policy makers. In 1974, the United Nations Commission on the Status of Women conducted a study in twenty-eight countries on how women are shown in the media and in advertising. They said,

> Women are shown primarily as housewives in commercials, although they comprise from thirty-five to fifty-five percent of the labor force of the different countries in the world. . . . Women are offered basically two roles, that of the beautiful but passive glamour girl and that of the housewife caring for the home and children. Both are shown as dependent on men and receiving their social identity not in themselves but through men. . . . Women seem to be obsessed with cleanliness . . . placing above normal emphasis on whiteness, brightness, and expressing a gamut of emotions at smelling the kitchen floor or the family wash.[42]

A few years later the National Advertising Review Board appointed a consultative panel representing diverse points of view to examine the situation and define a policy for the American advertising industry.[43] To a great extent their conclusions paralleled those of the United Nations report. They, too, found that women for the most part are shown as either housewives or glamor girls. Women are shown in stereotyped ways, either as being overly obsessed with cleanliness or not competent to cope with minor, everyday chores without the condescending explanations of a male announcer. Housewives are depicted as having a "warped sense of values," either mean and catty or boastful and envious. Alternatively, they are shown as sex objects. The report commented that this is "especially cheapening when the product is totally unrelated to the female body." It further said that there is almost no reflection of woman's role in life outside the kitchen or the bedroom, in the world of work or in community affairs.

The panel offered guidelines for the industry in the form of a checklist of questions for advertisers and agencies to consider as they develop their advertising executions. The checklist includes a number of negative portrayals of women for advertisers to avoid and positive portrayals for them to consider. Many of the points on the list seem self-evident. In the dozen or so years since it was first issued, much has changed in the advertising business including the way that women are shown in advertising. Nonetheless, I think the checklist is a sensible one and I commend it to anyone engaged in the business of communicating to women.[44]

Clearly, this is not solely an American issue. After all, the first major document on how women are portrayed in advertising was issued by an international body, the United Nations. The same concern about how women are portrayed in advertising has surfaced in other parts of the world. In Canada, a continuing dialogue among consumer activists, the government, and the advertising industry evolved into a self-regulatory group called the Advertising Advisory Board's Advisory Committee on Sex Role Stereotyping. This was established in 1980 and it goes beyond such attempts in other parts of the world. The group issued a set of guidelines and has taken an active role in communicating the need for challenging traditional assumptions about women. Among other activities taken was the creation of a film designed to educate the advertising industry on changes in women's lives and the challenge to reflect those changes in advertising. The film, called "Women Say the Darndest Things," has been an important element in sensitizing members of the advertising community to the problem.

The self-regulatory group in Great Britain is called the Advertising Standards Authority. It is an independent body: its chairman and two-thirds of its council members have no connection with the advertising industry. In 1982, they sponsored a major research study of how consumers perceive the treatment of women in advertising. Entitled "Herself Appraised," the study suggests that only a minority of women in Britain find advertisements offensive and most of their responses are bland or neutral. Nonetheless, that the study was undertaken suggests that there has been come concern about the way women are shown in advertising. The research presented here supports this. The women quoted here indicate a much greater intensity of feeling about the way women are shown in advertising.

The context is somewhat different in Australia. The Advertising Standards Council was formed in 1973 by a number of Australian advertising and media organizations. Its main function is to serve as the senior body in the advertising self-regulatory system to provide direct public access for complaints about offensive advertisements. Several consumer activist groups have attempted to have sexist advertising included in the self-regulatory process. To date this has not happened, but a set of guidelines entitled "Fair Exposure: Guidelines for the Constructive and Positive Portrayal and Presentation of Women in the Media" was issued by the Office of the Status of Women, Department of the Prime Minister and Cabinet. The dialogue on this issue continues in Australia.[45]

This is far from a comprehensive review of the extent to which people are challenging the stereotyping of women around the world. The concern is first voiced by consumer activists, and if an industry self-regulatory process is not in place, a group is formed either to study or to develop guidelines for the industry. It is only in Canada that the government has taken a more active role, and perhaps for this reason the process is somewhat further advanced in that country.

Missing from all of this discussion is the simple fact that advertising and marketing are most effective when they are relevant to their target audience. Certainly, the attitudes of women around the world expressed here are clear indication that women want to be treated with respect, resent condescension, and don't necessarily want to be defined only in terms of their family roles. It is a basic principle of marketing and communications that the best way to sell to customers is to talk to them in their own terms. It is simply bad marketing and bad advertising practice to alienate or insult consumers. Therefore, although consumer activists may, in fact, represent a minority and not the mass of women in their countries, the issues they have identified are extremely relevant to most women.

Stereotyping is not limited to advertising. Indeed, many consumer activists have strong stereotypes about advertising and its practitioners. And many advertising practitioners have had a knee-jerk reaction to activist criticism, claiming that these groups do not speak for the "real consumer." The reality is that the best-educated and most sophisticated consumers, the career women, are particularly skeptical about business in general and advertising in particular.

Yet, these are the very women who represent the most desirable prospects for many products and services. I suggest that it is simply good business practice and good advertising practice to keep in touch with the wants and needs and perceptions of our target consumers. If advertisers build the New Demographic and life-cycle perspective into their marketing procedures, they will not develop advertising that is insulting or alienating to the consumers they want to reach.

The solution is less an ideological one than a professional one. To quote the NARB report, "fairness to women may turn out to be an intelligent marketing decision." In fact, it might be the most intelligent marketing decision that any marketer who wants to reach the changing women's market will make.

A Final Word . . .

I HAVE attempted to chart some of the ways that women in the ten countries
resemble each other and the ways in which they differ. I regard the demographics and attitudes reported by each country as indicators of the nature and
direction of the women's market in each of those countries. Nevertheless, I am
aware that this is a brief excursion into ten very different cultures. It is not a
substitute for a more substantive cultural or anthropological analysis of evolving
mores.

The nature of the information varies from country to country. As discussed
earlier, definitive governmental statistics on some of the demographic aspects
were not available from some countries. Each country dealt with parallel subject
areas, but the specific manifestations of those topics varied from country to
country. In some ways the issues selected for discussion reflect a projective
expression of the concerns and interests of people in those countries, or at least
the interests of the reporting researchers.

Within these parameters certain distinctive patterns emerged. These were
the increase in women's presence in the work force, the link between the level
of women's education and their propensity to work, and women's increased
participation in higher education.

Women's motivations to work, both the economic motives of necessity and
income supplementation, and the psychic rewards of social stimulation, an enhanced sense of self and personal achievement, were found in varying degrees
in each country. The reasons why women don't work and don't want to work
were linked to their perception that the proper role for a woman is to be a wife
and mother. Some young housewives, who were out of the work force, yearned
for a connection with the outside world that they think work will bring them.
Again, these attitudes were quite pervasive.

The New Demographic typology of the stay-at-home housewife reflects the traditional homemaker's perception of her role; that of the plan-to-work house-wife reflects the aspirations of some young housewives to enter the work force. Similarly, the differentiation between just-a-job working women and career women reflects the achievement orientation and ambition of career women. Although the proportions of the New Demographic segments vary from country to country, they reflect a spectrum of values ranging from the most traditional attitudes, held by stay-at-home housewives, to the most nontraditional perspectives, expressed by career women. In many cases the plan-to-work housewives were far more like the two segments of working women than their stay-at-home counterparts.

The demographic realities, as well as women's attitudes and values, provide a snapshot of the state of the women's market in each country. Some of their responses provide intriguing glimpses into possibly strong cultural differences. The frustration in dealing with this kind of material is that it is suggestive but not definitive. Some of the observations, however, are clues that marketers and researchers on the scene might wish to pursue.

North America

United States

By some measures the United States might be perceived as the most advanced of the ten countries in terms of women's actual participation in the work force and the attitudes that go with it. Fifty-five percent of all American women go to work. Among active women, 65 percent are working women and 35 percent are housewives, a ratio of almost two to one. American women have the highest level of combined secondary and postsecondary education of women in any of the countries we examined. Currently, more than half of the students enrolled in colleges and universities in the United States are women.

Although housewives represent a small proportion of the active women's population, more of them are the traditional stay-at-home type than say they plan to go to work. Part of the reason for this is that the plan-to-work segment is a dynamic group, whose members tend to enter the work force as soon as their children are of school age, and sometimes before, whereas stay-at-home housewives are older and less well educated. Since they have no intention of working, their proportion in the population tends to be fairly stable. Conversely, although 27 percent of all active women in the United States are career-oriented working women, more working women see their work as "just a job."

American women endorse a partnership marital relationship over the traditional form of marriage. In a partnership marriage the husband and wife share the financial and household responsibilities equally. In practice, however, wives tend to do more of the household chores, although the husbands of working wives share tasks to a certain extent. Working couples are far more likely to share in financial and purchase decisions than they are to share in doing the housework.

This brief summary of the situation of American women does not include many aspects of their lives, social, occupational, and political. For example, the flow of women between the home and the workplace and the pressure of jug-gling work responsibilities with those for their children underline the need for day care. I believe that day care will be a basic social issue for the rest of this decade and into the 1990s. The question of day care is of concern to both the public and private sectors; and will become increasingly important in the years to come.

By definition, career women are ambitious and motivated to achieve; but many corporate women simply do not seem to get past a certain rung on the corporate ladder. This phenomenon is known as the "glass ceiling." This is a complex issue of entrenched attitudes and assumptions on the part of manage-ment and male colleagues. Some women have managed to break through the barrier, but only a few have done so. Many women have opted to move out of corporate life to entrepreneurship, as a way of circumventing the invisible bar-rier.

The focus of this book is on marketing, not on politics. Nonetheless, as women's participation in the workplace has increased, their participation in po-litical life has also been on the rise. It is five years since my book *The Moving Target* was published. In those few years we have seen a woman astronaut successfully fly into space, and we have seen another woman astronaut tragi-cally die in an accident. We have seen woman candidate for vice-president. We have seen more women run for political office and more women in positions of power on the staffs of political candidates.

In the past few elections, women have begun to vote differently from the men in their families, and politicians are beginning to recognize the gender gap. A few years ago I made the point that women began to be taken seriously as a political force in the United States when news of women's issues moved from the fashion page to the front page of the *New York Times*. I am now informed that there is no such thing as a "family page"; every story relating to women is part of the general news section and is selected for publication on the basis of its news worthiness rather than for its unique interest to women.

Canada

Canadian women are second to women in the United States in their work force participation. Fifty-two percent go to work. This represents a dramatic incre-ment of 73 percent over their 1960 level of participation. There are proportionately more housewives in Canada than in the United States. Among active women, 58 percent are working women and 42 percent are housewives. In part this reflects the fact that fewer nonworking women in Canada than in the United States are out of the mainstream.

There was also a dramatic gain in the number of women enrolled in colleges and universities. In 1965, 33 percent of college students were women. In 1985 they dominated college enrollment (55 percent). This represents a 67 percent rate of growth in twenty years.

The expansionary direction of Canadian women as reflected by their college enrollment is also reflected in the proportion of the New Demographic segments in that country. There are more plan-to-work housewives than stay-at-homes in Canada, which augurs increased participation in the work force by Canadian women in the near future.

Canada reported the highest proportion of career-oriented working women of any of the countries studied. More working women in Canada are career oriented than feel their work is "just a job." This dramatic emphasis on aspiration and ambition suggests that the quiet revolution has not yet run its course in Canada.

The attitudes of Canadian women are intriguing. A dramatic two out of three believe that women can live a satisfactory life without having children, but almost an equal proportion say that children are a source of women's greatest satisfaction. By two to one they reject the notion that woman's place is in the home. A dramatic 86 percent believe that a single woman can have a happy life.

Canadian women overwhelmingly support all aspects of partnership marriage. More than nine out of ten believe that if a woman works, her husband should share in child care; husbands and wives should share in major purchase decisions; women should know the amount and location of the family finances; and they should have some money of their own beyond the household requirements.

Finally, all Canadian women, both housewives and working women, have a strong sense of their own self-worth. They believe that their families respect what they do regardless of what that is. Almost universally they believe that their sons and daughters should have equal educational opportunities and an equal amount of independence. They believe that in today's society a woman must be able to support herself and her children. Their strong sense of self is expressed in their desire to go beyond derived status and to have an identity in their own right beyond that of wife and mother.

This bursting forth of Canadian women seems to have occurred in a few short years. George Clements, an international vice-president of the J. Walter

Thompson Company and national director of strategic planning of Canada, is an Englishman who lives and works in Canada and has spent time in the Far East. He believes that one of the underlying causes of the change is economic, "although it is a case of several issues merging rather than one single trend." He points out that "Canada has been a frontier country to a much greater extent than the U.S. for example. Because it has in recent historical times lived close to the subsistence level there has been a need for women to work." He also observes that "Canada has become increasingly urban, leading to higher incomes and greater independence of women."[1]

He also believes that "the most important issue currently is the high level of taxation. Canada is one of the most heavily taxed countries in the world. By itself this isn't necessarily significant, but because Canadians are exposed to the considerably higher U.S. standards of living, their wants cannot be supplied by a single earner. Hence, to afford the trip to Florida, the house renovation, the second car, and the third television set, the wife goes to work. The husband encourages the wife to work because he understands that he alone cannot earn enough to provide them with the living standards they want so there has been a long tradition of working which over the past few years has been intensified because of standard of living wanted. And once women work all the attitude changes fall into line in a predictable pattern."[2]

Marion Plunkett, director of research at the Ogilvy & Mather advertising agency in Toronto, points out that Canadian women "were a little slower to be participants in the labour force compared to our U.S. counterparts." On the other hand, she believes that the social climate in Canada is more supportive of working women: "We have Medicare . . . women have had seventeen weeks maternity leave by law, with paid unemployment insurance and guaranteed jobs for about ten years. In the U.S. women are still fighting for this. . . . In Canada the new abortion laws . . . protect women's constitutional rights more than ever before . . . in contrast to the defeat of the E.R.A. in many U.S. states." Therefore, she thinks that for Canadian women "the decision to return to work is a personal one, perhaps contributing to a greater sense of security."[3]

The Far East

Japan

Just under half of all women in Japan go to work. But this 49 percent workforce participation represents a decline since the 1950s and 1960s. At its peak, 57 percent of Japanese women were working women.

There are two reasons for this. There has been a major structural change in the nature of women's work. In the fifties and sixties women were largely in-volved in agriculture and family businesses; since then, there was an increase in conventional paid employment. Thus, although the absolute level is down, the quality of Japanese working women is rising. In addition, because the pop-ulation in Japan is growing older, there are fewer women of working age to participate in the work force.

Among active women, 60 percent are working women and 40 percent are housewives. The proportion of women in Japan who have completed secondary or postsecondary education is 53 percent. This is a conservative estimate, since it doesn't include junior college or graduate school education. Women's enroll-ment in colleges and universities rose by 50 percent in the twenty years be-tween 1965 and 1985. The rise was from 16 percent of students to 24 percent, which is not as great an increase as in other countries, perhaps a reflection that junior college and graduate study are not included in the numbers.

The proportion of the New Demographic segments in Japan has a more traditional bent than observed in Canada, for example. Twice as many Japanese housewives prefer to stay at home than plan to go to work. Twice as many working women say their work is "just a job" as consider themselves career women. Women in each of the New Demographic segments were very com-fortable with their choices. Stay-at-home housewives enjoy the traditional life style, but they respect the working woman's option to live differently. Career women in Japan are exuberant about their lives. They find their work rewarding and they enjoy their recreation with equal enthusiasm.

Japanese women are evenly split on whether women's place is in the home, but one in five Japanese women ventured no opinion on this question. Twice as many Japanese women believe that working women are not pressured to stay at home as think they are. Again, one in four gave no opinion. Fewer Japanese women believe that husbands would be happier if their wives didn't work as say that they would not. Again, a sizable proportion ventured no opinion.

Japanese women endorse some aspects of partnership marriage. Nine out of ten Japanese women believe that wives should share in all major purchase decisions made in the household. Three out of four think that husbands and wives should share in caring for young children. Just under seven in ten think that the wife should be responsible for handling the family finances. Although this may sound like an expression of liberation, in fact, it represents the tradi-tional Japanese custom. It is customary for the husband to turn his paycheck over to the wife, who determines how the money is to be spent. On the other hand, many corporations give working men sizable bonuses, which are not part of their salaries. The men spend these at their discretion.

Although Japanese women believe in partnership in purchase decisions and child care, they are less likely to want their husbands to share in household chores, either cleaning the house or shopping for groceries. Many Japanese women seem to feel that their own identities are linked to the care of the home. This point of view was expressed by working women as well as full-time home-makers.

Judgment on the potential of the changing role of women in Japan is mixed. An article in the February 1988 *Harvard Business School Bulletin* quoted Eiko Koizumi, a graduate of the Harvard Business School in the mid-1970s and now president of her own consulting firm in Tokyo, who thinks change is occurring more rapidly in Japan than in the United States "because it was close to explosion. Housework is easy now because so much is automated. We have an equal education system up through the university and women are usually more diligent students, so ability-wise they are there. They need something to help them feel that they are contributing to society. If you can finish your housework in two or three hours, what will you do with the rest of your day until your husband comes home at midnight? What do you look for in life? They needed something."[4] Her comments reinforce the aspirations of the plan-to-work housewives reported here.

On the other hand, Katsuhiko Betsushima, the director of strategic planning of J. Walter Thompson Company Japan, wonders whether the change is really basic. He confirms that "the beliefs and behaviors of Japanese women are changing significantly." He cites "the increase in the divorce rate, the decrease in arranged marriages, the increase in purchase of stockings and the decrease in the Japanese socks or 'tabi.'" He raises an important question: "When plan-to-work housewives enter the work force, will they continue to emulate the beliefs and behaviors of career women or will they become disappointed in their work and begin to share the frustrations of those women who see their work as just a job?" He speculates that "if they adopt the attitudes of career women to social change, then in the future the majority of Japanese women will reflect the beliefs and behaviors of that small group of women who are leading the kimono revolution today. But, if plan-to-work housewives continue to hold their conservative attitudes toward social change, the kimono revolution will certainly sputter."[5]

Robert Wilk, managing director of Marplan in Japan, believes that the change is real. "The first major trend and development that has had an enormous impact in marketing in Japan is the new Japanese woman. I believe the major event that finally allowed this to happen was the passing finally of the Equal Opportunity Law in 1986. Now among the very rule-respecting Japanese the creation of a new rule on equality of opportunity has ended major discussion on this issue and was more or less immediately accepted by everyone (with varying degrees of enthusiasm, as might be expected) but, importantly, accepted as the new rule."[6] The law has meant several changes for businesses in Japan. It "has forced companies to create managerial career paths for women. A survey by the Japanese Ministry of Labor found that seventy-nine percent of all major corporations recruited 1987 college graduates without regard to sex, up from thirty-six percent the previous year. More to the point, the social taboos against female executives are eroding as women prove themselves to be capable managers."[7]

Japanese women have traditionally had limited opportunities in corporate life, but that is changing quickly. IBM "launched a major long-term PR campaign over ten years ago specifically aimed at universities to present themselves as a company that appreciates and respects young talent, especially young female talent." The campaign has succeeded. "Last year in a yearly poll of the most favorite companies that female university graduates want to work for most, IBM was the Number One choice."[8] Other companies have followed suit.

Eiko Koizumi marvels at the change: "It's incredible. When I returned to Japan ten years ago, I would not have envisioned the current level of women's activities. I thought it would take thirty to fifty years to accomplish what we are doing today. You can see so many changes, not only in women's activities but in men's acceptance of women's work, especially among younger men." She believes that change is inexorable: "Companies realize these days that they can't avoid the strength of women. The sociological trend is here and if you're not out of touch, you can see it. The so-called male-dominated industries are all in decline. Many of the growing industries, especially in the service sector, have a lot of women to start with. These are quite astonishing changes."[9]

Australia

Forty-six percent of Australian women are in the work force. This represents a 59 percent increment over their work force participation in 1961. Among active women, 59 percent are working women and 41 percent are housewives. Although the educational system of Australia is quite different from that of some of the other countries, it is estimated that 57 percent of Australian women have achieved secondary or postsecondary education. Currently, 46 percent of college students are women. This represents a 53 percent rate of growth since 1970, when only 30 percent of college students were women.

Two studies of Australian women were conducted in 1984. The first was confined to women in the two major urban centers, Sydney and Melbourne, and the second included women in the five mainland cities. There were differences in their proportions of the New Demographic segments. In Sydney and Melbourne there were equal proportions of plan-to-work and stay-at-home housewives, and more working women saw their jobs as careers than as just a job. In the second study, however, there were higher proportions of stay-at-home housewives and just-a-job working women. Certainly, in the major urban centers at least, the aspirations of housewives and the ambitions of career women seem to be on the rise.

Australian women believe that children are important. More of them say that a woman should experience having a child than say that the experience is not necessary. On the other hand, by three to one they reject the traditional definition of woman's role, that her only responsibility should be her home and family. An equal proportion assert that a woman has the right to spend time on herself as well as on her family.

They endorse the partnership approach to marriage. Three out of four say that a husband and wife should share in earning a living. An overwhelming 96 percent say husbands and wives should share financial responsibilities, and 94 percent say they should share in major purchase decisions. They carry the partnership approach to the domestic sphere as well. Large majorities of Australian women believe that husbands and wives should share child care and household chores, such as shopping for groceries and cleaning the house.

Australian women show a strong desire for financial independence. Even stay-at-home housewives would prefer to have income in their own names and a high proportion of women believe that half of the spouse's income should legally belong to them. Approximately 40 percent of both traditional housewives and working women agree on this issue.

In the 1970s, the attitudes of a frontier society still lingered in Australia: Husbands at the very lowest economic level were perfectly willing to have their wives work because it was a matter of economic necessity. Then, as men rose to the middle class, they took it as a point of pride that they could support their wives. They voiced the attitude that "no wife of mine has to go to work."[10] Ironically, many of the middle-class women who became full-time homemakers sought broader horizons. They saw to it that their daughters achieved higher education. As wives and daughters became educated, they also sought something more in life than the limited role of wife and mother. This naturally led to a dissonance between the attitudes of men and the aspirations of women.[11]

In several visits to Australia over the past decade I have observed real changes. These are necessarily impressionistic. In 1977, I had a distinct feeling that Australia was a suburban, middle-class society. I was typically entertained at barbecues on the lawns of suburban homes outside the city. When I returned in 1984, Sydney seemed much more vibrant and much more urban. I was entertained by two-income couples living in Sydney. In one case the husband was very active in serving the dinner.

The occasion of my 1984 visit was to speak at a first-ever conference on "Women and Management." I could feel the electricity and dynamism in the audience of that symposium. The women were intensely involved and committed to expanding their professional opportunities. The kind of ambition reflected by career orientation was palpable in that room.

George Clements, an international vice-president of the J. Walter Thompson Company, spent some time in Australia as director of strategic planning. He has concluded that two issues are fueling the quiet revolution in Australia. The first of these is male domination.

For whatever historical reason Australia has traditionally been a male dominated society. The barefoot and pregnant in the kitchen syndrome. Australian women are finally breaking out from under this domination with a classic swing of the pendulum effect—because it was so far one way it has swung to the opposite extreme. A backlash effect. I think it has finally happened as a cumulative effect, a catching up to North America, just like a dam breaking, first a trickle and then a flood. We must remember that Australia isn't cut off from the rest of the world in the way it was. Once the Western World became a global village, Australian women became exposed to outside influences, e.g., U.S. television, travel, magazines, and you've got the classic hole in the dyke.[12]

The second issue is economics: "In recent years, Australia has suffered a depressed economy, high taxation, high rates of inflation, etc., hence there has been a greater need for women to work to maintain living standards. Coupled with this is the urbanization of Australia—I think it is even more urban than Canada. So you get the greater expectations that come from urban living and a depressed economy leading to the inevitable second income family. Unlike Canada, men do not necessarily endorse women working, and women try to overcompensate by becoming super-moms. Hence Australia is a country in transition, while Canada has arrived."[13]

Europe

Great Britain

Forty-seven percent of women in England are in the work force. Although their work-force participation has increased since the 1960s, the gain was slightly less dramatic than that in Canada and Australia, rising from 37 percent in 1961.

The ratio of working women to housewives is close, almost equal. Forty-six percent of British women have achieved either secondary or postsecondary education. There has been a marked increase in their enrollment in colleges and universities. In 1965, 27 percent of college students were women; in 1982 women's enrollment rose to 41 percent. This represents a more than 50 percent rate of growth in women's participation in advanced education.

The patterns of the New Demographic segments in Great Britain have a traditional cast. More than twice as many housewives would prefer to stay at home than aspire to go to work. More working women see their work as "just a job" than as a career.

An intriguing element in their attitudes is the way they feel about children. By an overwhelming 84 to 14 percent they feel that it is not necessary for a woman to have a child in order to be fulfilled. On the other hand, 52 percent believe that children are an important element in a happy marriage.

When considering the ideal life style for a married couple, fewer than one in four votes for the traditional form of marriage. Although the majority endorse a marriage in which both husband and wife work, more of them favor the transitional mode in which the husband has the more important job and the wife takes on more household and child-care responsibilities. Thirty-five percent favor a partnership marriage in which the husband and the wife take equal responsibility for earning money and running the household.

British men and women also differ on the question of whether wives should work. Sixty-five percent of women in Great Britain say that wives should go to work; only 37 percent of men endorse this. The attitudes of British housewives and just-a-job working women toward career women were startling. Stay-at-home housewives feel that a housewife is perceived as a second-class citizen. They feel defensive about their role and are sharply critical of career women as hard and overly ambitious. In other countries housewives and just-a-job working women admitted that they did not have the ambition or skills to aspire to careers, but they respected and appreciated women who do. In Great Britain, however, housewives and some just-a-job working women expressed a deep resentment of career women.

Judie Lannon, vice-president and director of research at J. Walter Thompson in London, believes there is a class element in this attitude:

> The more subtle resistance to talking about what people "do" is the snobbish and now very old-fashioned one. The upper class which was the role model, of course, didn't *do* anything. They *were* and they *owned*. But even now . . . the country gentleman and his lady and home are still more attractive figures than the captain of industry and his wife . . . perhaps an enviable person but not an admired one. The sort of tough minded (perfectly groomed) perfectionism so admired in the States seems only acceptable in the Prime Minister![14]

Perhaps another reason why British women think that the term *career women* is a pejorative is "that to place too much emphasis on your job suggests an only partially formed character, a limited sort of person. If anything, the question is what is she like rather than what does she do?"[15]

Audrey Slaughter, a journalist and editor, agreed, saying, "We still haven't shrugged off our class consciousness. There is a surface egalitarianism, but it doesn't go very deep. So for this reason there is a certain defensiveness about having a career among women over thirty-five. Leftover pride from 'I don't need to work, my husband is successful' days when only poor women worked because they jolly well had to."[16] According to Dr. Elizabeth Nelson, chairman of the Taylor Nelson Group, derived status still exists, but it is "perhaps less true now than previously and it is particularly not true for the under twenty-fives. Women are beginning to value their work and it is adding to their status without referral to their husband's status."[17]

One of the fascinating findings was that British women do not feel they need to have children for their own personal fulfillment but they do put a high value on the importance of children for a happy marriage. Judie Lannon believes that this is because of the value the British place on "familism": "It is impossible to overestimate the influence of the public example of the Royal Family. It is constantly in the news . . . it symbolizes how society should be structured . . . the traditional rites of passage are regularly, sentimentally, and publicly celebrated. This cannot help but contribute to a sense that families are the only proper way to live." She points out that Diana's educational qualifications "do not even amount to a high school diploma" and this is not important to most of the country. The British feel that "her job of working in a playschool with children was more important."[18]

Lannon suggests that the influence of the royal family also supports the values of domesticity over achievement: "Another characteristic of the Royal Family is their preoccupation with country matters, houses, dogs, and horses. And over fifty percent of people in Great Britain would choose to live in a country village rather than a large city." She points out that "country villages are where you raise children, garden, organize domestic life. It is hardly where you climb up the corporate ladder."[19]

Dr. Nelson agrees on the importance of familism, but adds that "there is a large body of women who wish to work in this country and whose aspirations are not unlike [those] in other countries."[20] Audrey Slaughter also believes that "British women have changed, at least superficially, and that most of them expect equal educational opportunities and that they do have the same rank as their husbands and that ownership of homes and goods may be divided fifty-fifty and that they may have, if they want it, a career." But the economic factor is a strong reason why women work: "It is virtually essential for a young woman to earn in order to help pay for a mortgage. . . . I fear most men would be happy to have a second salary but not too many employer demands are made on the woman to prevent her from . . . running the home." For the younger women, the problems have been deferred rather than solved. "In the younger age range, women just leaving universities, have not yet come up against the problems of combining family with career and the emotional pulls that that entails nor have had to solve the problem of whose career comes first, husband's or wife's, should there be a relocation."

Slaughter quotes Sir John Harvey-Jones, until recently chairman of ICI— the international industrial company, who said that recruitment among young women was very very healthy and showed a big increase. She said that he forecasts that as they work through it at least a third of the more senior managers will be women. She points out that until last year they didn't even make one percent. He is also the chancellor of Bradford University and reports that for the first time 30 percent of the new science and engineering enrollment are women.[21]

West Germany

Thirty-nine percent of women in West Germany were in the work force in 1980, a decline since 1961, when 41 percent of women went to work. There are two reasons for this: first, the structure of women's work changed during that period. They were less likely to be employed in family businesses and more likely to be paid employees in the public and private sectors. Second, there was a change in age composition. The population in West Germany is getting older, and many of the younger women are staying in school longer to improve their qualifications rather than entering the work force without any particular training. Germany has a retirement age of sixty, so there are fewer women of working age than in the past. Nevertheless, there has been a gain in the proportion of employed women among women of working age.

Among active women, 52 percent are working women and 48 percent are housewives. Just 36 percent of German women have completed the equivalent of secondary and postsecondary education, but there has been an increase in their enrollment in colleges and universities. In 1972, 28 percent of college students were women; in 1984, this rose to 38 percent, which represents a 36 percent rate of growth.

In West Germany the pattern of the New Demographics is strongly conservative. By more than two to one housewives would prefer to stay at home instead of go to work. Working women are far more likely to see their work as "just a job" than a career.

Although more German women believe that it is not necessary for a woman to have children in order to feel fulfilled than think children are necessary, they are less extreme in this attitude than British women. On the other hand, Ger-man women are more likely to say that children are important to a marriage than to think they are not.

German women are just slightly more likely to define women's role in con-temporary rather than traditional terms. Forty-five percent believe that a wife should devote herself to her home and her family because that's her job; 55 percent disagree.

More German women than women in the other two European countries choose a traditional marriage, but the majority choose some form of two-paycheck marriage either the transitional form or a partnership marriage. In addition, more German women than men believe that wives should work, though they are far less likely than women in Britain and Italy to endorse wives' participation in the work force. Half of all German women believe that house-work should be done by women and one in three thinks a man should have the last work in important decisions.

According to Robert Schutzendorf, a director of J. Walter Thompson in West Germany and director of account planning, the role of women in West Germany is changing profoundly.

> In our governments there are now Ministers for women's issues. Women's is-sues are determining factors in the discussion about the economic organization of the workplace, wages, working time, and paths to professional development. Articles on women's changing life situations appear frequently in important German magazines. A recent exhibition about the image of women in modern European painting received a lot of attention. Female musicians, writers, paint-ers, and architects have emancipated themselves from their male colleagues long ago.
>
> Marketing people have at last begun to think about products and advertis-ing concepts that are more relevant to women today. This, of course, has a strong influence on us being an advertising agency. We can hardly remember a topic that raised such intense interest among our clients as a series of presen-tations we did on the new female role model. And it has an effect on us as employers, as well. There are often more well-qualified female than male appli-cants for jobs in the middle management level.[22]

Yet not all women in Germany subscribe to the changes. "The trends do not affect all women in the same way. The women of the two post-war genera-tions are the main protagonists of change. This has a consequence that the changes do not happen that fast and are not so consciously targeted as one would possibly expect: since the starting position is not the same for all women, their objectives are still widely divergent."[23]

A Final Word . . .

He believes that it is difficult to predict the ultimate impact of the changing role of women, "but we may certainly say that the social trends that have caused these changes are irreversible: the demand for a better school education, the demand for a profession, and the demand to be able to combine job and family will continue. . . . Women are definitely undergoing a process of insight and clarification which the male half of society will have to face."[24]

Italy

Thirty-three percent of Italian women go to work, a 44 percent rate of growth since 1961, when 23 percent of women were in the work force. Among active women, 43 percent are working women and 57 percent are housewives. Just 15 percent of Italian women have completed secondary or postsecondary education.

Although very few Italian women go to college, women's share of the college enrollment is not low and it has increased. In 1970, 38 percent of all students enrolled in colleges and universities in Italy were women; this rose to 44 percent in 1982, a 16 percent rate of growth.

Stay-at-home housewives predominate in Italy. A substantial proportion of housewives plan to go to work. More than twice as many working women see their work as "just a job" than as a career. Italian women are more likely than women in the other two European countries to believe that a woman should have children in order to be personally fulfilled. On the other hand, slightly more of them reject than endorse the notion that children are necessary for a woman's personal fulfillment.

Compared to women in Great Britain and West Germany, there was more consonance in the way Italian women feel about the importance of children to their own fulfillment and the value of children in a marriage. Fifty-three percent believe that children are important to a marriage; 16 percent disagree.

Italian women are overwhelmingly in favor of partnership marriage. Forty-seven percent of them say that in the ideal marriage, husband and wife share financial and household responsibilities. Less than one in four chose a traditional marriage as the ideal; and 27 percent believe that the wife should work but the husband's job is more important and the wife should undertake the greater share of the household chores. One aspect of their support of partnership marriage is that more than four out of five Italian women believe it is fair for husbands and wives to divide the housework.

A dramatic three out of four Italian women believe that wives should go to work; just 43 percent of Italian men endorse the idea. There is a greater disparity between men and women in Italy than between men and women in either of the other two European countries.

281

Italian women express an emerging sense of self. More than four out of five believe that even though a woman has to care for her children and family, she has a right to her own aspirations, that a woman should have friendships, interests, and activities independent of those of her husband, and that the word *obey* should never be used in a relationship between a man and a woman. Nine out of ten believe that sons and daughters should be treated equally, both in opportunities for education and in learning household chores.

The distinguished Italian journalist, Benedetta Barzini, believes that there have been substantial changes among Italian women.

> Women, all over the country, in a homogeneous way, are aiming at a higher education and more qualified job positions. The strong issues substantially raised by the women's movement in the past few years have left a strong imprint on Italian society. There is an overall greater awareness of the woman's role both in professional areas and in domestic life.
>
> On the professional scene, women now can count on a government commission for equal opportunities that has just finished a nationwide training course for special professional roles. It is called "counselor for equal rights" whose main concern is to supervise that women are not being discriminated at work or in hiring procedures.[25]

Italian women in our study gave the distinct impression that although they seek broader horizons and self-realization, they are very comfortable with themselves as women. Benedetta Barzini confirms this. "In Italy, by equal rights, we do not mean to equate a woman's life with a man's. We wish to fight for respect of the fundamental differences that occur between the two sexes. A difference in methods, approaches, rhythms. A sexual difference."[26] Anna Scotti, president of J. Walter Thompson Italy, also thinks women have a distinctive approach to their work: "Women bring to their work certain elements of distinction: more devotion to the job and less personal ambition; competence and professionality are merged with human values and seasoned with a more personal approach."[27]

Barzini believes that the new awareness has affected family life as well. "As far as family life is concerned, women are gaining more emotional autonomy and represent sixty percent of the population that [initiated] claims for separations or divorces. Women are clearly less dependent on male protection . . . being 'single' is no problem even in Italy."[28]

She confirms that Italian working women share the universal conflict between children and work. "Raising children still remains a crucial problem and no general solution for working women can be considered successful. This is one of the main reasons that induces women to start their own business. This blooming of private companies run by women has been erroneously considered by the establishment as a sign of success. Women in Italy are profoundly aware of the real meaning of such 'success.'"[29]

Anna Scotti thinks that full-time homemakers have also changed dramatically.

> Housewives are a category of women who, today more than in the past, have chosen to drop out (or never dropped into) the working market. They enjoy their free time also by paying more attention to themselves (sports, beauty centers, etc.). They have acquired a good degree of education. Their critical capacities of analyzing, for instance, both the goods and the messages in the market have obliged the advertising world to evolve in the nature and the quality of any kind of campaign. Tired of stereotypes typical of national traditions, for instance, the "angel of the household," the spirit of sacrifice, the devoted mother and wife—the contemporary housewife could be often compared to an excellent critic or an impartial judge of facts and fiction in today's environment.[30]

Latin America

Venezuela

Thirty-one percent of women in Venezuela were in the work force in 1984, a dramatic 82 percent rate of growth over the 17 percent who worked in 1961. Among active women, 37 percent are housewives and 63 percent are working women. Only 6 percent of women in Venezuela have completed either secondary or postsecondary education. Although a very small proportion of Venezuelan women have achieved advanced education, in 1970, 40 percent of students enrolled in colleges and universities were women.

Venezuelan housewives are more likely to prefer to stay at home than aspire to go to work. Conversely, although only a small portion of women are in the work force, more of them are career oriented than see their work as "just a job."

Venezuelan women believe strongly in the importance of children. Ninety-five percent say that every couple should experience having a child. Although they are more likely to endorse the traditional perspective of men's and women's roles, they are less intense in this than they are in their enthusiasm for children. Sixty-two percent believe that men prefer women to stay at home and care for the house and family; 17 percent disagree. There is a closer vote on the question of whether men should be responsible for support of the family. Forty-six percent believe that they should; 39 percent disagree.

In spite of this traditional emphasis, two out of three Venezuelan women believe that a woman deserves to spend as much time on herself as on her family. Both men and women in Venezuela strongly endorse two aspects of partnership marriage. Ninety percent of women and 83 percent of men say that household tasks should be shared by the husband and wife. Ninety-four percent of men and of women believe that husbands and wives should share in making major purchase decisions.

Mexico

Twenty-eight percent of Mexican women go to work. This represents an increase of 75 percent over the 16 percent who were working in 1961. Five percent of women in Mexico have completed either secondary or postsecondary education. Although a tiny proportion of Mexicans were attending college in 1982, just about one in three college students was a woman. In 1979, 30 percent of college students were women, a 30 percent rate of growth in three years.

Although stay-at-home housewives are in the majority among Mexican women, a substantial proportion of full-time homemakers say they plan to go to work. More of the working women in Mexico see their work as a job than as a career.

Mexican women believe strongly in the importance of children, although not as intensely as women in Venezuela. Eighty-three percent say that every couple should experience having a child. They are more likely than their Venezuelan neighbors to endorse the traditional viewpoint that men prefer women to stay at home and care for the house and family. They are also slightly more likely to endorse the traditional notion that it is the man's responsibility to support the wife and family.

Although more of them approve than disapprove of a woman's having the right to spend time on herself, they are less intense than Venezuelan women in their attitude on this issue. In spite of their slightly more traditional orientation, Mexican men and women strongly endorse two aspects of partnership marriage. Seventy-nine percent of the women and 77 percent of the men believe that household tasks should be shared by husbands and wives. Eighty-nine percent of women and 87 percent of men believe that husbands and wives should share in making major purchase decisions.

Brazil

In 1980, 27 percent of women in Brazil were in the work force, a 59 percent rate of growth over the 17 percent who were working in 1960. Nine percent of women in Brazil have achieved secondary or postsecondary levels of education. Although a very small proportion of people in that country attend college, in 1970 women's share of college enrollments was 38 percent.

A dramatically high proportion of Brazilian housewives plan to go to work rather than stay at home. More of the working women in Brazil see their work as "just a job" than as a career.

Like their neighbors in the other Latin American countries, Brazilian women believe strongly in the importance of children. Ninety-two percent say that every couple should experience having children. They also tend to endorse the traditional definition of the male and female roles. Seventy-five percent believe that men prefer women to stay home and care for the house; 22 percent do not agree. More of them say that it is the man's responsibility to support the wife and family than disagree. Nevertheless, their endorsement of husbands' financial responsibilities is not nearly as strong as their emphasis on the importance of children.

Conversely, Brazilian women believe very strongly that women have a right to spend as much time on themselves as on their families. An overwhelming 84 percent feel this way; 13 percent disagree. A majority of both women and men in Brazil agree that household tasks should be shared by husbands and wives. Eighty-nine percent of women and 79 percent of men endorse the partnership approach.

According to Mercedes Pulido de Briceno, assistant secretary-general and coordinator for the Improvement of the Status of Women in the Secretariat of the United Nations and a distinguished Venezuelan psychologist and former university professor, "Since the 1960s many changes have taken place [in Latin America] due to the impact of urbanization and the improvement of modern services in each country." Education has played a pivotal role. "The accessibility of education to all levels of the population has . . . created the most impact." She attributes "the revolution of expectations" to urbanization and education. "The beginning of modernization facilitated the emergence of new attitudes toward the role of women, as well as an increase in women's sense of self-esteem." Ironically, she believes that the economic situation in the region makes it necessary for women to work but that "the present economic crisis will curtail accessibility of women to the labor force."[31]

In her view, "the family structure continues to be perceived as a conservative entity and women as being primarily responsible for child rearing." She thinks this is particularly true of lower-income groups, who "still regard motherhood and economic support of the family as the sole responsibility of women. The family structure in these groups is basically organized around the role of the mother with several small children without a permanent partner."[32]

One of the surprising findings here was the strong endorsement of shared responsibilities among men and women in the three Latin American countries. Senora de Briceno confirms this dramatic change in attitudes. Both husbands and wives work "to achieve better living standards." Because of this they are moving toward a partnership approach to marriage: "Men and women share the same responsibilities and, therefore, the family is seen as a joint venture and not within the traditional 'machista' division of roles."[33]

If I had to use one word to describe the state of the women's market in the ten countries studied, I would choose *diversity*. Women are not a monolithic group. In every country there is a diverse spectrum of segments representing a range of values and attitudes and a range of marketplace behavior.

Some universal elements transcended national boundaries, and distinctive cultural nuances differentiated women in each country from women in other countries. Women are not only not a monolithic group, they are not unidimensional. Even women in those countries that were most supportive of traditional values were also surprisingly in favor of nontraditional behaviors and life styles.

New values and old values coexist in varying proportions in every country we studied. Those values and the behavior that reflects them appear to be changing rapidly. In the course of this book I have suggested some ways that international marketers can address those changes in their marketing procedures.

The only constant in the world of the international advertiser is change. Consumers are changing. Markets are changing. And the cultural context is changing. On the other hand, the flip side of change is an opportunity for the marketer with the courage and vision to seize the challenge.

Notes

Preface

1. Professor Eli Ginzberg, chairman of the National Commission for Manpower Policy, interview with Carolyn Biro, *Working Woman* magazine, December 1976, p. 5.
2. "Target Australia: Women, the Quiet Revolution," J. Walter Thompson Australia, Survey Research Group Australia Pty. Ltd. 1984; Robert Langtry and Maxine Krige, "National Survey," January/February 1984, "Sydney/Melbourne Survey," January/February 1984.
3. Private communication from Datin Akiko Aw, chairman of Timas Pte. Ltd., Singapore, May 1981.

One

1. Rena Bartos, *The Moving Target: What Every Marketer Should Know about Women* (New York: Free Press, 1982), p. 3.
2. U.S. Bureau of the Census, Current Population Survey 1985, age base 16+; Canada, Population Census 1981, age base: 15+.
3. Japan, Population Census 1985, age base: 15+; Great Britain, Population Census 1981, age base: 16+; Australia, Population Census 1981, age base: 15+.
4. West Germany, Population Census 1980, age base: 15+.
5. Italy, Population Census 1981, age base: 14+.
6. Venezuela, Population Census 1984, age base: 15+; Mexico, Population Census 1980, age base: 12+, Brazil, Population Census 1980, age base: 10+.
7. Canada, Population Census 1961/1981, age base: 15+.
8. U.S. Bureau of the Census, Current Population Survey 1960/1985, age base: 16+.
9. Australia, Population Census 1961/1981, age base: 16+.
10. Great Britain, Population Census 1961/1981, age base: 16+.
11. Italy, Population Census 1961/1981, age base: 10+/14+.
12. Venezuela, Population Census 1961/1984, age base: 10+/15+.
13. Mexico, Population Census 1961/1980, age base: 8+/12+.
14. Brazil, Population Census 1960/1980, age base: 10+.
15. Japan, Population Census 1960/1985, age base: 15+.
16. West Germany, Population Census 1961/1980, age base: 15+.
17. Statistiches Bundeamt, *Statistische Jahrbuecher*, Wiesbaden, West Germany, 1950/1986.
18. Japan, Annual Report on Labour Force Survey, 1950/1985.
19. Germany, Population Census 1980/Trendmonitor, Basisresearch, 1985.

20. Italy, ISTAT Census 1981.
21. Australia, Population Census 1981; "Beyond the Stereotypes," Reark Research Pty. Ltd. for Clemenger Network of Advertising Agencies, 1984.
22. Japan, Annual Report on the Labour Force Survey; Japan, Population Census 1985.
23. Venezuela, Population Census 1981/1984, in the *Statistical Yearbook*.
24. U.S. Bureau of Labor Statistics, *Employment and Earnings*, January 1987.
25. Canada, Population Census 1981; "Women in the Marketplace," Thompson Lightstone & Company, Ltd., 1984.
26. Great Britain, Population Census 1981.

Two

1. Newspaper Advertising Bureau. Inc. "Women, Work, and Markets of the 80s," December 1979, p. 16.
2. The Roper Organization, Inc., "The 1985 Virginia Slims American Women's Opinion Poll," p. 73.
3. Commission of the European Communities, "European Men and Women 1983," the European Omnibus Survey coordinated by Helene Riffault.
4. "Beyond the Stereotypes," Reark Research Pty. Ltd. for Clemenger Network of Advertising Agencies, 1984, p. 14.
5. "Women: The Moving Target in the U.K.," J. Walter Thompson Ltd., 1986.
6. Ibid.
7. "The Moving Target in Japan," J. Walter Thompson Japan; Japan Market Research Bureau, Inc., 1986.
8. Japan Market Research Bureau, Inc., 1986.
9. Ibid.
10. "Beyond the Stereotypes," Reark Research Pty. Ltd. for Clemenger Network of Advertising Agencies, 1984, p. 12.
11. Ibid.
12. "Women in the Marketplace," Thompson Lightstone & Company, Ltd., 1984.
13. Ibid.
14. "The Changing Market: Aspects of Life, the World of Women," prepared by MRB Italia srl for J. Walter Thompson Italy, 1987.
15. "Women in Germany: The Moving Target," J. Walter Thompson West Germany, 1986.
16. "Target Venezuela," J. Walter Thompson Venezuela, 1986.
17. "Target Mexico," J. Walter Thompson Mexico, 1986.
18. "Target Brazil," J. Walter Thompson Brazil, 1986.
19. Ibid.
20. The Roper Organization, Inc., The 1985 Virginia Slims American Women's Opinion Poll, p. 74.
21. Commission of the European Communities, "European Men and Women 1983," the European Omnibus Survey coordinated by Helene Riffault, pp. 71, 72, 73.
22. "Women: The Moving Target in the U.K.," J. Walter Thompson Ltd., 1986.
23. Ibid.
24. "The Moving Target in Japan," J. Walter Thompson Japan, Japan Market Research Bureau, Inc., 1986.
25. Ibid.
26. "Beyond the Stereotypes," Reark Research Pty. Ltd. for Clemenger Network of Advertising Agencies, 1984, p. 14.
27. "Women in the Marketplace," Thompson Lightstone & Company, Ltd., 1984.
28. "The Changing Market: Aspects of Life, the World of Women," prepared by MRB Italia srl for J. Walter Thompson Italy, 1987.
29. "Target Venezuela," J. Walter Thompson Venezuela, 1986.

Notes

30. "Target Mexico," J. Walter Thompson Mexico, 1986.
31. "Target Brazil," J. Walter Thompson Brazil, 1986.
32. Ibid.

Three

1. This pattern showed an amazing consistency even though I did not have data for every country and even though educational systems vary from country to country. U.S. Bureau of the Census, Current Population Survey, March 1985; Canada Labour Force Annual Averages, 1983; Japan, Statistics Bureau, Management and Coordination Agency, 1982; Great Britain, Office of Population Censuses and Surveys; "Target Australia: Women, the Quiet Revolution," J. Walter Thompson Australia, Survey Research Group Australia Pty. Ltd.; Audits of Great Britain, 1984; Statistisches Bundeamt, *Statistische Jahrbuecher*, Wiesbaden, West Germany, 1950 and 1986; Italy, ISTAT Census 1981.
2. Center for International Research of the United States, Bureau of the Census; *Yearbook Australia 1985*. It should be noted, however, that Australia was not included in the Census Bureau's international comparisons. The educational data for Australia were obtained from *Yearbook Australia 1985*. The "completed secondary" group in Australia is a combination of "completed compulsory requirements," that is, remained in school through age fifteen, and "post-school qualifications," that is, went on to some vocational training such as secretarial school. Therefore, the Australian "completed secondary" group is not comparable to those of the other countries.
3. U.S. Department of Education, National Center for Educational Statistics, Digest of Educational Statistics, 1965/1982, 1984/1985; Canada Statistics, 1971/1982; Japan, Ministry of Education, The School Basic Survey, 1965/1985; United Kingdom Education Statistics, 1965/1966, 1984/1985; Statistisches Bundeamt, *Statistische Jahrbuecher*, Wiesbaden, West Germany, 1950 and 1986.
4. U.S. Department of Education, National Center for Educational Statistics, Digest of Educational Statistics, 1965/1982.
5. U.S. Department of Education, National Center for Educational Statistics, U.S. Bureau of the Census, Population Reports 1988.
6. Canada, Statistics 1965/1985. Includes graduate and undergraduate students full and part time; Japan, Ministry of Education, The School Basic Survey, 1965/1985; United Kingdom Education Statistics 1965/1982; *UNESCO Yearbook 1984;* Statistisches Bundeamt, *Statistische Jahrbuecher*, Wiesbaden, West Germany, 1950 and 1986; *UNESCO Yearbook 1984*.
7. *UNESCO Yearbook 1984*.
8. Ibid.
9. "American Women Today and Tomorrow," study directed by Dr. Barbara Everitt Bryant for Market Opinion Research for the National Commission on Observance of International Women's Year, 1977.
10. The Roper Organization, Inc., The 1985 Virginia Slims American Women's Opinion Poll, pp. 64–67.
11. "Beyond the Stereotypes," Reark Research Pty. Ltd. for Clemenger Network of Advertising Agencies, 1984, p. 20.
12. "Women in the Marketplace," Thompson Lightstone & Company, Ltd., 1984.
13. "Women: The Moving Target in the U.K.," J. Walter Thompson Ltd., 1986.
14. Ibid.
15. Ibid.
16. Ibid.
17. "The Moving Target in Japan," J. Walter Thompson Japan, Japan Market Research Bureau, Inc., 1986.
18. Ibid.
19. Ibid.

Notes

20. Commission of the European Communities, "European Men and Women 1983," the European Omnibus Survey coordinated by Helene Riffault, p. 79.
21. "The Changing Market: Aspects of Life, the World of Women," prepared by MRB Italia srl for J. Walter Thompson Italy, 1987.
22. Ibid.
23. Ibid.
24. "Target Brazil," J. Walter Thompson Brazil, 1986.
25. "Target Mexico," J. Walter Thompson Mexico, 1986.
26. "Target Venezuela," J. Walter Thompson Venezuela, 1986.

Four

1. The Roper Organization, Inc., The 1985 Virginia Slims American Women's Opinion Poll; Commission of the European Communities, "European Men and Women 1983," the European Omnibus Survey coordinated by Helene Riffault; "Beyond the Stereotypes," Reark Research Pty. Ltd. for Clemenger Network of Advertising Agencies, 1984.
2. "Women in the Marketplace," Thompson Lightstone & Company, Ltd., 1984.
3. "The Moving Target in Japan," J. Walter Thompson Japan, Japan Market Research Bureau Inc., 1986.
4. Ibid.
5. "Beyond the Stereotypes," Reark Research Pty. Ltd. for Clemenger Network of Advertising Agencies," 1984, p. 22.
6. "Women: The Moving Target in the U.K.," J. Walter Thompson Ltd., 1986.
7. Ibid.
8. Ibid.
9. Ibid.
10. Ibid.
11. "The Changing Market: Aspects of Life, the World of Women," prepared by MRB Italia srl for J. Walter Thompson Italy, 1987.
12. Ibid.
13. "Target Brazil," J. Walter Thompson Brazil, 1986.
14. "Target Mexico," J. Walter Thompson Mexico, 1986.
15. "Target Venezuela," J. Walter Thompson Venezuela, 1986.

Five

1. "Target Latin America," J. Walter Thompson Latin America, 1986.
2. "Target Australia: Women, the Quiet Revolution," J. Walter Thompson Australia, Survey Research Group Australia Pty. Ltd.
3. Gallup Report on European Values, Social Surveys (Gallup Poll) Ltd., London, England, 1987.
4. Ibid.
5. Ibid.
6. "Women in the Marketplace," Thompson Lightstone & Company, Ltd., 1984.
7. Gallup Report on European Values, Social Surveys (Gallup Poll) Ltd., London, England, 1987.
8. Ibid.
9. Ibid.
10. Ibid.
11. "Women in the Marketplace," Thompson Lightstone & Company, Ltd., 1984.
12. The Roper Organization, Inc., The 1985 Virginia Slims American Women's Opinion Poll, p. 43.
13. "The Italian Woman Facing the '80s," Arnoldo Mondadori/McCann-Erickson Italy, 1981.

Notes

14. "Target Latin America," J. Walter Thompson Latin America, 1986.
15. Ibid.
16. "The Moving Target in Japan," J. Walter Thompson Japan, Japan Market Research Bureau, Inc., 1986.
17. "Women in Germany: The Moving Target," J. Walter Thompson West Germany, 1986.
18. The Roper Organization, Inc., The 1985 Virginia Slims American Women's Opinion Poll, p. 8.
19. Commission of the European Communities, "European Men and Women 1983," the European Omnibus Survey coordinated by Helene Riffault.
20. Ibid.
21. Ibid.
22. Ibid.
23. Ibid.
24. Ibid.
25. Ibid.
26. Ibid.
27. "Women in the Marketplace," Thompson Lightstone & Company, Ltd., 1984.
28. "Target Australia: Women, the Quiet Revolution," J. Walter Thompson Australia, Survey Research Group Australia Pty. Ltd., 1984.
29. "Women in the Marketplace," Thompson Lightstone & Company, Ltd., 1984.
30. The Roper Organization, Inc., The 1985 Virginia Slims American Women's Opinion Poll.
31. Ibid.
32. "The Italian Woman Facing the '80s," Arnoldo Mondadori/McCann-Erickson Italy, 1981.
33. Ibid.
34. Ibid.
35. "Women in the Marketplace," Thompson Lightstone & Company, Ltd., 1984.
36. The Roper Organization, Inc., The 1985 Virginia Slims American Women's Opinion Poll.
37. "Target Latin America," J. Walter Thompson Latin America, 1986.
38. "Target Australia: Women, the Quiet Revolution," J. Walter Thompson Australia, Survey Research Group Australia Pty. Ltd., 1984, pp. 119, 120.
39. Ibid.
40. "The Italian Woman Facing the '80s," Arnoldo Mondadori/McCann-Erickson Italy, 1981.
41. "Women in the Marketplace," Thompson Lightstone & Company, Ltd., 1984.
42. Ibid.

Six

1. The sources of these data are the most recent census of the population in each country. The date of each report and the age on which the female population is based are as follows:

United States	1985	16+
Canada	1981	15+
Japan	1985	15+
Great Britain	1981	16+
Australia	1984	16+
West Germany	1985	14+
Italy	1981	14+
Venezuela	1974	15+
Mexico	1970	12+
Brazil	1980	15+

2. Regrettably, we do not have any census data or other government statistics on the proportion of women who have children in the three Latin American countries. It should be noted that the sample for "Target Latin America" was based on female heads of households who were

overwhelmingly likely to be married. Given the definition of the sample, it is not surprising that the women in the three Latin American countries who participated in the consumer study were also likely to have children. The data cannot be projected to the total female population in those countries, but only to those women who are heads of households and living in urban areas. Therefore, we have not included these three countries in the analysis in this chapter. We have also excluded Italy from the life-cycle analysis. Although we have data on the proportion of Italian women who are married and the proportion of Italian households that contain children, at the present time there is no information on the proportion of married and unmarried women with and without children under the age of eighteen.

3. See note 1.
4. Ibid.
5. Ibid.
6. Ibid.
7. Ibid.
8. Ibid.

Seven

1. "Women in the Marketplace," Thompson Lightstone & Company, Ltd., 1984.
2. "Beyond the Stereotypes," Reark Research Pty. Ltd. for Clemenger Network of Advertising Agencies, 1984, p. 10.
3. Ibid.
4. Ibid., p. 8.
5. "Women in Germany: The Moving Target," J. Walter Thompson West Germany, 1986.
6. Ibid.
7. Ibid.
8. "Beyond the Stereotypes," Reark Research Pty. Ltd. for Clemenger Network of Advertising Agencies, 1984, p. 4.
9. "Women: The Moving Target in the U.K.," J. Walter Thompson Ltd., 1986.
10. Ibid.
11. Ibid.
12. "The Moving Target in Japan," J. Walter Thompson Japan, Japan Market Research Bureau, Inc., 1986.
13. Ibid.
14. "Women: The Moving Target in the U.K.," J. Walter Thompson Ltd., 1986.
15. Commission of the European Communities, "European Men and Women 1983," the European Omnibus Survey coordinated by Helene Riffault.
16. "Women: The Moving Target in the U.K.," J. Walter Thompson Ltd., 1986.
17. "Women in Germany: The Moving Target," J. Walter Thompson West Germany, 1986.
18. "American Women Today and Tomorrow," study directed by Barbara Everitt Bryant for Market Opinion Research for the National Commission on Observance of International Women's Year, 1977.
19. Commission of the European Communities, "European Men and Women 1983," the European Omnibus Survey coordinated by Helene Riffault, p. 66.
20. Ibid., p. 68.
21. Ibid., p. 76.
22. Ibid., p. 69.
23. Ibid.
24. "Women in Germany: The Moving Target," J. Walter Thompson West Germany, 1986.
25. Ibid.
26. "Beyond the Stereotypes," Reark Research Pty. Ltd. for Clemenger Network of Advertising Agencies, 1984, p. 57.

Notes

27. "The Changing Market: Aspects of Life, the World of Women," prepared by MRB srl for J. Walter Thompson Italy, 1987.
28. "Women: The Moving Target in the U.K.," J. Walter Thompson Ltd., 1986.
29. Ibid.
30. Ibid.
31. "Beyond the Stereotypes," Reark Research Pty. Ltd. for Clemenger Network of Advertising Agencies, 1984, p. 58.
32. Ibid., p. 59.

Eight

1. "The Moving Target in Japan," J. Walter Thompson Japan, Japan Market Research Bureau, Inc., 1986.
2. "Women in the Marketplace," Thompson Lightstone & Company, Ltd., 1984.
3. "Target Australia: Women, the Quiet Revolution," J. Walter Thompson Australia, Survey Research Group Australia Pty. Ltd., 1984; Audits of Great Britain, 1984.
4. "Target Latin America," J. Walter Thompson Latin America, 1986.
5. "American Women Today and Tomorrow," study directed by Dr. Barbara Everitt Bryant for Market Opinion Research for the National Commission on Observance of International Women's Year, 1977.
6. "Target Latin America," J. Walter Thompson Latin America, 1986.
7. "Beyond the Stereotypes," Reark Research Pty. Ltd. for Clemenger Network of Advertising Agencies, 1984, p. 28.
8. The Roper Organization, Inc., The 1985 Virginia Slims American Women's Opinion Poll, pp. 86, 87.
9. Ibid., p. 84.
10. "Women in the Marketplace," Thompson Lightstone & Company, Ltd., 1984.
11. "The Moving Target in Japan," J. Walter Thompson Japan, Japan Market Research Bureau, Inc., 1986.
12. "Women in the Marketplace," Thompson Lightstone & Company, Ltd., 1984.
13. Commission of the European Communities, "European Men and Women 1983," the European Omnibus Survey coordinated by Helene Riffault.
14. Ibid.
15. Ibid.
16. Ibid.
17. Ibid.
18. Ibid.
19. Ibid., pp. 93–97.
20. "The Moving Target in Japan," J. Walter Thompson Japan, Japan Market Research Bureau, Inc., 1986.
21. "Target Australia: Women, the Quiet Revolution," J. Walter Thompson Australia, Survey Research Group Australia Pty. Ltd., 1984.
22. The Roper Organization, Inc., The 1985 Virginia Slims American Women's Opinion Poll.
23. "Beyond the Stereotypes," Reark Research Pty. Ltd. for Clemenger Network of Advertising Agencies, 1984, p. 28.
24. Commission of the European Communities, "European Men and Women 1983," the European Omnibus Survey coordinated by Helene Riffault.
25. Ibid., p. 98.
26. The Roper Organization, Inc., The 1985 Virginia Slims American Women's Opinion Poll, pp. 89, 90.
27. Ibid., pp. 90, 91.
28. "Women in the Marketplace," Thompson Lightstone & Company, Ltd., 1984.
29. Ibid.

30. Ibid.
31. "Target Australia: Women, the Quiet Revolution," J. Walter Thompson Australia, Survey Research Group Australia Pty. Ltd., 1984; Audits of Great Britain, 1984.
32. "The Moving Target in Japan," J. Walter Thompson Japan, Japan Market Research Bureau, Inc., 1986.
33. "Target Australia: Women, the Quiet Revolution," J. Walter Thompson Australia, Survey Research Group Australia Pty. Ltd., 1984; Audits of Great Britain, 1984.
34. "The Moving Target in Japan," J. Walter Thompson Japan, Japan Market Research Bureau, Inc., 1986.
35. "Target Latin America," J. Walter Thompson Latin America, 1986.
36. Ibid.
37. Ibid.
38. Ibid.
39. "Women in the Marketplace," Thompson Lightstone & Company, Ltd., 1984.

Nine

1. The Yankelovich Monitor, conducted by Yankelovich, Shelly and White, 1971.
2. "Women: The Moving Target in the U.K.," J. Walter Thompson Ltd., 1986.
3. "Women in Germany: The Moving Target," J. Walter Thompson West Germany, 1986; "The Moving Target in Japan," J. Walter Thompson Japan, Japan Market Research Bureau, Inc., 1986.
4. "Target Mexico," J. Walter Thompson Mexico, 1986; "Target Venezuela," J. Walter Thompson Venezuela, 1986.
5. The Yankelovich Monitor, conducted by Yankelovich Clancy Shulman, 1986.
6. Abacus Richerche Di Mercata E Sondozzi D'Opinine, Italy.
7. "Target Brazil," J. Walter Thompson Brazil, 1986.
8. "Women in the Marketplace," Thompson Lightstone & Company, Ltd., 1984.
9. "Target Australia: Women, the Quiet Revolution," J. Walter Thompson Australia, Survey Research Group Australia Pty. Ltd., 1984, p. 3.
10. "Beyond the Stereotypes," Reark Research Pty. Ltd. for Clemenger Network of Advertising Agencies, 1984, p. 7.
11. "Target Venezuela," J. Walter Thompson Venezuela, 1986.
12. "Women in the Marketplace," Thompson Lightstone & Company, Ltd., 1984.
13. "Target Australia: Women, the Quiet Revolution," J. Walter Thompson Australia, Survey Research Group Australia Pty. Ltd., 1984; Audits of Great Britain 1984, p. 3.
14. "Beyond the Stereotypes," Reark Research Pty., Ltd. for Clemenger Network of Advertising Agencies, 1984, p. 7.
15. The Yankelovich Monitor, conducted by Yankelovich Clancy Shulman, 1986.
16. "Women: The Moving Target in the U.K.," J. Walter Thompson Ltd., 1986; "Target Brazil," J. Walter Thompson Brazil, 1986; "Target Mexico," J. Walter Thompson Mexico, 1986.
17. "The Moving Target in Japan," J. Walter Thompson Japan, Japan Market Research Bureau, Inc., 1986.
18. Abacus Richerche Di Mercata E Sondozzi D'Opinine, Italy.
19. "Women in Germany: The Moving Target," J. Walter Thompson West Germany, 1986.
20. "Target Brazil," J. Walter Thompson Brazil, 1986; Brazil, Population Census 1980.
21. "Women in the Marketplace," Thompson Lightstone & Company, Ltd., 1984; Canada, Population Census 1985; "Target Australia: Women, the Quiet Revolution," J. Walter Thompson Australia, 1984; Australia, Population Census 1981.
22. "Target Venezuela," J. Walter Thompson Venezuela, 1986; Venezuela, Population Census 1984.
23. The Yankelovich Monitor, conducted by Yankelovich Clancy Shulman, 1986; U.S. Bureau of the Census, Population Survey 1986.

Notes

24. "Target Mexico," J. Walter Thompson Mexico, 1986; Mexico, Population Census 1980; "The Moving Target in Japan," J. Walter Thompson Japan, Japan Market Research Bureau, Inc., 1986; Japan, Population Census 1985; "Target Australia: Women, the Quiet Revolution," J. Walter Thompson Australia, 1984; Australia, Population Census 1981.
25. "Women in Germany: The Moving Target," J. Walter Thompson West Germany, 1986; West Germany, Population Census, 1980.

Ten

1. "Target Venezuela," J. Walter Thompson Venezuela, 1986.
2. "Target Brazil," J. Walter Thompson Brazil, 1986.
3. "Target Mexico," J. Walter Thompson Mexico, 1986.
4. "Target Australia: Women, the Quiet Revolution," J. Walter Thompson Australia, Survey Research Group Australia Pty. Ltd., 1984, p. 119.
5. Ibid., p. 116.
6. "Women in Germany: The Moving Target," J. Walter Thompson West Germany, 1986.
7. "Women in the Marketplace," Thompson Lightstone & Company, Ltd., 1984.
8. Ibid.
9. Ibid.
10. Ibid.
11. The Roper Organization, Inc., The 1985 Virginia Slims American Women's Opinion Poll.
12. Ibid.
13. "Target Latin America," J. Walter Thompson Latin America, 1986.
14. "Target Australia: Women, the Quiet Revolution," J. Walter Thompson Australia, Survey Research Group Australia Pty. Ltd., 1984, p. 118.
15. Ibid., p. 50.
16. "The Moving Target in Japan," J. Walter Thompson Japan, Japan Market Research Bureau, Inc., 1986.
17. The Roper Organization, Inc., The 1985 Virginia Slims American Women's Opinion Poll.
18. "Target Latin America," J. Walter Thompson Latin America, 1986.
19. Ibid.
20. "Women in the Marketplace," Thompson Lightstone & Company, Ltd., 1984.
21. The Roper Organization, Inc., The 1985 Virginia Slims American Women's Opinion Poll.
22. "Women in the Marketplace," Thompson Lightstone & Company, Ltd., 1984.
23. "The Moving Target in Japan," J. Walter Thompson Japan, Japan Market Research Bureau, Inc., 1986.
24. "Women in the Marketplace," Thompson Lightstone & Company, Ltd., 1984.
25. "Beyond the Stereotypes," Reark Research Pty. Ltd. for Clemenger Network of Advertising Agencies, 1984.
26. The Roper Organization, Inc., The 1985 Virginia Slims American Women's Opinion Poll.
27. "Target Latin America," J. Walter Thompson Latin America, 1986.
28. "Target Australia: Women, the Quiet Revolution," J. Walter Thompson Australia, Survey Research Group Australia Pty. Ltd., 1984; Audits of Great Britain, 1984.
29. "The Moving Target in Japan," J. Walter Thompson Japan, Japan Market Research Bureau, Inc., 1986.
30. Ibid.
31. "Target Australia: Women, the Quiet Revolution," J. Walter Thompson Australia, Survey Research Group Australia Pty. Ltd. 1984; Audits of Great Britain, 1984.
32. The Roper Organization, Inc., The 1985 Virginia Slims Women's Public Opinion Poll.
33. Ibid.
34. "Target Latin America," J. Walter Thompson Latin America, 1986.
35. "Target Venezuela," J. Walter Thompson Venezuela, 1986.
36. "Target Mexico," J. Walter Thompson Mexico, 1986.

Notes

37. "The Moving Target in Japan," J. Walter Thompson Japan, Japan Market Research Bureau, Inc., 1986.
38. "Target Australia: Women, the Quiet Revolution," J. Walter Thompson Australia, Survey Research Group Australia Pty. Ltd., 1984.
39. "The Moving Target in Japan," J. Walter Thompson Japan, Japan Market Research Bureau, 1986.
40. "Target Australia: Women, the Quiet Revolution," J. Walter Thompson Australia, Survey Research Group Australia Pty. Ltd., 1984.
41. "Target Venezuela," J. Walter Thompson Venezuela, 1986.
42. "Target Brazil," J. Walter Thompson Brazil, 1986.
43. "Target Mexico," J. Walter Thompson Mexico, 1986.
44. "Target Brazil," J. Walter Thompson Brazil, 1986.
45. "Target Mexico," J. Walter Thompson Mexico, 1986.
46. "Target Venezuela," J. Walter Thompson Venezuela, 1986.

Eleven

1. "Women: The Moving Target in the U.K.," J. Walter Thompson Ltd., 1986.
2. Ibid.
3. Ibid.
4. Ibid.
5. "The Moving Target in Japan," J. Walter Thompson Japan, Japan Market Research Bureau, Inc., 1986.
6. Ibid.
7. Ibid.
8. Ibid.
9. "Women in the Marketplace," Thompson Lightstone & Company, Ltd., 1984.
10. "Beyond the Stereotypes," Reark Research Pty. Ltd. for Clemenger Network of Advertising Agencies, 1984, pp. 19, 21.
11. Ibid., p. 22.
12. Ibid., p. 24.
13. "The Changing Market: Aspects of Life, the World of Women," prepared by MRB Italia srl for J. Walter Thompson Italy, 1987.
14. Ibid.
15. Ibid.
16. "Target Brazil," J. Walter Thompson Brazil, 1986.
17. "Target Mexico," J. Walter Thompson Mexico, 1986.
18. "Target Venezuela," J. Walter Thompson Venezuela, 1986.
19. "Women in the Marketplace," Thompson Lightstone & Company, Ltd., 1984.
20. "Beyond the Stereotypes," Reark Research Pty. Ltd. for Clemenger Network of Advertising Agencies, 1984.
21. "Women: The Moving Target in the U.K.," J. Walter Thompson Ltd., 1986.
22. Ibid.
23. Ibid.
24. Ibid.
25. Ibid.
26. Ibid.
27. "The Moving Target in Japan," J. Walter Thompson Japan, Japan Market Research Bureau, 1986.
28. Ibid.
29. Ibid.
30. Ibid.
31. Ibid.

Notes

32. "The Changing Market: Aspects of Life, the World of Women," prepared by MRB Italia srl for J. Walter Thompson Italy, 1987.
33. Ibid.
34. "Target Australia: Women, the Quiet Revolution," J. Walter Thompson Australia, Survey Research Group Australia Pty. Ltd., 1984, p. 42.
35. "Beyond the Stereotypes," Reark Research Pty. Ltd. for Clemenger Network of Advertising Agencies, 1984, p. 12.
36. Ibid., p. 14.
37. Ibid.
38. "Women in the Marketplace," Thompson Lightstone & Company, Ltd., 1984.
39. Ibid.
40. The Roper Organization, Inc., The 1985 Virginia Slims American Women's Opinion Poll.
41. Ibid.
42. "Target Venezuela," J. Walter Thompson Venezuela, 1986.
43. "Target Mexico," J. Walter Thompson Mexico, 1986.
44. "Target Brazil," J. Walter Thompson Brazil, 1986.
45. Ibid.
46. Ibid.
47. "Women in Germany: The Moving Target," J. Walter Thompson West Germany, 1986.
48. Ibid.
49. "Women: The Moving Target in the U.K.," J. Walter Thompson Ltd., 1986.
50. Ibid.
51. Ibid.
52. Ibid.
53. Ibid.
54. Ibid.
55. Ibid.
56. "The Moving Target in Japan," J. Walter Thompson Japan, Japan Market Research Bureau, Inc., 1986.
57. Ibid.
58. Ibid.
59. Ibid.
60. Ibid.

Twelve

1. "Target Latin America," J. Walter Thompson Latin America, 1986.
2. Ibid.
3. Ibid.
4. "Women in the Marketplace," Thompson Lightstone & Company, Ltd., 1984.
5. "Women in Germany: The Moving Target," J. Walter Thompson West Germany, 1986.
6. "The Moving Target in Japan," J. Walter Thompson Japan, Japan Market Research Bureau, Inc., 1986.
7. "Target Australia: Women, the Quiet Revolution," J. Walter Thompson Australia, Survey Research Group Australia Pty. Ltd., 1984, pp. 117, 118.
8. "Women in Germany: The Moving Target," J. Walter Thompson West Germany, 1986.
9. "Women in the Marketplace," Thompson Lightstone & Company, Ltd., 1984.
10. Ibid.
11. "Target Latin America," J. Walter Thompson Latin America, 1986.
12. Ibid.
13. Ibid.
14. "Women in the Marketplace," Thompson Lightstone & Company, Ltd., 1984.

15. "Target Australia: Women, the Quiet Revolution," J. Walter Thompson Australia, Survey Research Group Australia Pty. Ltd., 1984, p. 116.
16. Ibid, p. 59.
17. "The Moving Target in Japan," J. Walter Thompson Japan, Japan Market Research Bureau, Inc., 1986.
18. Ibid.
19. "Target Australia: Women, the Quiet Revolution," J. Walter Thompson Australia, Survey Research Group Australia Pty. Ltd., 1984, p. 54.
20. Ibid., p. 56.
21. Ibid., p. 55.
22. Ibid., p. 57.
23. Ibid., p. 56.
24. Ibid., pp. 54–57.
25. "Women in the Marketplace," Thompson Lightstone & Company, Ltd., 1984.
26. "Home Truths," Reark Research Pty. Ltd. for Clemenger Network of Advertising Agencies, 1986, p. 31.
27. Ibid.
28. Ibid., p. 33.
29. Ibid.
30. Ibid.
31. Ibid.
32. "Target Brazil," J. Walter Thompson Brazil, 1986.
33. Ibid.
34. Ibid.
35. "Target Mexico," J. Walter Thompson Mexico, 1986.
36. Ibid.
37. "Target Venezuela," J. Walter Thompson Venezuela, 1986.
38. Ibid.
39. "Target Australia: Women, the Quiet Revolution," J. Walter Thompson Australia, Survey Research Group Australia Pty. Ltd., 1984, p. 63.
40. Ibid., p. 64.
41. "Home Truths," Reark Research Pty. Ltd. for Clemenger Network of Advertising Agencies, 1986, p. 32.
42. Ibid., pp. 32, 33.
43. "Target Mexico," J. Walter Thompson Mexico, 1986.
44. Ibid.
45. Ibid.
46. "Target Venezuela," J. Walter Thompson Venezuela, 1986.
47. Ibid.
48. "Target Brazil," J. Walter Thompson Brazil, 1986.
49. Ibid.
50. "Target Australia: Women, the Quiet Revolution," J. Walter Thompson Australia, Survey Research Group Australia Pty. Ltd., 1984, p. 86.
51. "The Moving Target in Japan," J. Walter Thompson Japan, Japan Market Research Bureau, Inc., 1986.
52. "Target Australia: Women, the Quiet Revolution," J. Walter Thompson Australia Survey Research Group Australia Pty. Ltd., 1984, p. 85.
53. Ibid., p. 86.
54. Ibid., p. 66.
55. Ibid., p. 67.
56. Ibid.
57. Ibid., p. 77.
58. Ibid., p. 78.

Notes

59. Ibid., pp. 79–81.
60. Ibid.
61. "Beyond the Stereotypes," Reark Research Pty. Ltd. for Clemenger Network of Advertising Agencies, 1984.
62. "The Moving Target in Japan," J. Walter Thompson Japan, Japan Market Research Bureau, Inc., 1986.

Thirteen

1. "The Changing Market: Aspects of Life, the World of Women," prepared by MRB Italia srl for J. Walter Thompson Italy, 1987.
2. Ibid.
3. Ibid.
4. Ibid.
5. "The Moving Target in Japan," J. Walter Thompson Japan, Japan Market Research Bureau, Inc., 1986.
6. Ibid.
7. "Women in Germany: The Moving Target," J. Walter Thompson West Germany, 1986.
8. "Beyond the Stereotypes," Reark Research Pty. Ltd. for Clemenger Network of Advertising Agencies, 1984, p. 44.
9. Ibid.
10. Ibid., p. 43.
11. Ibid.
12. "Target Australia: Women, the Quiet Revolution," J. Walter Thompson Australia, Survey Research Group Australia Pty. Ltd., 1984, p. 89.
13. Ibid., p. 90.
14. Ibid.
15. Ibid., p. 91.
16. Ibid., p. 93.
17. Ibid., p. 91.
18. Ibid., p. 94.
19. Ibid., p. 92.
20. Ibid.
21. Ibid., p. 95.
22. "Women: The Moving Target in the U.K.," J. Walter Thompson Ltd., 1986.
23. Simmons Market Research Bureau, Special Analysis by JWT Communications Development, 1986.
24. Ibid.
25. Ibid.
26. "Target Australia: Women, the Quiet Revolution," J. Walter Thompson Australia, Survey Research Group Australia Pty. Ltd., 1984, p. 95.
27. Ibid., p. 96.
28. Ibid., p. 97.
29. Simmons Market Research Bureau, Special Analysis by JWT Communications Development, 1986.
30. Ibid.
31. Ibid.
32. "Target Australia: Women, the Quiet Revolution," J. Walter Thompson Australia, Survey Research Group Australia Pty. Ltd., 1984, p. 94
33. Simmons Market Research Bureau, Special Analysis by JWT Communications Development, 1986.
34. Ibid.

35. Ibid.
36. "Target Venezuela," J. Walter Thompson Venezuela, 1986.
37. "Target Brazil," J. Walter Thompson Brazil, 1986.
38. Ibid.
39. Ibid.
40. "Target Mexico," J. Walter Thompson Mexico, 1986.
41. Ibid.
42. Ibid.
43. Jobson, "Special Report on Spirits, Wine & Beer," 1987; M. Shanken, "Communications Impact," 1987.
44. Ibid.
45. Nancy Harmon Jenkins, "Stocks Are Down, Gin Is Back and So Is the Cocktail Party," and Frank J. Prial, "Reviving the Dry Martini," *New York Times*, October 28, 1987.
46. "The Moving Target in Japan," J. Walter Thompson Japan, Japan Market Research Bureau, Inc., 1986.
47. Ibid.
48. Ibid.
49. Ibid.
50. Ibid.
51. Ibid.
52. "Target Venezuela," J. Walter Thompson Venezuela, 1986.
53. Ibid.
54. "Target Mexico," J. Walter Thompson Mexico, 1986.
55. Ibid.
56. "Target Brazil," J. Walter Thompson Brazil, 1986.
57. Ibid.
58. Ibid.
59. Ibid.
60. "Women in Germany: The Moving Target," J. Walter Thompson West Germany, 1986.
61. The Yankelovich Monitor, conducted by Yankelovich Clancy Shulman, 1987.
62. Ibid.
63. Simmons Market Research Bureau, Special Analysis by JWT Communications Development, 1986.
64. Ibid.
65. Ibid.
66. "Women: The Moving Target in the U.K.," J. Walter Thompson Ltd., 1986.
67. "The Moving Target in Japan," J. Walter Thompson Japan, Japan Market Research Bureau, Inc., 1986.
68. Ibid.
69. Ibid.
70. Ibid.

Fourteen

1. "Women: The Moving Target in the U.K.," J. Walter Thompson Ltd., 1986.
2. Ibid.
3. Ibid.
4. Ibid.
5. Ibid.
6. Ibid.
7. Ibid.
8. Ibid.
9. Ibid.

10. Ibid.
11. Ibid.
12. Ibid.
13. Ibid.
14. Ibid.
15. Ibid.
16. "The Moving Target in Japan," J. Walter Thompson Japan, Japan Market Research Bureau Inc., 1986.
17. Ibid.
18. Ibid.
19. Ibid.
20. Ibid.
21. Ibid.
22. Ibid.
23. Ibid.
24. Ibid.
25. Ibid.
26. Ibid.
27. Ibid.
28. Ibid.
29. Ibid.
30. "Target Australia: Women, the Quiet Revolution," J. Walter Thompson Australia, Survey Research Group Australia Pty. Ltd., 1984, p. 102.
31. Ibid., p. 101.
32. Ibid., p. 68.
33. "Women in Germany: The Moving Target," J. Walter Thompson West Germany, 1986.
34. Ibid.
35. Ibid.
36. "The Changing Market: Aspects of Life, the World of Women," prepared by MRB Italia srl for J. Walter Thompson Italy, 1987.
37. Ibid.
38. Ibid.
39. Ibid.
40. Ibid.
41. Ibid.
42. Simmons Market Research Bureau, Special Analysis by JWT Communications Development, 1986.
43. Ibid.
44. John Molloy, *Dress for Success* (New York: Warner Books, 1976).

Fifteen

1. "Women: The Moving Target in the U.K.," J. Walter Thompson Ltd., 1986.
2. Ibid.
3. Ibid.
4. Ibid.
5. Ibid.
6. Ibid.
7. Ibid.
8. Ibid.
9. "The Moving Target in Japan," J. Walter Thompson Japan, Japan Market Research Bureau, 1986.
10. Ibid.

11. Ibid.
12. Ibid.
13. Ibid.
14. Ibid.
15. Ibid.
16. Ibid.
17. Ibid.
18. "The Changing Market: Aspects of Life, the World of Women," prepared by MRB Italia srl for J. Walter Thompson Italy, 1987.
19. Ibid.
20. Ibid.
21. "Women in Germany: The Moving Target," J. Walter Thompson West Germany, 1986.
22. Simmons Market Research Bureau, Special Analysis by JWT Communications Development, 1986.
23. Ibid.
24. "Target Australia: Women, the Quiet Revolution," J. Walter Thompson Australia, Survey Research Group Australia Pty. Ltd., 1984, pp. 103, 104, 105.
25. Ibid., p. 105.
26. Ibid., p. 107.

Sixteen

1. "Target Venezuela," J. Walter Thompson Venezuela, 1986.
2. "Target Australia: Women, the Quiet Revolution," J. Walter Thompson Australia, Survey Research Group Australia Pty. Ltd., 1984, pp. 51, 52.
3. "Women in the Marketplace," Thompson Lightstone & Company, Ltd., 1984.
4. "The Moving Target in Japan," J. Walter Thompson Japan, Japan Market Research Bureau, Inc., 1986.
5. "Target Mexico," J. Walter Thompson Mexico, 1986.
6. "Women in Germany: The Moving Target," J. Walter Thompson West Germany, 1986.
7. The Roper Organization, Inc., The 1985 Virginia Slims American Women's Opinion Poll, p. 44 plus custom analysis of New Demographic segments.
8. "The Moving Target in Japan," J. Walter Thompson Japan, Japan Market Research Bureau, Inc., 1986.
9. Private conversation with Tom Sutton, former director of the Far East division of J. Walter Thompson, 1987.
10. "Target Australia: Women, the Quiet Revolution," J. Walter Thompson Australia, Survey Research Group Australia Pty. Ltd., 1984.
11. Ibid., p. 119.
12. "Target Latin America," J. Walter Thompson Latin America, 1986.
13. Ibid.
14. Ibid.
15. "Target Australia: Women, the Quiet Revolution," J. Walter Thompson Australia, Survey Research Group Australia Pty. Ltd., 1984, p. 51.
16. The Roper Organization, Inc., The 1985 Virginia Slims American Women's Opinion Poll, p. 44 plus custom analysis of New Demographic segments.
17. Ibid., p. 91.
18. Ibid., plus custom analysis of New Demographic segments.
19. Ibid.
20. Simmons Market Research Bureau, Special Analysis by JWT Communications Development, 1986.
21. Ibid.
22. Ibid.

23. Ibid.
24. Ibid.
25. Ibid.
26. Ibid.
27. "Women: The Moving Target in the U.K.," J. Walter Thompson Ltd., 1986; Target Group Index, custom analysis of New Demographic segments.
28. Ibid.
29. Ibid.
30. Ibid.
31. "Women: The Moving Target in the U.K.," J. Walter Thompson Ltd., 1986.
32. Ibid.
33. Ibid.
34. Ibid.
35. Ibid.
36. Ibid.
37. Ibid.
38. "Women in Germany: The Moving Target," J. Walter Thompson West Germany, 1986.
39. Ibid.
40. Ibid.
41. Ibid.
42. Ibid.
43. Ibid.
44. Ibid.
45. "Beyond the Stereotypes," Reark Research Pty. Ltd. for Clemenger Network of Advertising Agencies, 1984, p. 37.
46. Ibid., p. 38.
47. Ibid., p. 45.
48. Ibid.
49. Ibid., p. 46.
50. Ibid.
51. Ibid.
52. Ibid., p. 48.
53. "Women in the Marketplace," Thompson Lightstone & Company, Ltd., 1984.
54. Ibid.
55. Ibid.
56. Ibid.
57. Ibid.
58. Ibid.
59. Ibid.
60. Ibid.
61. Ibid.
62. "Target Brazil," J. Walter Thompson Brazil, 1986.
63. "Beyond the Stereotypes," Reark Research Pty. Ltd. for Clemenger Network of Advertising Agencies, 1984, p. 23.
64. Ibid.
65. Ibid., p. 24.

Seventeen

1. "Women: The Moving Target in the U.K.," J. Walter Thompson Ltd., 1986; Target Group Index, custom analysis of New Demographic segments.
2. Ibid.
3. Ibid.

Notes

4. Ibid.
5. Ibid.
6. Ibid.
7. Ibid.
8. Ibid.
9. Ibid.
10. Ibid.
11. Ibid.
12. Ibid.
13. Ibid.
14. Ibid.
15. "Beyond the Stereotypes," Reark Research Pty. Ltd. for Clemenger Network of Advertising Agencies, 1984, p. 47.
16. Ibid.
17. "The Changing Market: Aspects of Life, the World of Women," prepared by MRB Italia srl for J. Walter Thompson Italy, 1987.
18. Ibid.
19. "Target Venezuela," J. Walter Thompson Venezuela, 1986.
20. Ibid.
21. Ibid.
22. Ibid.
23. "Target Brazil," J. Walter Thompson Brazil, 1986.
24. Ibid.
25. Ibid.
26. Ibid.
27. Ibid.
28. "Target Mexico," J. Walter Thompson Mexico, 1986.
29. Ibid.
30. Ibid.
31. Ibid.
32. Simmons Market Research Bureau, Special Analysis by JWT Communications Development, 1986.
33. Ibid.
34. Ibid.
35. Simmons Market Research Bureau, Value Index by JWT Communications Development, 1986; U.S. Bureau of the Census, 1986; The Yankelovich Monitor, conducted by Yankelovich Clancy Shulman, 1987.

Eighteen

1. "The Italian Woman Facing the '80s," Arnold Mondadori/McCann-Erickson Italy, 1981.
2. Simmons Market Research Bureau, Special Analysis by JWT Communications Development, 1986.
3. Ibid.
4. Ibid.
5. Ibid.
6. Ibid.
7. Ibid.
8. Ibid.
9. Ibid.
10. Ibid.
11. "Women: The Moving Target in the U.K.," J. Walter Thompson Ltd., 1986.
12. Ibid.; Target Group Index, custom analysis of New Demographic segments.

Notes

13. Ibid.
14. Ibid.
15. Ibid.
16. Ibid.
17. Ibid.
18. Ibid.
19. Ibid.
20. "Beyond the Stereotypes," Reark Research Pty. Ltd. for Clemenger Network of Advertising Agencies, 1984, p. 50.
21. Ibid.
22. Ibid.
23. Ibid.
24. Ibid.
25. Ibid.
26. Ibid.

Nineteen

1. Simmons Market Research Bureau, Special Analysis by JWT Communications Development, 1986.
2. Ibid.
3. Canada, Print Measurement Bureau, Readership Survey, 1986.
4. Ibid.
5. Ibid.
6. "Women: The Moving Target in the U.K.," J. Walter Thompson Ltd., 1986; Target Group Index, custom analysis of New Demographic segments.
7. Ibid.
8. "Women in Germany: The Moving Target," J. Walter Thompson West Germany, 1986; Trendmonitor, Basisresearch, custom analysis of New Demographic segments, 1985.
9. "Target Brazil," J. Walter Thompson Brazil, 1986.
10. "Target Mexico," J. Walter Thompson Mexico, 1986.
11. "Target Venezuela," J. Walter Thompson Venezuela, 1986.
12. "The Moving Target in Japan," J. Walter Thompson Japan, Japan Market Research Bureau, Inc., 1986.
13. "Beyond the Stereotypes," Reark Research Pty. Ltd. for Clemenger Network of Advertising Agencies, 1984, p. 53.
14. "Target Australia: Women, the Quiet Revolution," J. Walter Thompson Australia, Survey Research Group Australia Pty. Ltd., 1984.
15. "Beyond the Stereotypes," Reark Research Pty. Ltd. for Clemenger Network of Advertising Agencies, 1984, p. 53.
16. Ibid., p. 54.
17. Ibid., p. 55.
18. Ibid.
19. Ibid., p. 54.
20. Ibid., p. 55.
21. Simmons Market Research Bureau, Special Analysis by JWT Communications Development, 1986.
22. Canada, Print Measurement Bureau, Readership Survey, 1986.
23. "Women: The Moving Target in the U.K.," J. Walter Thompson Ltd., 1986; Target Group Index, custom analysis of New Demographic segments.
24. "Women in Germany: The Moving Target," J. Walter Thompson West Germany, 1986; Arbeitsgemeinschaft Media-Analyse E.V. (AG.MA), Media-Analyse.
25. "Target Brazil," J. Walter Thompson Brazil, 1986.

26. "Target Mexico," J. Walter Thompson Mexico, 1986.
27. "Target Venezuela," J. Walter Thompson Venezuela, 1986.
28. "Beyond the Stereotypes," Reark Research Pty. Ltd. for Clemenger Network of Advertising Agencies, 1984, p. 52.
29. Ibid., p. 53.
30. "Target Australia: Women, the Quiet Revolution," J. Walter Thompson Australia, Survey Research Group Australia Pty. Ltd., 1984.
31. "Beyond the Stereotypes," Reark Research Pty. Ltd. for Clemenger Network of Advertising Agencies, 1984, p. 52.
32. Simmons Market Research Bureau, Special Analysis by JWT Communications Development, 1986.
33. Canada, Print Measurement Bureau, Readership Survey, 1986.
34. "Women: The Moving Target in the U.K.," J. Walter Thompson Ltd., 1986; Target Group Index, custom analysis of New Demographic segments.
35. Ibid.
36. "Women in Germany: The Moving Target," J. Walter Thompson West Germany, 1986; Arbeitsgemeinschaft Media-Analyse E.V. (AG.MA), Media-Analyse.
37. "Women in Germany: The Moving Target," J. Walter Thompson West Germany, 1986; Trendmonitor, Basisresearch, 1985.
38. "Beyond the Stereotypes," Reark Research Pty. Ltd. for Clemenger Network of Advertising Agencies," 1984, p. 51.
39. "Target Australia: Women, the Quiet Revolution," J. Walter Thompson Australia, Survey Research Group Australia Pty. Ltd., 1984.
40. Japan Market Research Bureau, Inc., National Omnibus Survey, 1984.
41. Ibid.
42. Ibid.
43. Ibid.
44. Ibid.
45. Ibid.
46. Simmons Market Research Bureau, Special Analysis by JWT Communications Development, 1986.
47. "Women in the Marketplace," Thompson Lightstone & Company, Ltd., 1984.
48. Ibid.
49. "Women: The Moving Target in the U.K.," J. Walter Thompson Ltd., 1986; Target Group Index, custom analysis of New Demographic segments.
50. "Women in Germany: The Moving Target," J. Walter Thompson West Germany, 1986.
51. "Target Venezuela," J. Walter Thompson Venezuela, 1986.
52. "Target Mexico," J. Walter Thompson Mexico, 1986.
53. "Target Brazil," J. Walter Thompson Brazil, 1986.
54. "Beyond the Stereotypes," Reark Research Pty. Ltd. for Clemenger Network of Advertising Agencies, 1984, p. 51.
55. "Target Latin America," J. Walter Thompson Latin America, 1986.
56. Ibid.
57. Ibid.
58. Ibid.
59. Ibid.
60. Ibid.
61. Ibid.
62. Ibid.
63. Ibid.
64. Ibid.
65. Ibid.
66. Ibid.

67. Ibid.
68. Ibid.
69. Ibid.

Twenty

1. "Women in the Marketplace," Thompson Lightstone & Company, Ltd., 1984.
2. "The Changing Market: Aspects of Life, the World of Women," prepared by MRB Italia srl for J. Walter Thompson Italy, 1987.
3. Ibid.
4. Ibid.
5. Ibid.
6. Ibid.
7. Ibid.
8. Ibid.
9. "The Moving Target in Japan," J. Walter Thompson Japan, Japan Market Research Bureau, Inc., 1986.
10. Ibid.
11. Ibid.
12. Ibid.
13. Ibid.
14. Ibid.
15. "Target Latin America," J. Walter Thompson Latin America, 1986.
16. Ibid.
17. Ibid.
18. Ibid.
19. Ibid.
20. Ibid.
21. Ibid.
22. Ibid.
23. Ibid.
24. Ibid.
25. Ibid.
26. "Women: The Moving Target in the U.K.," J. Walter Thompson Ltd., 1986.
27. Ibid.
28. Ibid.
29. Ibid.
30. Ibid.
31. Ibid.
32. Ibid.
33. Rena Bartos and Theodore F. Dunn, "Advertising and Consumers—New Perspectives" (New York: American Association of Advertising Agencies, 1976), p. 84.
34. Rena Bartos, *The Moving Target: What Every Marketer Should Know about Women* (New York: Free Press, 1982), pp. 254–257.
35. Ibid., p. 258.
36. Ibid., pp. 260, 261.
37. Ibid., pp. 262, 263.
38. Ibid., pp. 264, 265.
39. Ibid., p. 266.
40. Ibid., p. 267.
41. Ibid., p. 269.
42. "Influence of Mass Communication Media on the Formation of a New Attitude towards the Role of Women in Present-Day Society," Report of the Secretary-General, United Nations

Notes

Commission on the Status of Women, 25th Session, Item 7 of the Provisional Agenda, January 1974.

43. "Advertising and Women: A Report on Advertising Portraying or Directed to Women," prepared by a consultive panel of the National Advertising Review Board, March 1975, pp. 7–10.

44. Robert G. Wyckham, "Self-Regulation of Sex Role Stereotypes in Advertising: The Canadian Experience," *Journal of Public Policy and Marketing* 6, 1987, pp. 76–92.

45. Sexism Complaints Checklist, Women's Electoral Lobby, Surrey Hills, N.S.W., Australia.

A Final Word . . .

1. Private communication from George Clements, international vice-president of the J. Walter Thompson Company, national director of strategic planning of Canada, March 3, 1988.

2. Ibid.

3. Private communication from Marion Plunkett, board director and director of research, Ogilvy & Mather Advertising, Toronto, Canada, March 11, 1988.

4. John Junkerman, "A Woman's Place," *Harvard Business School Bulletin* (February 1988) p. 49.

5. "The Kimono Revolution," by Katsuhiko Betushima, director of strategic planning, J. Walter Thompson Japan, May 1, 1987.

6. Robert Wilk, "The New Japanese Consumer: Five Major Trends for Marketing in Japan Today," a speech given at the 50th World Marketing Conference of the American Marketing Association, May 1987, from the session, "The Marketing Challenge: What We Can Learn from the Japanese." Robert Wilk is managing director of Marplan Japan.

7. Junkerman, "A Woman's Place," p. 42.

8. Wilk, "The New Japanese Consumer."

9. Junkerman, "A Woman's Place," p. 43.

10. "The Moving Target," a proprietary study by the J. Walter Thompson Company, 1974.

11. Ibid.

12. Private communication from George Clements, international vice-president of the J. Walter Thompson Company national director of strategic planning of Canada, March 3, 1988.

13. Ibid.

14. Private communication from Judie Lannon, vice-president and director of research, J. Walter Thompson Company Ltd., September 24, 1987.

15. Ibid.

16. Private communication from Audrey Slaughter, editor and journalist, formerly of *Working Woman*, October 21, 1987.

17. Private communication from Dr. Elizabeth Nelson, chairman of the Taylor Nelson Group, September 30, 1987.

18. Private communication from Judie Lannon, vice-president and director of research, J. Walter Thompson Company Ltd., September 24, 1987.

19. Ibid.

20. Private communication from Dr. Elizabeth Nelson, chairman of the Taylor Nelson Group, September 30, 1987.

21. Private communication from Audrey Slaughter, editor and journalist, formerly of *Working Woman*, October 21, 1987.

22. Private communication from Robert Schutzendorf, director of J. Walter Thompson West Germany and director of account planning, March 16, 1988.

23. Ibid.

24. Ibid.

25. Private communication from Benedetta Barzini, journalist, March 16, 1988.

26. Ibid.

Notes

27. Private communication from Anna Scotti, president of J. Walter Thompson Italy, March 16, 1988.
28. Private communication from Benedetta Barzini, journalist, March 16, 1988.
29. Ibid.
30. Private communication from Anna Scotti, president of J. Walter Thompson Italy, March 16, 1988.
31. Private communication from Mercedes Pulido de Briceno, assistant secretary-general and coordinator for the Improvement of the Status of Women in the Secretariat of the United Nations, March 22, 1988.
32. Ibid.
33. Ibid.

Index

motivations for working in, 20, 21, 25–26
part-time work option for women in, 76–77
roles of men and women in, 55, 86
European Economic Community (EEC) study, 24, 87
European women, 276–283
Evening series programs (television), 239
Ewing, David, 5
Extravagance, 89–90

F

Family
  full-time housewife and, 77–78
  importance of, 106–107, 278–279
  work and, 75–79, 80–90
Far Eastern women, 271–276
Fashion, 174–185
Female heads of household. *See* Unmarried women, with children
Financial activity of women, 202–212
Financial independence, 27–28, 205, 209, 210, 213, 214, 275
Financial responsibility
  family finances and, 199–202
  roles of men and women and, 53–57, 108–111
  working vs. traditional wives and, 67–68
Flexible working arrangements, 77
Food, women and
  beverages and, 166–171
  diet and nutrition and, 163–165
  dining habits and, 160–163
  health and grocery shopping and, 165–166
  smoking and, 171–172
Fragrance. *See* Grooming

G

Gallup Poll, 93
Game shows, 239
Generics, 157–159
"Glass ceiling," for career women, 269
Great Britain. *See* United Kingdom
Grocery shopping
  health and, 165–166, 173
  responsibility for, 153–156
Grooming, 186–191
Guilt, feelings of, 83

H

Hairdressers, 187, 188
Harvey-Jones, John, 279

Health, 165–166, 173
Higher education, 267
  Brazilian women and, 284, 285
  Canadian women and, 270
  German women and, 279
  Italian women and, 281, 282
  Mexican women and, 284
  Venezuelan women and, 283
  women's involvement in, 30–32
Holiday travel, 225–231
Homemaking magazines, 245
"Home Truths" study, 150–152
Hotels and motels, 227
Household budget, 210–211
Household tasks
  advertising and, 259
  feelings about, 34, 144–145
  shared responsibility for, 145–150, 275, 285–286
Housewife. *See also* Plan-to-work housewife; Stay-at-home housewife
  feelings about going to work and, 95–96
  full-time, and family responsibilities, 77–78
  motivations of, 39–45
  negative connotation of term, 122–123
  vs. nonworking woman, 7, 15–17
  vs. working woman, 2, 7, 17–18
Husbands
  attitudes of, 83–88, 275
  household tasks and, 145–153, 272–273
  nonworking women and, 39–40
  travel decisions and, 226–227
  women's feelings about work and, 115–118

I

Ideal life style, 32–38, 58, 75–76, 277
Identity of women, 59–61, 270
Income
  New Demographic segments and, 102–103
  size of wife's, 85–86
Industry standards, and consumers, 156–157
Insurance, 203–204, 206–207, 209–210, 212
Investment, 203, 204, 207, 211
Investment dressing, 184
Italy
  aspirations of women in, 37
  attitudes toward work in, 125, 130
  cultural characteristics of women in, 281–283
  desirability of wife working in, 83, 84
  dining habits in, 160–161
  fashion and grooming in, 182–183, 190
  housewives' feelings about working in, 96
  importance of children in, 50
  just-a-job working women in, 130
  life-cycle profile in, 48